Robert Stiffler's
Gardening

In Southeastern Virginia &
Northeastern North Carolina

The Best Of 20 Years
Of Gardening Advice

Edited by Aimee Cunningham Batten

D1537460

The Virginian–Pilot   Norfolk

Robert Stiffler
Copyright © 1995 The Virginian–Pilot

Second Edition, Revised December 1995

Published by The Virginian–Pilot, 150 W. Brambleton Avenue, Norfolk, Virginia 23510

Cover Design by Jose Barcita, Virginia Beach, Virginia
Book Design and Typography by Cheryl Dozier, Virginia Beach, Virginia

Printed in the United States of America by Byrd Press,
Cadmus Communications, Richmond, Virginia

Library of Congress Cataloging–in–Publication Data

Stiffler, Robert
Gardening in Southeastern Virginia–Northeastern North Carolina/ Robert Stiffler

ISBN 0–9648308–1–7

"Time began in a Garden"

-the sundial at Filoli Estate Garden, Woodside, California

THE AUTHOR

Robert Stiffler, a native of Iowa, began poking around his grandparents' garden when he was a boy. He also pursued his hobby in Ohio before settling in Virginia. A regular contributor to The Virginian–Pilot since 1974, he writes a three–part gardening column consisting of a plant feature, weekly reminders and answers to reader questions. He retired in 1987 after 33 years in the agricultural and horticultural marketing business. Along with the late Fred Heutte, founder of the Norfolk Botanical Garden, Stiffler helped start the Men's Garden Club of Tidewater in 1974. He was a Botanical Garden board member for 12 years and president for three. Membership in plant societies continues to help him hone the fine art of gardening. Stiffler was named Horticulturist of the Year in 1988 by the Tidewater Nurserymen's Association. He lives in Virginia Beach, where he tends a 2–acre garden filled with perennials, trees, shrubs, vines, annuals, vegetables, roses and plenty of squirrels, rabbits and raccoons.

THE EDITOR

Aimee Cunningham Batten was Stiffler's editor at The Virginian–Pilot before retiring to become a mother. A free–lance journalist living in Norfolk, she is a graduate of the University of Missouri–Columbia School of Journalism. She sorted through 20 years of Stiffler's writing to select the best for this book.

Thanks...

No garden writer could exist without a lot of help from friends who are better gardeners. I particularly want to thank those who have helped me, starting with the late Fred Heutte, a French gardener who dreamed big ideas, including the founding of the Norfolk Botanical Garden.

To the many who gave me advice, as well as plants, Zelma Crockett and Louisa Venable Kyle head the list.

Those who were or are with the Virginia Tech extension service have been and continue to be invaluable in answering difficult reader questions. These include Drs. Charles Elstrodt, Dan Milbocker, Bonnie Appleton and Peter Schultz. Plus Virginia Beach extension agent Randy Jackson as well as retired Botanical Garden superintendent Bob Matthews. And knowledgeable members of plant societies whom I've been able to count as friends have helped immensely. Thanks to them all. And a special thanks to my good friend and editor, Aimee Cunningham Batten, for making my words sound better than when I wrote them.

–Robert (Bob) Stiffler

Table of Contents

January

Plan Garden Carefully 1
Hollies Brighten Winter Landscape 2
Trim Up the Garden 3
Basic Pruning Techniques 5
Gardening Reminders 6

February

Let Camellias Do All the Work 9
Good Bugs Can Control the Bad Ones 11
New Roses Require Less Care 12
Planting Method for Roses 14
Gardening Reminders 15

March

Love at First Bloom: Azaleas 19
Looking Ahead to Late Summer 21
Soil Enrichment 22
Spring Basics for Lawns 23
How Grasses Stand Up 24
Mulch Now to Protect Plants 25
Why Bulbs Don't Bloom the Second Year 25
Gardening Reminders 26

April

Faithful Dogwood 31
Vines Worth Clinging To 33
Fruit Trees: A Feast For the Eyes 34
Fussy Boxwood Sometimes Requires Extra Care 36
More About Boxwood 37
Fertilizer Basics 38
Gardening Reminders 39

May

Earthly Plot: The Summer Vegetable Garden 43
Save Money Growing Your Own Vegetables 44
Weeds and Vegetables Don't Mix 45
Square–Foot Vegetable Gardening 45
Herbs Add Flavor to Home Gardens 46
An Ounce of Prevention Produces Pounds of Tomatoes 48
Summer Annuals Give Your Garden a Splash of Color 50
Gardening Reminders 51

June

Preparing Your Garden For Summer 53
Fragrance Makes a Scents–ible Garden 54
Day by Day, Enjoy the Glory of Daylilies 55
The Essence of Organic Gardening 56
Gardening Reminders 58

Table of Contents

July

Saving Water By Xeriscaping 61
Summer Savior: The Crape Myrtle 63
List of Crape Myrtle Cultivars 65
Options Abound For Seaside Gardening 66
A Look Inside 7 Private Beach Gardens 67
Flowers Made to Last 69
Tips for Gardeners With Arthritis 70
Gardening Reminders 71

August

Feeling at Home in a Native Garden 73
Proper Pruning of Hydrangea Types 77
Webworms, Caterpillars Make a Mess of Trees 78
Preparing a Fall Vegetable Garden 79
Gardening Reminders 81

September

Caring For Your Cherished Lawn 85
Easy Does It: Low–Care Plants Replace Old Favorites 88
Mums Extend the Season 89
Growing Garlic 90
Plants For Wet Places 90
Be Secure With Your Shrubs 91
Gardening Reminders 92

October

Versatile Perennials Provide Months of Color 95
Harvesting Broccoli and Cauliflower 97
Put Down Some Tree Roots 98
10 Steps in Proper Tree Planting 99
Tree Growth in 10 Years 100
Gardening Reminders 101

November

Spring Bulbs Bring Joy to Garden 105
Great Coverups Replace Lawns 108
Forcing Paper–whites for Christmas 109
Gardening Reminders 110

December

Winterize Your Garden 113
African Violets: Friend or Foe 114
For the Birds 115
Indoor Blooms Brighten Dull Winter Months 117
Gardening Reminders 11

Reader Questions

Birds and Butterflies 123
Bulbs 125

Table of Contents

Reader Questions (continued)

Fruits and Berries 126
    Apples 126
    Berries 126
    Citrus 127
    Grapes 127
    Peaches 128
    General 130
Herbs 130
House plants 131
Lawn Care 134
Moles, Voles and Other Varmints 138
Perennials, Biennials and Annuals 142
Pest, Disease and Weed Control 144
Rose Care 151
Seaside Gardening 154
Trees and Shrubs 158
    Azaleas 158
    Boxwood 158
    Camellias 158
    Crape myrtle 160
    General 163
Vegetables 169
    Tomatoes 169
    General 171

J A N U A R Y

Plan Garden Carefully

Catalogs spill from your coffee table. Catalogs hawking vegetables, annuals, herbs, perennials, flowering shrubs, shade and fruit trees.

You finally locate a pencil, dull of point and with worn eraser, and begin to make a meager, bare–bones list of things you must have. Enough to plant Central Park: $847.45 worth. You scratch out a few items (remember, the eraser's shot), and you're down to $795.60.

Now, throw away the list.

Have you forgotten so quickly? About how last year you stacked zucchini in cords? And how that fast–growing hybrid poplar caused angry words from the utility people? And how 17 varieties of marigolds were a few too many? And how that miracle "pomato" bush had potato leaves and tomato roots?

Before you jump for those super–bargains, those once–in–a–lifetime deals, make your garden plans – carefully. Be realistic about how much time you have to spend in the garden.

Avoid flamboyant claims. Purchase from reliable companies only. Remember that if a plant is supposed to work miracles, it will be a miracle if it works at all. If a claim sounds too good to be true, it probably is.

Trees, shrubs and perennials should have both common and Latin names listed. For example, "cardinal bush" could be any of four or five different plants. But *Weigelia* cv. *Vanicekii* can be only that.

Ask gardening friends for recommendations on where to buy. Find out which mail-order sources are reliable. Also, read catalog descriptions carefully. Look at hardiness, height, flower color, texture, time to harvest and other plant characteristics. If you do not want a substitute when an item is sold out, state so clearly. Order early to avoid disappointment, and look for and understand the guarantee policy.

You might go ahead and find yourself a favorite local garden center you can rely on. If you want an unusual variety, ask them now, and they may be able to order it for you.

January is a good time for planning ahead because it will save headaches later.

Hollies Brighten Winter Landscape

Nothing pierces the bleakness of winter better than a cheerful holly. Its versatility in a garden can't be beat. Hollies come in many sizes and colors. Some grow into tall trees. Others hug the ground throughout their lifetime.

Colorwise, you can find anything from a variegated green–and–yellow holly to a blue one. The blues have a bluish–green foliage and although attractive have not become popular. They usually cost more than other hollies, and they don't grow well in Southeastern Virginia–Northeastern North Carolina.

You can even buy a holly that sheds its leaves, so you can see its bright–red berries all winter. Sparkleberry (*Ilex serrata x verticillata*), which sports large red berries, is one of the best of these deciduous plants. More homeowners should be enjoying its striking beauty in their gardens. Be sure to buy both a female and male. The female has berries but needs a male for pollination.

A favorite of many homeowners and landscapers is the Fosteri holly (*Ilex cassinex opaca*), usually sold as Foster's No. 2. It was conceived from a cross of the Dahoon and native American holly (*Ilex opaca*) about 25 years ago. It makes an excellent specimen plant or hedge. The outstanding feature of the Foster is its many berries. By fall every year, it is covered with hundreds of pea–size red berries, which show off because its foliage is small and narrow. Usually by spring, the birds have removed the berries, but they don't strip it immediately, giving you a bright garden ornament for several months.

Planting and care

When you buy any holly, ask if it needs a pollinating mate to produce berries. Most male hollies do not have berries and many other hollies require pollination. The Foster holly is pollinated by the native American holly, so make sure there is one in your area before planting.

Hollies should be planted or transplanted between November and March when the plant is dormant. Dig a hole twice as big as the container and set the plant at the same level that it grew in the container. Backfill around it with the same soil you took out of

Popular hollies

	Carissa (*Ilex cornuta carissa*)	Nellie R. Stevens (*Ilex cornuta x rotondofolia*)	Sparkler (*Ilex aquifolium*)	Blue Prince Holly (*Ilex meserveae*)	Yellowfruit American Holly (*Ilex D'or*)
WHAT TO PLANT	A low-growing Chinese holly. It's extremely dense with glossy foliage and is excellent for foundations, low hedges or in a planter.	A holly much prized for its Christmas greenery. It grows tall to become a tree, loaded with large berries.	An English holly that is exceptionally robust. It's an upright grower that branches readily with shiny dark–green foliage. It produces a prolific crop of glistening red berries at an early age.	A hardy ornamental of upright habit. It has small, glossy, dark–green leaves and is a good pollinator for all hollies that need a male to produce berries. Many do, so be sure to ask your nursery about that when making your selections.	A choice plant with golden berries.

the hole. Do not fertilize until the second year. Hollies like an acid soil, so do not use any lime around the plant. Mulch around it with pine straw, bark or decayed oak leaves, and water it well.

Hollies benefit from a yearly fertilization in early spring with a good holly food (10–10–10), or a tree and shrub acid–forming fertilizer. Watch for insect damage, especially from the holly leaf miner. That insect tunnels through the leaves, causing a permanent mark. If seriously damaged, the leaf will drop off. Cygon is the chemical spray recommended for control of leaf miner.

All hollies should be watered weekly during drought periods. A newly set holly needs water every three or four days until late fall, if rain doesn't do it for you.

If your hollies have yellow leaves in spring, it may be caused by a shortage of nutrients spent on producing a large crop of berries, according to experts at North Carolina State University. Try fertilizing it well in spring. If that doesn't correct the problem, there may be an iron shortage, so give it a shot of soluble iron.

Holly flowers

FEMALE

MALE

When you buy any holly, ask if it needs a pollinating mate to produce berries. Most male hollies do not have berries and many other hollies require pollination.

Trim Up the Garden

Probably the most common fault in American home landscapes is overgrowth. Foundation plantings often are done by the lowest bidder and then forgotten. You can drive most anywhere and see evergreen shrubs that cover a second–story window.

Late winter is an ideal time to prune most shrubs and trees. Little else can be done in the garden, so go to work on those overgrown plants.

Start with sharp, durable tools. For proper pruning, you'll need hand shears, lopping shears and pruning saws. Use shears to cut twigs and small branches. For larger branches up to an inch or so in diameter, loppers usually are best. Use a pruning saw for branches too large to cut with loppers.

Regrettably, it seems the one pruning tool most people have – and take great pride in – is hedge clippers. If they were all thrown away, the landscaping around most homes would improve. Too many plants are butchered with hedge clippers instead of being selectively pruned with hand shears. It takes a little longer to do the job right, but the result is beautiful. Don't use hedge trimmers for anything but hedges. Stop giving your good bushes a crewcut and spoiling their natural beauty.

The National Arborists Association recommends that shrubs be "thinned" by re-moving about one-third of the old stems each year, allowing new stems to take their place. They agree that all too often, shrubs are mere-ly sheared at some convenient level. This care-lessness produces a bushy-topped shrub with bare lower branches.

Evergreens are best pruned from now un-til early spring. Branches to be shortened among the needled varieties, such as pine and spruce, should be pruned back to a side branch or bud, if one is present. If there is no branch or bud, remove the entire limb.

Arborvitae, juniper, cedar and yew all may be pruned or sheared at any time, but it's best done at this time of year. Then new growth in the spring will quickly cover the pruning wounds.

Don't be afraid to be severe. Stand back and look at your foundation plantings. If they are overgrown in proportion to your house, cut them back. Healthy plants, like children, have a remarkable ability to recover fast. To help keep out insects and disease, you might want to cover the severed ends of larger branches with pruning paint. Some experts say this practice hurts more than it helps, but many gardeners still prefer treating the un-sightly wounds.

A glance at the old gardens in Williams-burg or England shows they were planted with a certain size and shape in mind. But most im-portantly, they have been carefully controlled and allowed to grow old gracefully by selec-tive pruning.

Prune at least twice a year, starting now. Do not, however, prune spring-blooming plants at this time. These shrubs include for-sythia, flowering quince, azaleas, pussy wil-low, flowering almond and any others that bloom early. You'll cut off flower buds if you trim them now. They should be thinned after blooming in spring.

A well-maintained tree is healthier and less hazardous. Remove dead, weakened or diseased branches that might fall down in storms. Thin and shape the crown of the tree to allow wind to pass through it, not against it. Thinning also means fewer branches to col-lect ice and snow, and stronger new growth next year.

The crotch of the tree, where the trunk branches out, may need bracing for greater strength. Narrow crotches high in the tree may need cabling to keep main branches from swaying too much.

Remove low, overhanging branches, es-pecially those over buildings. Even if the branches do not tear loose, they can damage roofs by rubbing against them in high winds.

Hire a qualified, professional arborist to trim your large trees. It's a dangerous job. Make sure they're bonded and certified.

The worst crime is "topping," whereby the tree is cut straight across the top, like a crew-cut. Not only does it look hideous, but it also ruins the tree's soundness and makes it vul-nerable to disease as many thick, strong limbs are cut flat across the top.

Letting plants develop into their natural shape, with a little help, is one of the many challenges of gardening. But once you get the hang of it, your garden will flourish.

TWO MAIN PRUNING CONCEPTS

Thinning: Makes a plant grow taller and more open.

Heading back: Increases plant den-sity and sturdiness.

The Cut In Relation To Buds

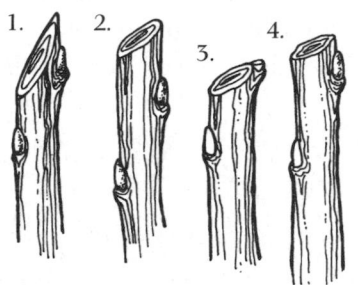

1. *Too slanted* – Exposes too much surface area to damage.
2. *Too long* – Can cause dieback of the stub.
3. *Too short* – Will interfere with bud growth.
4. *Ideal* – Cut from opposite the base of the bud slanting upward to the top.

Choosing The Correct Bud

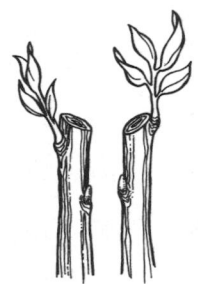

Prune near a lateral (side) bud that is pointing in the direction that you want the subsequent branch to grow. Cutting of a terminal (end) bud will cause the nearest lateral bud to inherit its strength and direction.

Pinching

Using the thumb and forefinger, frequently pinch back soft growth throughout the growing season to avoid future pruning, to redirect growth, and to increase the density of the plant. Pinching is also useful for disbudding flowers and thinning fruit.

Pruning Deciduous Shrubs

Remove all broken, diseased and crisscrossing branches. Remove a part of each long shoot that may spoil the shape of the shrub, and prune down to ground level about one-third of the oldest branches.

The Ideal Hedge Shape

Prune hedges narrow at the top to allow sunlight to reach the bottom foliage.

Removing Heavy Limbs

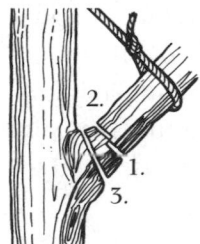

Use a 3–cut technique to avoid damage to a tree by splitting. Cut at (1) under the limb, then at (2) above and further out to remove the limb, and at (3) to remove the stub. The heaviest limbs may be supported by a rope. Always use proper safety procedures.

A Proper Cut

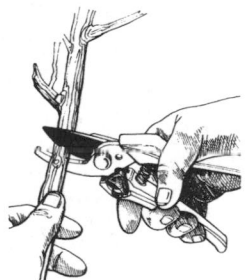

Support the branch below where the cut is to be made. Cut at a slant in the direction you want the new branch to grow.

Cut Close

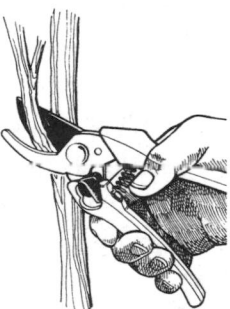

Cut an unwanted branch in such a way as to leave the shortest possible stub.

BASIC PRUNING TECHNIQUES

Reprinted with permission from Ames® Lawn & Garden Tools, Grow America Series, Box 1774, Parkersburg, WV 26102

Gardening
Reminders for
January

Early month

Fertilize

➤ Put wood ashes on your garden. They contain minor amounts of plant food and are a good soil conditioner.

Lawn care

➤ Give your lawn a cleanup on a warm day by raking all the leaves and fallen limbs and twigs. Don't walk on it when the grass is frozen.

Miscellaneous

➤ Make sure bark mulch does not have a strong, acrid odor. It's an indication that the pH of the bark is below 4.5, which can cause problems and even kill plants.

➤ Water all evergreens thoroughly, especially those planted under an overhang where they fail to get enough rain. They constantly lose water through their foliage in winter, especially during strong winds. Roots cannot replace lost water quickly enough. Leaves may turn brown and the plant will wilt.

Pruning

➤ Call a certified tree-care company if you need work done on large trees. Prices are usually lower in winter when leaves have fallen and limbs are bare.

Midmonth

House plants

➤ Clip some greens from cedar, yew or pines and stick them in the pot around your poinsettia to replace the green leaves that proba-

bly have dropped by now. Blooms on most of the hybrids will last another month or two. If kept in the sun, however, poinsettias won't lose their leaves. Also continue to water each plant thoroughly once a week and fertilize monthly.

Lawn care

➤ If the weather's warm, go out and scratch up those bare places in your lawn that annoy you. Scatter some seed and a little fertilizer. Then slightly cover it. It will be there ready to germinate and grow on the first warm days of spring when you may be too busy to do anything about it.

Miscellaneous

➤ Request seed and nursery catalogs. Then spend cold winter evenings and weekends reading them. You can learn a lot about planning your garden.

➤ Remove leaves and other debris from gutters one more time to eliminate the possibility of overflow during winter or spring rains.

Pest control

➤ Apply horticultural, or dormant, oil spray. Pick a day when the temperature is above 40 degrees F (and below 90) and will remain so for 48 hours. There are two types of sprays: oil and lime-sulphur. Determine which you need, and follow directions carefully. Keep dormant oil away from fir and spruce. Do not apply oil on thin-bark trees such as beech, sugar and Japanese maple, walnut or butternut. Used on apple, peach, pear, plum and cherry trees, as well as roses, oil sprays smother overwintering scale insects, aphids, mealybugs and mites, as well as certain diseases. One oil spray a season is sufficient.

Planting

➤ Take advantage of any mild day when the ground is not frozen and plant the trees and shrubs you want to add to your landscape. In our area, you can plant all winter and still give the plant a much better chance for survival than when planting just before hot weather.

Pruning

➤ Prune deciduous trees, shrubs and vines. You can easily see what needs to be pruned out now that they've shed their leaves.

Late month

Fertilize

➤ Fertilize your trees beyond the spread of the limbs, or "drip line." Radial root spread for poplar, willow, elm and most *prunus* (fruit bearing trees and shrubs) is 1½ to 2 times the height of the tree. The root spread for sycamore, oak, ash, horse chestnut, apple, pear and black locust is about 1½ times their height. Trees can be fertilized any time weather permits, up through late spring.

➤ Pecan trees need fertilizer for a big crop. Use 4 pounds of 10–10–10 per inch of trunk diameter. If this amount doesn't produce 6 or more inches of new terminal twig growth each year, additional nitrogen is needed. Also remember that pecans often need minor elements such as zinc, manganese or boron.

House plants

➤ Move your indoor plants around in the winter to give them more light. Winter changes the environment in your home, and adjustments should be made to keep house plants healthy. Because of the plants' position in the room, they may not be getting enough direct or indirect light.

Miscellaneous

➤ Keep water out for the birds. They need help finding water during winter. Also keep feeders filled, and check them regularly.

➤ Take advantage of any warm day to clean up flower borders by removing spent annuals and frozen tops of perennials. Chrysanthemums should be left with 6 inches of stalk remaining. Begonias, cannas and other perennials and annuals should be cut off at the top of the ground and the tops discarded. Beds should be mulched if not already done.

Planting

➤ Get on hand all the things you need for starting seed indoors. This includes peat pots, planting trays, growing soil and seed. Perhaps a small table–top greenhouse too. Some seeds should be started in the next 30 days.

➤ Stake young trees and grapevines to prevent damage during strong winds. Severe cold gusts can break trunks and limbs of small ornamentals and fruit trees.

➤ Propagating hardwood cuttings is one of the least expensive and easiest methods to get new trees and shrubs. Cuttings can be taken now from deciduous plants, which are dormant in winter. Plants that root easily include members of the rose, honeysuckle and privet families. To root, cut vigorous, mature, 1–year–old wood that has strong, easily seen, growth buds. Remove the tip of each shoot, making a cutting 4 to 10 inches long. Willow and honeysuckle can be planted outside and kept moist. Some, such as plums, can be bundled together and wrapped in moist sphagnum moss until spring planting. Roses and others can be planted in the ground or in a container filled with potting mix. Cover with a clear glass or plastic jar and they'll soon be rooted.

Planting

➤ Plant small fruits such as raspberries, blackberries, blueberries and dewberries now while the plants are dormant. They may be difficult to find at local nurseries, but don't be discouraged. Choose varieties adapted to local growing conditions.

➤ If you have to prune your azaleas every year to control their size, transplant them now, or whenever the ground is not frozen, to an area where they can grow larger. By moving them away from the foundation of your house or back from a walkway, they can grow into a natural form that requires less maintenance. If you're setting out new azaleas, keep in mind how tall and wide they'll be when mature. Avoid a hodgepodge of colors. Group plants of a single color together.

F E B R U A R Y

Let Camellias Do All the Work

The camellia was made for brown thumbs. Flower–laden in fall, winter or spring, resistant to most bugs and green all year long, it requires little attention to bear flawless blooms.

While most gardeners are pruning and pulling weeds until their fingers turn numb, camellia growers let their plants do all the work. Their subjects love shade and thrive with less pesticide spraying and fertilizer than most plants. Abundant bouquets spill from them during bloom season.

Probably the toughest chore is picking up spent blooms. Left lying around, rotting flowers will contract diseases and transfer them to the plant.

By comparison, the rose, our national flower, requires monthly fertilization and weekly insect spraying to look its best. Its growers fret over pest–ridden foliage and lackluster petals, while camellia growers have none of these problems.

Camellias belong to the tea family and are native to China and Japan. George Joseph Kamel, a Jesuit missionary, is credited with being the first to carry cuttings into Europe, so the plant is named in his honor. Reportedly, tea traders believed they were transporting small tea plants, but instead had been given specimens of the closely related camellia.

Camellias were introduced into the United States in the late 1700s and flourished in the South. But during the War Between the States, many beautiful varieties disappeared. Camellia reticulata, or Chinese camellia, was brought to England in 1742 by a sea captain named Rawes. It had dull–green leaves and large flowers. It is again available but usually not hardy in our climate.

In Southeastern Virginia and Northeastern North Carolina, camellias fare well. Until the dogwood and azalea blooms pop out in early spring, camellias can be depended upon to provide color. The plant is native to wooded areas, where it grows under or among trees, according to landscape horticulturist Henry Smith of North Carolina State University. It will grow vigorously in residential areas if given light shade, friable organic soil that is slightly acid and sufficient air and moisture.

To get started, prepare a planting bed two months before setting out plants, Smith recommends. If the soil is heavy clay, add organic loam by incorporating sharp sand and organic matter such as pine bark or well rotted, shredded leaves. If the soil is light and sandy, work large amounts of organic matter into it to help hold moisture.

Test the soil. Add sulfur if you need to make it more acid, or apply lime to raise the pH value. A pH of 5.5 to 6.5 is best.

Robert Matthews, a revered horticulturist and retired superintendent of the Norfolk Botanical Garden, offered this advice in a garden bulletin:

"Plant properly…not too deep. Leave the ball of soil at least 1 inch above its original planting, drawing the soil up to it. This will permit the plant to settle a bit without being smothered with excessive soil over its root system. Apply a 3-inch-deep mulch of pine bark, pine needles or anything you have. It doesn't make that much difference. The main thing is to retain moisture on the roots and keep weeds out."

Correct spacing also is important. Experts recommend placing bushes 6 feet to 8 feet apart.

Beginning camellia growers would do well with any of the following varieties:

• **Pink Perfection**, which looks like a pink carnation with perfect blooms. Other pinks include Magnoliaeflora, Bernice Boddy, Elegans and Lady Clare.

• **Ville de Nantes**, a dark-red variegated flower with serrated petals.

• **Blood of China**, a hardy plant that blooms late in the season with a red flower. Other reds include onekelarii and Kumasaka.

• **Herme**, a red-and-white variegated bloomer. Daikagurai also has red-and-white variegated flowers.

• **Mathotiana**, a large, flat double with purplish-red blooms. Also available as Alba, with white blooms.

Grover "Bud" Miller of Norfolk, who grew camellias for more than four decades, recommended growing the bushes under pine trees for the right amount of filtered light. Other tips from Miller include:

➤ Spray with Scalecide in early May, after flowering, and again in late October or November. Scalecide is an oil-and-sulfur mixture that thwarts red spider mites, scale and other crawling insects that pester the plant. Apply only when the temperature is above 40 degrees F, but no higher than 90 degrees. Be sure to coat the undersides of leaves.

➤ If you move a camellia, prune large plants back to 2 feet wide and 3 feet tall to make them manageable. "It will not bloom that year," Miller said, "but the second year it will be loaded with buds." Don't fertilize until the second year.

➤ To produce larger and earlier blooms, inject a few drops of gibberellic acid into a growth bud near the bloom. It's called "gibbing." Be careful not to overstimulate the plant, making it weak.

➤ During a hot, dry summer, water regularly.

➤ Fertilize in March with 10-10-10 and again in late September or October.

"People look at this and think it's a lot of work," Miller said of his 1,500 camellia bushes. "But it's not. I only fertilize and spray twice a year."

Good Bugs Can Control the Bad Ones

Rather than use pesticides, some gardeners have turned to birds and beneficial insects to help maintain flowers and vegetables.

Such creatures feed on insects that harm garden plants. A variety of insects are sold by many mail-order companies and garden centers.

The theory is that nature works in harmony with itself. The food chain consists of plants, plant eaters and eaters of plant eaters. The latter attack the "bad" bugs that eat our crops.

Birds are the best natural guardians. Unfortunately, they eat peaches, apples and tomatoes. But they also devour hundreds of insects. Invite birds to your garden and you'll have fewer pest problems.

As for other "good" bugs, the main difficulty is keeping them at home. There's no guarantee they'll stay on your property if they find better eating across the street. Many beneficial insects are tiny and require humidity to restore lost moisture and to keep them active. Create a moist, shaded environment by placing plants close together; however, you must be careful not to create disease problems by overcrowding. Misting or drip irrigation also helps.

Beneficial insects must eat, so don't release them until you have an infestation of bad insects. Between meals, you can feed them a product called Bug Chow, available by mail or at garden centers.

Good bugs to welcome to your garden include:

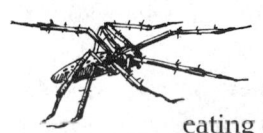

Spiders. Many folks jump at the sight of a spider, but spiders live by eating other bugs. Don't destroy them in your garden.

Ladybugs. Most gardeners are familiar with the benefits of ladybugs. They feed on

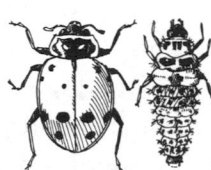

aphids, scale, mites, whiteflies and the eggs of some other insects. But their appetites are limited, so they alone cannot keep serious pest infestations at bay. If you buy ladybugs, don't release them until you see aphids. Also, don't release them early in the day. At sundown, they're more likely to stay in your garden. Be gentle when releasing them because they don't like to be agitated. Also, water the area first to provide a cool, damp, inviting home.

Soldier beetles. These beetles resemble burned-out fireflies. They feed on grasshopper eggs, cucumber beetles and caterpillars.

Ambush bugs. Mites, scale and thrips provide a gourmet diet for ambush bugs, which even attack wasps and bees.

Assassin bugs. Many a caterpillar, aphid, Mexican bean beetle, Colorado potato beetle, Japanese beetle, leafhopper or hornworm has met its fate between the bristly front legs of a hungry assassin bug. They'll even bite you if you're not careful. Sunflowers attract them.

Damsel bugs, or damsel flies. Their innocent-sounding name is misleading. They eat mites, aphids, leaf-hoppers and other insects.

Soldier bugs. These small brown bugs search stalks of broccoli for cabbage loopers and worms. They also feast on Mexican bean beetles.

Tachinid flies. These bristly little bugs resemble house flies. They are probably the most important pest-control parasite, says Rhonda Hart in her book, "Bugs, Slugs and Other Thugs – Controlling Garden Pests Organically." The flies feed on beetles, caterpillars, cutworms and army worms and Japanese and Mexican beetles.

Praying mantis. Next to the ladybug, the praying mantis is the most recognizable insect predator. Up to 5 inches long, it is fascinating to watch. It eats aphids, beetles, bugs, leaf hoppers and caterpillars. Unfortunately, it also eats butterflies, bees, wasps and other praying mantis. The larger it grows, the more likely it is to take on bigger game. It's attracted to cosmos and raspberry canes. Hart, the author, says vendors overrate the mantis as a pest control. Its lack of aggressiveness makes it less effective than many smaller insects.

Beneficial nematodes. This microscopic worm is primarily recommended for controlling grubs and cutworms in soil. They are more expensive than some controls.

Other bug-eating visitors that you should welcome in your garden include toads, salamanders and frogs.

New Roses Require Less Care

Are you one of the many who are tired of spraying roses? Surveys indicate the average homeowner either doesn't have time to spray or wants to cut back on chemical use. Are roses really worth the effort?

The toxic ingredients in common fungicidal sprays are causing concern among the public. So, over the past couple of years, rose breeders have responded to these qualms by developing plants that require little or no spraying.

The trend toward intense care of roses was brought about primarily by "medal seekers," who spray and spray and spray and concoct various potions to create prize-winning roses. The resulting flowers were beautiful but fragile, requiring continual care.

The late George Ferguson, who worked for years to create the excellent Bicentennial Rose Garden at the Norfolk Botanical Garden, labored throughout his lifetime to make rose growing simple for amateurs. But without much luck.

Most serious rosarians continued their quest for the perfect long-stemmed hybrid tea rose. They became slaves to schedules for watering, spraying, fertilizing, deadheading and pruning.

But now, for those willing to forgo the faultless fresh-cut rose, new plants are being introduced to beautify your garden. Some, such as the revolutionary 'Flower Carpet,' which made its debut in August 1995, are marketed as ground covers.

'Flower Carpet' was developed over a 25-year period by a German breeder, and it has been launched with the most expensive and expansive advertising program ever behind a rose. It has cranberry-colored, semi-double blooms and comes in a distinctive pink pot with six months' worth of fertilizer. The breeders recommend using it as a ground cover, with three plants per square yard. It sells for around $16 a plant, which adds up to $50 to cover a 3-by-3-foot area. You can buy them for less, however, by checking around.

Not wanting to sit out the rose revolution, the All America Rose Selection committee has picked 'Carefree Delight' as one of its 1996 selections. It blooms profusely with upright, arching canes and free-branching habit that spreads to 5 feet to become a ground cover. Clusters of up to 10 buds open to carmine-pink petals with a creamy white center. The foliage is dense and dark green with 2-inch single flowers. It was bred by House of Meilland in France, which also gave us the 'Peace' rose. 'Carefree Delight' will be introduced by the Conard-Pyle Co. in spring 1996. It is touted as highly resistant to mildew, black spot and rust.

Another 1996 All America rose is 'Livin' Easy,' a constant-blooming floribunda with apricot-orange flowers. It shows excellent black-spot resistance and has glossy green foliage. It comes from Weeks Roses and has medium-long stems, suitable for cutting. I test grew it in 1995, and its color is excellent, although it did not bloom as much as most floribundas. Because it was planted with my tea roses, it was sprayed along with them, about once every two weeks.

From Young's American Rose Nursery in Ohio comes a new series called the 'Towne & Country' selections, which include low-spreading ground cover and compact border roses. These roses supposedly bloom continually throughout the summer and into fall. They were bred in Denmark and do not require preventive spraying of insecticides and fungicides. They also are virtually self-cleaning, meaning petals fall off by themselves. They cost around $10 each.

This series of six starts with 'Aspen,' a ground cover that changes from deep to pastel yellow, and concludes with 'Napa Valley,' a border rose with bright-red flowers.

The best shrub rose I've ever grown is 'Sevillana,' from Meilland and Conard-Pyle. I planted two bare-root the first week of May, very late for bare-root planting of roses in this area. Each grew to 4 feet tall, and they were filled with brilliant red blooms all summer. The bushes have never been sprayed or deadheaded and were fertilized only once. It should be available in spring '95 in garden centers.

Another easy-to-care-for plant is the Butterfly rose (*Rosa chinensis* 'Mutabilis'). It has flowers of dainty, single petals that open to pale yellow, turn pink, then darken to deep rose, giving a kaleidoscope of color on a single plant. The butterfly rose is a large grower, so give it ample room to show off. It can survive with little fertilizer and little spraying.

You may have read that old-fashioned, or heritage, roses are carefree because they're purer and hardier, not to mention wonderfully fragrant. But that's not always the case. My experience has been that some heritage roses must be sprayed just as often as the fussy hybrids, especially to prevent mildew.

Planting and care

Whatever type of rose you choose to grow, your options are wide open. Whether you plant in fall or spring is a personal decision. I used to believe that fall planting was best, but in recent years, I've lost many that were started in fall. Now I plant only in spring.

Roses require excellent drainage and plenty of sunshine, at least five hours a day. If drainage is in doubt, raise the bed 6 to 8 inches. They also don't like wind, so try to locate them near a windbreak such as a fence, hedge or wall, but don't crowd them.

Dig a generous hole, about 2 feet wide and almost as deep. Add about one-third to one-half humus material to good garden soil. This can be peat, compost or well-rotted manure. Roses like a slightly acid soil with a pH of 6.5 to 7, so have the soil tested if necessary and fertilize accordingly.

When planting, it helps to create a mound of soil inside the planting hole over which you can spread the roots so they won't be mashed. The bud union of the rose should be level with the top of the bed.

Buy only the finest plants available. They are a bargain in the long run. Do not allow plants to dry out before planting. Group roses in one area of the landscape, and make the bed no more than two rows wide for ease of maintenance and picking. Avoid using a commercial fertilizer until new growth appears. Prune new bushes back, leaving one-third to one-half of the top and remove all damaged roots before planting.

Immediately after you open the package, bare-root roses should be soaked in a bucket of water spiked with a root stimulator. A small amount of bleach added to the water helps kill any disease organisms. You can soak it for up to a day. Plant it quickly after removal.

Here are more tips on rose care from the Garden Club of Virginia Rose Test Committee:

➤ Don't grow weak, "chemically dependent" varieties.

➤ Select hardy, disease-resistant varieties.

➤ Even though old-fashioned roses get black spot and other diseases, they don't die from them. Don't rush to spray them.

➤ Don't try to grow roses in shade.

➤ Don't water late in the day, which encourages fungal growth.

➤ Don't grow them close together. Lack of air circulation and evening dampness – without relief from warm morning sun to dry them – is a recipe for disaster.

➤ Keep plants healthy by good housekeeping. Weed and clean beds and feed roses well and regularly. Strong plants are more disease resistant.

➤ Water deeply. A soaker hose is ideal. Do not water every day; instead, once or twice a week is enough.

➤ Feed the birds all year long. They help keep insect populations in check.

➤ Try organic products instead of chemical sprays.

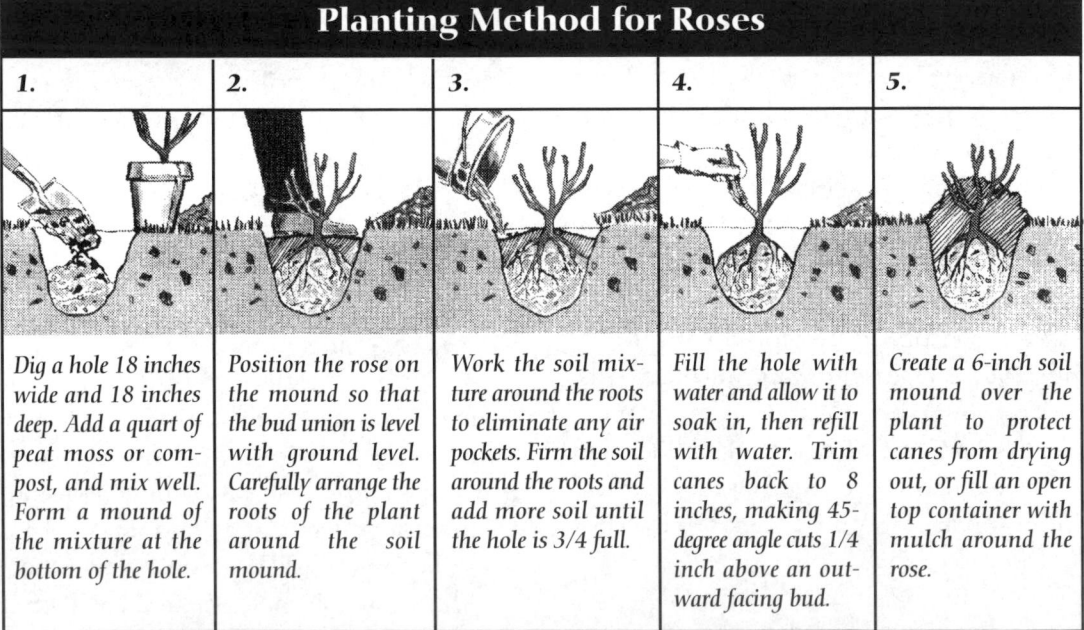

Planting Method for Roses

1.	2.	3.	4.	5.
Dig a hole 18 inches wide and 18 inches deep. Add a quart of peat moss or compost, and mix well. Form a mound of the mixture at the bottom of the hole.	Position the rose on the mound so that the bud union is level with ground level. Carefully arrange the roots of the plant around the soil mound.	Work the soil mixture around the roots to eliminate any air pockets. Firm the soil around the roots and add more soil until the hole is 3/4 full.	Fill the hole with water and allow it to soak in, then refill with water. Trim canes back to 8 inches, making 45-degree angle cuts 1/4 inch above an outward facing bud.	Create a 6-inch soil mound over the plant to protect canes from drying out, or fill an open top container with mulch around the rose.

Illustrations reprinted with permission by All-America Rose Selections, Inc.

Gardening Reminders for February

Early month

Lawn care

➤ The best advice this time of year is to stay off your lawn if it's frozen because you will damage grass and leave tracks in the lawn. You can put out seed now if needed. Make sure there are no leaves covering and choking out the grass.

➤ Control wild onions and garlic in lawns early by mowing them short three times or more to kill them. Or, spray with a glyphosate (Roundup or Kleenup). Be careful not to let it touch healthy grass. It may take two sprayings about 10 days apart to be effective.

Maintenance

➤ Shear liriope before new growth begins. Use a lawn mower at its highest setting if you have numerous plants. Don't cut too deep, or you'll harm young shoots in the crown.

➤ Cut down weak or problem trees around your home. Better yet, hire professionals for the job. The task is easier now when there are no leaves on the trees. Stack the logs to use in your fireplace.

Miscellaneous

➤ Don't use salt to melt ice on walkways bordered by plants because the salt will burn plants. Instead, try sand. Some gardeners use granular or pelleted fertilizer, which feeds plants as it soaks into the ground.

➤ Don't be surprised if your camellias drop buds after a cold spell. If they lose buds for three or four years in a row, consider moving the bushes to a semishaded spot, where they will be protected from cold winds and the sun and wind won't burn their leaves.

➤ If we get extremely cold weather for several days, accompanied by strong wintry winds, expect plant problems. Snow isn't harmful because it acts as an insulator. But a quick, severe drop in temperatures, accompanied by high winds, could spell disaster for plants that are budded or blooming. Mulch thoroughly, and keep plants well-watered. Spraying broadleaf plants with an anti-transpirant (Wilt-Pruf) would be good insurance. Leaves dry out in windy weather, and the roots can't replenish moisture quickly enough. It's usually loss of water that kills plants during cold snaps. Buds can be picked and brought inside to bloom if the forecast is for severe weather.

Pest control

➤ It made me ill when I discovered that rabbits had pruned the leaves off my small azaleas. The ones I propagated myself! Then I looked at the Indian hawthorn (*Rhaphiolepis umbellata*) and really got sick. Immediately I stirred up this concoction the University of Maryland recommends for discouraging rabbits from eating evergreens: 1 tablespoon Tabasco or Louisiana Hot Sauce in 1 gallon water. Add 4 tablespoons Wilt-Pruf to make it stick to the leaves all winter. Spray all parts of the plant susceptible to injury. Do this when temperatures are above 40 degrees. This spray won't bring back foliage, but it should prevent further snacking.

Planting

➤ If you like to grow your plants from seed, it's time to get them started. Check the back of the package for the time required, usually four to six weeks before they're large enough to set in the garden.

House plants

➤ Wash the dust and grime off your house plants so they can breathe. Put them in the shower where they can drain without too much mess.

➤ If you can raise the humidity in your home, your plants will benefit. Group plants together on a table or in a corner. Misting is only a temporary fix. The best method is to place a shallow, water–tight tray filled with a few inches of crushed stone or sand under your pots. The stone or sand should be kept moist, but don't allow the plants to sit directly in water. Also, pans of water placed on radiators will increase the room's humidity as the water evaporates.

Midmonth

Disease control

➤ Pull off browned, spoiled and partially opened blooms from your camellias. Don't let them collect under the plant, where they could spread disease.

Fertilize

➤ Pansies planted last fall could use some water–soluble fertilizer now.

➤ If a warm January forced many plants, especially shrubs and roses, ahead of their normal growth schedule, hold off fertilizing until March. A late freeze could kill them.

➤ You can fertilize trees most any time of the year when the soil is soft. But remember that 99 percent of a tree's roots are in the top 3 feet of soil, so apply fertilizer on the surface or use spikes instead of drilling holes that may damage roots. In some soil, the important, fine absorbing roots are concentrated in the upper 4 to 8 inches. Root spread is up to seven times the width of the drip line (edge of branches).

House plants

Valentines Day roses will stay fresh for about a week if you keep the vase filled with fresh water. Some folks add Sprite or 7–Up to the water as a preservative. If they're arranged in floral foam, which tends to inhibit water intake, why not transfer them to a vase where they can spread out naturally? Trim off about an inch of the stems under water as soon as you get them home. Place the vase in a cool spot, away from direct sunlight or radiators. If they wilt, place the bouquet – stems and all – in a long, deep pan (a bathtub will do) and cover them with water until they liven up, from five to 30 minutes. Then recut stems under water before returning them to the vase.

Miscellaneous

➤ If you buy plants by mail, use only reputable, long–established companies. Avoid splashy ads and extravagant claims.

➤ If rabbits bother your apple trees, prune the trees early and leave limbs on the ground for the little varmints. Maybe they'll get so full they won't bother the tree. In orchards, trunks are wrapped for protection.

Planting

➤ As long as the soil is soft and wet, it's ideal for early planting of shrubs and trees or transplanting others.

Pruning

➤ Hold off pruning roses and other shrubs if they're growing ahead of schedule because of a warm winter. A freeze could cause severe dieback after pruning. If you have energy to burn, prune your trees.

➤ Hydrangeas can be pruned anytime during the next few weeks if you didn't do it last fall. But be careful: The large buds you see on stalks will produce flowers and foliage this summer. These plants must have last year's growth to bloom. The deeper you prune, the fewer blooms you'll have. Some gardeners prune after hydrangeas finish blooming in late summer.

Late month
Disease control

➤ Apply dormant oil spray, also called horticultural oil. Many homeowners have written about black smudge on foliage of gardenias and camellias. It's "sooty mold," which results from a scale or aphid infestation. Inspect holly, osmanthus (especially vulnerable), euonymus, camellias, roses and dogwood trees in particular. The spray smothers scale and helps clean the leaves.

House plants

➤ Put house plants outside on warm days to condition them for a summer vacation outdoors. Be sure to bring them in on cold days and nights so they don't suffer shock.

Lawn care

➤ Avoid raking grassy areas or you'll pull the grass out by its roots. Your lawn is moist and tender this time of year.

Maintenance

➤ Walk your property and pick up all the sticks, branches and stones that storms have scattered.

Miscellaneous

➤ Don't feed your outdoor pond fish yet, even though they surface, acting hungry, on warm days. Their metabolism is still slow, and feeding could harm them, according to experts at East–West Specialties in Norfolk. They don't need anything to eat until March or April, and then only greens or wheat germ.

➤ To soften and heal dry, cracked, peeling hands, I use Bag Balm. It's messy but the very best. Cover your hands with it at night and wear rubber gloves to seal in moisture while you sleep.

Planting

➤ If you grow your own peppers, it's time to start seed indoors. Don't plant them outdoors before May 1.

Pruning

➤ Late February to early March, when trees are dormant and haven't thrown out new leaves is ideal. Use hand–held pruners or long–handled loppers for branches up to 1 inch in diameter. Beyond that, use a saw. Keep the flat side of the shears facing the trunk of the tree for the closest cut. Some people dip their shears in bleach to prevent the spread of disease; however, bleach is highly corrosive to metal. Instead, try Lysol, which is just as effective.

M A R C H

Love at First Bloom: Azaleas

They seem so perfect, so demure. Like Southern belles, blooming azaleas always look presentable and can nearly unglue the Confederacy at first blush.

It must be good breeding. Azaleas were conceived in the Orient centuries ago and sent to Europe, where they became cultured. Some dallied in England, France and Belgium before arriving on American plantations in the mid–1800s.

The first import graced Middleton Place Plantation, an 18th century estate near Charleston, S.C., in 1846, says public relations director Donna Owens. "We don't have any documentation to prove that though," Owens concedes, "because of the burning of the house in 1865."

But her report does suggest that some azaleas died during the War Between the States, an honor that ensures acceptance at any Southern country club for these members of the *Rhododendron* family.

The first rule of courtship with these shallow-rooted plants is to never underestimate them. Take a stroll on any Norfolk Botanical Garden path in spring, and before you can say

"Azalea Festival," you're swooning.

Robert Matthews, retired superintendent and granddaddy of 250,000 bushes planted at the Garden since 1936, once attested to their mass appeal. You must treat them right, urged Matthews. Azaleas prefer good soil, slightly acid. Beds should be fluffed with compost.

Proper drainage is a must. Raise their beds if you have to. But take care not to suffocate them in a deep hole, where they will pout and wither. It is better to set plants on the ground and build topsoil and compost around their roots for security. Tuck them in with pine-needle or bark mulch to help avert weeds and retain moisture. Water regularly so they may glow, Southern-style.

Not one of hearty appetite, the azalea should be fed lightly each spring with 10-10-10 or a special azalea fertilizer. Doting admirers prefer feeding mature plants small amounts three times a year, in March, May and October. Prune only after blooming, but never demean the genus by shaping bushes into gumdrops or sugar cubes. Reach down into the center of the plant and remove a few stems entirely.

And remember, well-bred azaleas avoid the midday sun. Plant them under pine or oak trees where their blooms will linger longer.

In a mild winter, eager bushes will bloom early. While they are in full dress, select the ones that suit your fancy.

Plant young azaleas immediately, but do not fertilize them yet; instead, treat them to a root stimulator that contains vitamin B1 and a small amount of plant food. To make a big splash, arrange one color in a mass. The clashing of purple, orange and red is best avoided lest your neighbors be shocked.

When it comes to popularity, the early blooming pink Coral Bells, Hershey's Red and White Snow are winners. But why limit yourself to just a few weeks of spring fever? An abundance of varieties will keep you in the pink from February through September.

Local favorites

Azaleas are everywhere, and everyone has favorites. The following four Hampton Roads azalea authorities were asked to name their top picks according to blooming season: Robert Matthews, retired superintendent of the Norfolk Botanical Garden; Peter Frederick, Botanical Garden director; Jo Anne Gordon, City of Norfolk horticulturist; and R.M. "Rusty" Averett, the azalea guru of Virginia Beach.

In describing azalea blooms, "hose-in-hose" means two rows of petals, or a bloom within a bloom. Unless noted, plant size is a normal 2 to 3 feet tall and just as wide at maturity.

Early bloomers

Matthews recommends Vitatta fortunei, which is a tall plant that can bloom as early as February with full bloom a month later. It's solid purple, to white, with many mixed patterns. Others are: Coral Bells, one of the Kurume hybrids; Southern Indica hybrids; and George Lindley Taber, which he suggested should be planted with pur-

ple Formosa for an outstanding show of color. Another favorite is Salmon Beauty, true to its name. He said to plant it with Poukanense, a native of Korea that loves sun or shade, is cold hardy and has pale-lavender blooms.

Frederick says Hinode Giri and Coral Bells are favorites of his and of visitors to the Botanical Garden.

Averett's favorites: Festive, a white pink-striped bloom that is fairly fragrant; Amoena, a tiny deep-purple hose-in-hose bloom; Koromo Shikibu, with long, graceful petals of delicate pink; and canescens, a deciduous pink azalea, native to Tidewater, that "puts out tiny leaves and then literally bursts forth with early blossoms." Averett and Gordon both also recommend Vitatta fortunei.

Gordon adds these: Hershey's Red; Hinode Giri with purple-red flowers; Hino-Crimson; White Snow, planted in masses; Delaware Valley, a large white spreading plant; Coral Bells; Pink Pearl; Pukanense, a pale lavender; and Flame.

Midseason bloomers

Averett recommended these: Ben Morrison, a variegated red-and-pink with white margins; Apple Blossom, a semidwarf, pink-and-white variegated bloom; Pink Ice, a delicate pink with tiny purple stripes here and there; Louise J. Bobbink, a red-purple, frilly blossom with a lighter throat; Redoing, a large, strong-red hose-in-hose ruffled blossom, which often is sold in garden centers as Red Ruffles or Red Bird; and Red Slippers, with a deep, vivid red bloom.

Other favorites of Averett that are slightly later to bloom are: Marian Lee, a beautiful red with white center; Albert-Elizabeth, with a red-and-white variegated, frilly blossom; Fawn, a purplish-pink with white center; Margaret Douglas, a large bloom with a light-pink center and deeper pink margin; and Kehrs White Rosebud, a full double white with a green throat.

Matthews suggested two more: Redoing, a hardy Belgian variety with 3-inch hose-in-hose, orange-red blossoms; and Martha Hitchcock, white with deep-lavender margins. "Plant it with Glacier, a white with chartreuse throat, for a breathtaking display," he urged.

Gordon named the following: Sunglow; Glacier, a large plant with deep-green foliage and large white blooms tinged with green; Rosebud, with deep-purplish-pink double flowers; George Lindley Taber; Formosa; Ben Morrison; and Martha Hitchcock. Frederick listed Formosa as his pick but said garden visitors prefer Sunglow, George Lindley Taber and Formosa.

Late bloomers

Matthews preferred all the Satsuki series, which bloom into June. Blooms are large, but plants are small, so they can be used in many locations. His next choice was Pink Gumpo, a compact, low-growing variety that has 3-inch frilly flowers and small leaves. "Rabbits love them," he warned, "so prepare for that problem."

Gordon named several: Macrantha Red; Gumpo White; Gumpo Pink; Lady Robin Eikan, with large yellow-pink blooms; and Meicho, with a large, flat, white blossom, red stripes and pink sectors. Frederick also listed Macrantha Red and Gumpo White, not only as his favorites, but also best loved by visitors.

Averett also is a Gumpo admirer. He described them as "tiny dwarf plants with large, single, frilled blossoms in colors of white, pink and rose." He also liked Meicho.

Last but not least

"In June and July," Gordon said, "the deciduous Exbury and Mollis hybrid azaleas become ablaze with brilliant oranges and yellows and have a place in most gardens."

Matthews suggested that gardeners not overlook prunifolia, a deciduous azalea, native to Georgia. It blooms from July to September with flowers of orange and red. It should be planted at the edge of an area shaded from the morning sun.

With this expert advice, you can't go wrong in planting azaleas in your garden. Every spring you'll be reminded of their worth.

Looking Ahead to Late Summer

Too often, we concentrate only on spring color. By late summer, most gardens seem drab in Southeastern Virginia and Northeastern North Carolina. Everyone's tired of the beach, crowds and heat, often accompanied by a lack of rain.

But there is a cure for this headache: Plant some late-summer flowering trees and shrubs now. You'll feel refreshed despite the soaring temperatures.

Following is a list of favorites that have similar growing requirements. The following choices are all sun-loving and need well-drained soil. They also can become weedy with age and are best when cut back in very early spring because all bloom on new growth.

Buddleia, or **Butterfly Bush**: This long-blooming tall shrub features flowers of white, blue or purple in arching spikes that attract butterflies. They are best grown in a mass or a perennial border. Give them plenty of room. A dwarf cultivar, Nanho Purple, is being marketed by Monrovia Nurseries and is available locally.

Caryopteris, or **Bluebeard**: This neat-looking 3- to 4-foot-tall, mounded shrub is much like Buddleia. But it is covered with blue flowers all summer. It maintains its neat form without summer pruning. Flowers are long-lasting when cut and provide an excellent contrast to its blue-gray fragrant foliage. It is excellent for foundations or perennial borders but does best in full sun.

Vitex, or **Chaste Tree:** Although it can become very tall and ungainly unless cut back hard in spring, Vitex will reward you with spikes of lavender flowers in midsummer. It will look very dead until late April but then will throw out new growth. One in my garden is used regularly with other flowers for summer bouquets. It is also available with blue or white blooms.

Abelia: This common shrub in our area often becomes ratty-looking with age. Several new cultivars merit consideration and are much better than the variety usually grown.

Prostrate is a dwarf, blooming in July with small, white, fragrant blossoms. Edward Goucher is a pink-flowering variety that gets about 4 feet tall.

Clethra alnifolia, or **Summer Sweet**: This fragrant summer-flowering shrub thrives in sun or shade, dry or wet soil, and even tolerates sand, making it ideal for beach gardens. Flowers are white or pink. It throws up suckers from its roots, which can become a problem. Bees love its flowers.

Sophora japonica: A member of the pea family, this tree requires lots of room because it has a tremendous spread and grows 75 feet tall. It has white blooms in July that bees adore, but it can be messy. After flowering, the petals drop, and the green pods come down in the fall. But it does cast a beautiful light shade and is tolerant of dry soils and air pollution. Because of its messy habits, however, it should be avoided except in very large lawn areas.

Soil Enrichment

Call it "dirt" if you want. But the only resemblance between the soil in your garden and what most people call dirt should be purely semantic.

"Soil" is your garden's staff of life. Whether you buy commercially prepared potting soil or mix it yourself, it is the primary source of nourishment that plants need. The more we observe how the best gardeners work, the surer we become that the most essential step is soil preparation.

The problem is that most of us are in a hurry and never enrich the soil as well as we should. Then we blame ensuing problems on the seed or plant, rather than ourselves.

Eventually, most gardeners should do a test to determine their soil's acidity or alkalinity (pH scale) and the amount of nitrogen, phosphorus, potassium and other nutrients present.

Simply buy one of the many kits available through garden centers, or have the soil professionally tested. A few local garden centers offer the service, which costs around $10. State universities also test soil, usually for a similar fee.

Garden mums, asters and most other perennials grow best in slightly acidic soil (pH 5.5 to 6.5). On a scale of 1 to 10, a low pH indicates that soil is too acidic. Six to 7 is close to neutral.

Improper watering – too much or not enough – kills more plants than anything else. Standing water also can be a problem.

Drainage can be as important as watering. Keep track of rainfall by measuring water, collected in coffee cans or other containers. Most outdoor plants need a minimum of 1 inch of water a week. Generally, one good soaking is best. With several light waterings, much of the moisture is likely to evaporate.

Clay increases the water–and nutrient–holding capacity of sandy soil, while sand helps lighten heavy clay. As a rule, medium loam contains 10 percent to 20 percent clay. Most plants grow best in medium to slightly sandy loam.

The best time to prepare soil is before planting: in summer for fall planting, and in fall for spring planting. Add compost, peat or other organic matter.

In preparing your garden, first remove foreign matter such as rocks, logs, pieces of metal or other debris that interferes with tillage and plant growth. Next, add lots of organic matter, such as leaves (preferably chopped up), peat moss, old sawdust, wood chips, bark, grass clippings, composted material or animal manure.

Soils that have been improved for years with regular additions of compost will not crust when formed into seedbeds. Unimproved clay or silt soils will run together like paste when watered and will dry hard as a brick. Some seeds may sprout, but the mortality is often severe. Organic materials will help improve water intake and reduce soil crusting and erosion.

Fertilize as needed, and keep your soil moist, but don't overwater. And don't walk in your garden when the soil is wet, or you'll compact the soil and create clods that won't break up before fall.

Spring Basics for Lawns

If you have a fescue lawn, as do most homeowners in this area, there's little maintenance in spring. Your lawn probably just needs some cleanup. A light raking or mowing with the blade set high, using a grass catcher, will pick up leaves and other debris.

By early April, your fescue should be fertilized once lightly with a high–nitrogen fertilizer, such as 25-5-10. Zoysia, St. Augustine and Bermuda need to be fertilized every month through August.

If you haven't limed your lawn in the past three years, it probably needs it. Use 50 pounds per 1,000 square feet. Buy granulated lime so you don't get covered with dust. If you're not sure what you need, get a soil test.

When it comes time to mow, cut fescue at 2 to 2-1/2 inches; while Bermuda, St. Augustine and Zoysia should be mowed at 1/2 to 1 inch, except in play areas where longer grass holds up better. If you have bare spots, reseed them, or, in the case of warm–season grasses, plant plugs or sprigs. The thicker you plant, the narrower the blade will be, which is desirable.

If you haven't aerated your lawn, do that early. It helps seed get started, aids penetration of fertilizer and water and helps grass roots breathe.

If you're seeding a new lawn, the recommended rate is 5 pounds of fescue per 1,000 square feet. The tag on the grass seed should guarantee 85 percent germination or better. Also, check for noxious weed content. You don't want to plant weeds in your lawn.

When weeds show up, and they will, spray with a weed killer but avoid fragile shrubs and the root area under trees or you will kill them too. Warm–season grasses such as St.

Augustine and zoysia are too sensitive for most weed killers, so make sure you read the warnings. Usable products recommended by Louisiana State University include Green Light Wipe-out, K Mart Broadleaf Weed Killer for Southern Grasses, Spectrum 33 Plus, Trimec, Fertilome Weed Out and Ortho Weed-B-Gon for Southern Lawns II.

If crabgrass is a problem, a preventer product should be applied when the forsythia is in bloom. You cannot, however, use crabgrass preventer and apply seed at the same time. There usually is a six-week waiting period, so you'll have to decide which is most needed.

For heavy traffic areas, use wear-resistant grass. Species and cultivars can make a big difference in how lawns stand up to heavy use. (See table below.) This choice is impor-tant if children or pets are playing on the lawn.

If you have established Bermuda grass or tall fescue in a play area, mow higher to help it survive. Fertilize regularly, but don't overdo it. Too much nitrogen reduces wear tolerance. Adding potash, up to 8 pounds per 1,000 square feet per year (even if your soil already is high in potassium), can improve wear tolerance. If your soil is sandy, add potassium in small doses throughout the growing season to minimize losses from leaching. A little bit of thatch can actually aid wear tolerance by providing a cushion for the grass, but too much is detrimental.

Most important, make sure your mower blade is sharp so you don't tear up the grass.

HOW GRASSES STAND UP		
Type of Grasses	*Wear Tolerance*	*Compaction Tolerance*
Bermuda	very high	very high to medium
St. Augustine	very high	high to medium
Zoysia	very high	high to medium
Fescue	very high to high	medium
Annual bluegrass	very low	high
Kentucky bluegrass	medium	high to medium
Annual rye grass	low	medium

New Grass Plants Need Water

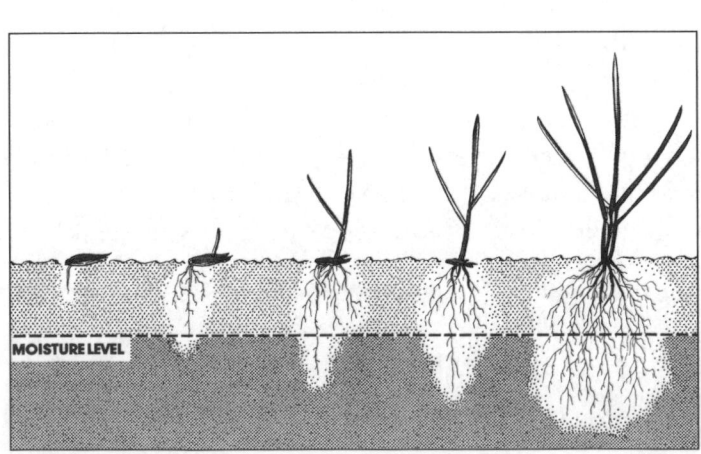

MOISTURE LEVEL

Drawing courtesy of O.M. Scott & Sons

Mulch Now to Protect Plants

March and April are ideal months to mulch shrubs and trees to help them through the hot, dry summer ahead. Heat often results in the death of newly planted trees and shrubs, even though homeowners believe they've watered properly during dry spells. Mulch helps plants retain moisture.

Three inches of mulch is the recommended depth. Bark mulch provides a material that slowly decomposes, thus adding to the organic content of the soil. Hardwood bark, usually more expensive, offers no advantages over pine bark. Bark allows proper penetration of rain, while also retaining sufficient cohesion so that erosion is significantly reduced. It also has low heat-conducting characteristics, so it results in lower soil temperatures, which enhances root growth. Mulch also reduces air temperatures above the plant.

Although stone can be used as a decorative mulch, it does not cool the soil or air like an organic or bark mulch. This is especially important around new plantings.

Other effective mulches are pine straw, ground-up leaves and compost. Peat moss does not make a good mulch and should be avoided.

All these mulches can be blown away by power tools (mowers, edgers, blowers), so keep that in mind.

Many area homeowners have the bad habit of adding new mulch every spring. Sometimes it can get as deep as 6 to 8 inches. This can be harmful to the plant. Do not add bark each spring, but instead rake and renew it. Replace only as needed to keep it 3 inches deep. In that way, it provides weed and temperature control all summer.

Why Bulbs Don't Bloom the Second Year

All bulbs demand a well-drained soil and will grow in full sun to part shade, say Louisiana State University specialists. There are several reasons why they fail to flower the second year after planting. Among them are: 1) Varieties not adapted to our climate, particularly tulips, Dutch hyacinths and some daffodils. 2) Foliage removed before it turns brown. 3) Disease and insect damage. 4) Planting in too much shade, and 5) Planting in poorly drained soil.

Daffodils and Narcissus that can be depended upon to bloom year after year in Southeastern Virginia and Northeastern North Carolina are:

Daffodils: Fortune (yellow-orange cup), Helios (yellow-orange edged cup), Brooksville (white-yellow cup), Geranium (white-orange cup), Ice Follies (white-yellow cup, Dick Wellband (white-yellow cup), Spring Glory (white-yellow cup), Mount Hood (pale cream), Carlton (yellow), February Gold (yellow), Peeping Tom (yellow) and Silver Chimes (white).

Narcissus: Thalia (white), Trevithian (yellow), Paper White (white), Pearl (white), Golden Sceptre (yellow jonquil).

Gardening Reminders for March

Early month

Fertilize

➤ Fertilize Burford Hollies if the foliage looks yellow. Virginia Tech experts say the berries suck protein out of the leaves, causing them to yellow. There's nothing a homeowner should do except feed the plant in early spring. Use half a cup of good shrub fertilizer per foot of height. Often after a heavy set of berries, the plant will not set berries for two years. Another possible problem may be defoliation if we have an early drought. So keep the holly sufficiently watered.

➤ Feed camellias with one cup of 10-10-10 fertilizer per square yard of surface area around the plant. If the plant has scale, spray with an oil spray before new growth begins. Cygon also can be used to control scale and should be used when new spring leaves are just fully expanded. Apply again in a month.

House plants

➤ Buy Easter lilies with lots of buds but only one flower open so they'll last longer. As each flower opens, reach down into the tube and pull out the yellow anthers before they disperse millions of golden pollen grains. Unfertilized flowers last longer. Place in indirect light. Keep the soil moist, and after it finishes blooming, plant it in a sunny spot in your garden where it will bloom again next year.

➤ Contrary to old advice, African violets can be watered from the top or bottom. Newly potted plants are better top-watered, which controls the amount of water the soil gets. If you water from the top, it washes nutrients to the bottom. If you alternate and water from the bottom, it drives nutrients upward. Watering on top washes nutrients back down. Alternating every few days seems to work best. Be careful not to water the foliage when watering from the top. And remember, too little water is always better than too much.

➤ Indoor foliage will use more water as our light intensity increases. Regardless of species, plants receiving more light need more water.

Lawn care

➤ If you had crabgrass problems in your lawn last year, apply a pre-emergent herbicide labeled for crabgrass control at the same time the forsythia bush blooms.

➤ Get rid of chickweed, wild onions and garlic in your lawn. Dig them up, making sure to get the bulb with a trowel or use recommended herbicides such as Roundup, Finale or Spectracide Grass and Weed Killer.

➤ There appears to be a connection between early spring fertilization and development of fusarium blight and brown patch in susceptible varieties of grass. So you may need to hold off fertilizing home lawns until May or even early June. Stronger root systems develop if nitrogen application is delayed. Plan to apply nitrogen in fall, rather than spring.

Maintenance

➤ Fertilize daffodils, crocus, tulips and hyacinths, just as their foliage appears above ground. Use 8-8-8, 10-10-10, or a special bulb fertilizer. Scatter it around the plant, but avoid spilling it on leaves because they will burn. If that happens, spray it off with water at once. They need no other fertilization until fall.

Miscellaneous

➤ Don't fret if a cold snap or snow beat down your daffodils and crocuses. Healthy spring-flowering bulbs will withstand extreme cold, snow or early warm spells. Bulbs don't need extra protection, additional mulch or covers. Snow seldom hurts any plant. It's really an insulator. What kills plants is severe cold accompanied by high winds, which robs them of moisture.

➤ Harbingers of spring are blooming throughout our area this month. You'll see mostly Bradford pear (white), flowering plum (pink), forsythia (yellow) and quince (white, orange and pink).

Planting

➤ Plant azaleas and rhododendrons during the cool season between fall and spring. These plants love acid soil and will grow in full sun or moderate shade. An ideal spot is under tall pines. Generally, they do best on the north or east side of your home, where they will be protected from hot afternoon sun. Avoid planting in clay soil. Work in large quantities of peat moss, leaf mold or other organic matter before planting. After planting, mulch with 3 to 4 inches of pine needles or pine bark.

➤ Plant cool-weather vegetable crops early in the month. Include snow peas, garden peas, Sugar Snap peas, carrots, turnips, lettuce, spinach, Swiss chard, radishes, beets and onion sets. Plant seed potatoes for early potatoes and transplant seedlings of cabbage, cauliflower, Brussels sprouts, broccoli and kohlrabi. But don't tramp around on the garden if it's mucky. You'll compact the soil and make it even more difficult for plants to flourish.

➤ Plant asparagus, Jerusalem artichokes and horseradish off to one side of the garden so they won't be in the way when you work up the rest of the garden for annual crops.

➤ The National Garden Bureau says the last killing frost in Norfolk is March 18, but the National Weather Service says March 23 is a more realistic date. The key is soil temperature, and that will vary year to year, depending on the season. If you prepare your seed indoors four to six weeks before the last killing frost date, you can set your transplants outside in a warm spot in the daytime. Bring them in at night until ready to go into the garden. That should prevent leggy plants. Most plants, except vegetable cole crops, are not going to do anything in a garden but sit and sulk until the soil warms up. The best gardening is

done by experience, rather than preset rules.

➤ It's time to plant bare-root roses, which most experts prefer because they have more roots than those pruned to fit into boxes or bags. You should plant roses on a pyramid of soil you create in the planting hole. Protecting them from the drying wind and sun is always a challenge. The days between the time you plant and when roses leaf out and establish themselves are critical. Spraying plants with an anti-transpirant can help. You can use a large, black plastic planter with the bottom cut out as a shelter from the wind. Put the pot around the rose after it is planted and fill the pot with pine straw, which allows sufficient sun for the rose.

Pruning

➤ Prune the dead tops off liriope with a lawn mower set high or pruning shears. Be careful not to mow too closely and damage the crown, where new growth is emerging.

Midmonth

Fertilize

➤ Fertilize trees now, while the ground is soft and moist. Trees should be fertilized annually: in fall for deciduous varieties after leaves drop and in late spring for evergreens.

➤ Feed perennial flowers with a garden or flower fertilizer or 8-8-8.

Maintenance

➤ Divide cannas, coreopsis, phlox, Shasta daisies and chrysanthemums before they begin to grow. Cannas are invasive, so dig them up and replant in another area or give them to a friend.

➤ Pinch spent flowers off pansies to help produce more blooms. They'll last until midsummer heat makes them wilt.

➤ Have your garden soil tested and follow recommendations on lime and plant nutrients.

➤ Every spring, most sidewalks need a good cleaning, especially if large trees overhang them. Pour straight laundry bleach on the sidewalk and leave it for three days without rain. You will be amazed at the difference.

➤ This is the month to graft camellias, but it can be tricky. First step is to get a good book and learn how. Many from the Brooklyn Botanic Garden are available at the Norfolk Botanical Garden. Or, get a book on grafting or plant propagation from your garden center or library. Camellias are in bloom now. Every yard should have at least three: a red, a white and a pink. One that never fails is R.L. Wheeler, featuring huge rose–pink blossoms.

Pest control

➤ Camellias, hollies and other evergreen shrubs should be sprayed now if they have scale. Use dormant, or horticultural oil when the temperature is above 45 F. Don't spray when the plant suffers from lack of moisture.

➤ A recipe for an organic spray for insects and diseases on indoor and outdoor plants comes from horticulturists Doc and Katy Abraham in Nursery Business magazine: "One cup Listerine mouthwash, 1 cup flea and tick shampoo with pyrethrum (for dogs) and 1 cup chewing tobacco. Pour 1 quart boiling water over four fingers of chewing tobacco. Let stand until cool, and use 1 cup of the tobacco "tea" in the above mixture. Pour 3 cups of the mixture into a 20–gallon hose–end sprayer, add warm water and fill the sprayer. Then spray your plants and bushes. Tobacco "tea" is toxic to humans and fish, so keep it away from children."

Planting

➤ Remember that tomatoes and peppers require magnesium at blossom time. If you had blossom end rot last season, you should have applied lime last fall in the area you planned to grow them this year. As an alternative, use any Tomato Blossom End Rot Spray. Or, spray the plants twice, 10 days apart, with a solution of 1 teaspoon Epsom salts in 1 quart warm water. Another method is to use 1 tablespoon Epsom salts in 1 gallon water, applied to the soil around each tomato or pepper plant. Roses will grow better if given the same

treatment each spring and fall.

➤ It's the season for transplanting and pruning trees and shrubs. The weather is ideal for giving them a good start. Prune trees before leaves hide what you're trying to accomplish.

➤ As soon as the soil is dry enough to work, get flower and vegetable gardens ready for planting. (If you squeeze a handful of soil and it crumbles when you release it, it's dry enough.) Spade or till in lime, if needed, plus fertilizer and organic matter.

➤ When danger of frost has passed, sow seeds of sweet alyssum, flowering tobacco, portulaca, petunia, bachelor's button, Browallia, calendula, California poppy, cosmos, and snapdragons. Cover the seeds lightly, if at all. If nights turn cold, protect plants with a blanket.

➤ Plant geraniums mid– to late month. Most local soils need large amounts of organic matter to make them suitable for geraniums. Leaf mold, compost and peat moss are good sources. While enriching the soil, mix in 2 to 4 pounds of 8–8–8 fertilizer for each 100 square feet of bed. Slow–release fertilizers are helpful during the growing season. Geraniums do best when potbound. They will grow in shade but have fewer flowers. Allow soil to dry out between waterings. Avoid splashing leaves because it encourages disease.

➤ North Carolina State University says that before planting raspberries, you should prepare the soil as you would when planting any vegetable. Space plants 4 feet apart, keeping rows 5 feet apart. Early spring is the best time to plant. When growth begins, fertilize with 8–8–8 or 10–10–10 and again in late summer or early fall. Mulching is recommended to prevent weeds and grass. In late winter or early spring, prune out the old canes that have fruited. They die anyway and can be a home for disease if not removed. Thin out unhealthy plants so there is a healthy cane every 10 inches. To ensure top–quality berries, harvest every day when they begin to ripen.

➤ Early–bird gardeners can start putting tomatoes in the ground, if they use wind and cold protection. Tomato plants should be spaced 18 to 24 inches apart. If they don't get enough sun, few blossoms will form and they may drop off before setting fruit. Vegetable specialists at Louisiana State University recommend pouring one cupful of a starter solution into the holes when you are transplanting tomatoes. Make your own by mixing one–half cup of 8-8-8 fertilizer in2-1/2 gallons of warm water. Commercial soluble fertilizers also are available. This feeding will encourage establishment of a strong root system and faster growth.

Pruning

➤ It's rose-pruning time. You will need a good set of hand shears, a sharp pruning saw (for large bushes), a pair of long-handled loppers, pruning paint, sealing wax or white glue, plus a pair of heavy leather gloves. Loppers should be used to cut large canes, but use shears for smaller branches. Cover all cuts and ends of canes with the pruning paint, white glue or sealing wax. Cut back top growth to 14 inches to 16 inches above ground. Retain four to six healthy canes arising from the graft or bud union. Remove all dead, diseased and injured twigs and branches. Also, cut out all thin, spindly growth frequently found at the base of old established bushes.

For climbing roses only, any cane more than 2 years old should be removed or cut back severely. This can be done after blooming, if you prefer.

After pruning, fertilize each bush with a cup of rose food scattered around each plant, then mulch with pine bark, pine straw or shredded leaves. Espoma is a good organic rose food.

It's also not too early to start spraying with a disease–control product such as Funginex. Most folks prefer to spray an insecticide and fungicide mixed, with the preferred blend being Orthenex. Organic formulas can be made at home. The one used most came from Cornell University and calls for 1 tablespoon of baking soda, 1 teaspoon Sunspray horticultural oil and 1 tablespoon liquid soap in 1 gallon of water. For good roses, you need to spray about every 10 days and fertilize once a month until Sept. 15.

➤ For pruning jobs, I like Fiskars pruning shears, though I used the Swiss–made Felco for years. Fiskars also makes those popular orange–handled kitchen shears. They're made in Switzerland, as well as the United States, under the name Wallace. The shears are sharp and seem to stay that way longer than others. They're lighter–weight than Felco, too.

➤ Prune back crape myrtles to encourage lush flowering. Cut as much as one–third of their height. Remove all suckers on the branches and around the base of the trunk.

➤ Prune and fertilize fruit trees with 8-8-8, 10-10-10 or any tree fertilizer.

➤ Prune nandina, sometimes called heavenly bamboo, severely but properly. The recommended method is to prune stalks at varying heights. For example, if a bush has three or more main stalks, prune one down to the ground, another halfway up, and on the third, take out just the top with its faded berries. Repeat every spring to produce new foliage from top to bottom. It's important to clean off the old leaf stem with your hands. Unless you do this, and break them off right down to the main stalk, new stems and leaves will not grow. Then you will have a tall stalk with only a few leaves at the top. After pruning, fertilize with half a cup of shrub plant food.

Late month
Planting

➤ Snap beans should be planted after the last frost, normally the end of March. Recommended varieties are Bush Blue Lake, Gator Green 15, Royal Burgundy, Provider, Top Crop, Peak, Atlantic, Strike, Javelin, Bronco and Contender. Many locals prefer Contender. Good flat-pod types are Pirate and Green Crop. One-half pound of seed is enough for a 100–foot row. Plant seeds about one-half inch apart. Beans give you more food per foot of garden space than any vegetable you can grow.

A P R I L

Faithful Dogwood

"Everybody loves the dogwood: spring tourists, autumn poets, squirrels, birds, landscape architects," says C. Ritchie Bell, retired director of the North Carolina Botanical Garden.

And its beauty is somewhat blinding. "Four or five Southern states have chosen it for their state flower," Bell says, "though it is a tree. And its white petal–like bracts are not flowers at all but modified leaves."

No matter what people see in Virginia's state flower, none can deny its ethereal influence on springtime. So if you've been longing to have a dogwood or add new ones, spring is the best time to plant or transplant.

Those seemingly innocent trees that brighten our spring are native dogwoods, or *Cornus florida*. The healthiest usually thrive right where nature deposited a seed. The entrance to the Alanton neighborhood of Virginia Beach, for example, is a bower of beauty in April, with dogwoods arching over the road-way and dropping petals like snow.

Although admired by homeowners, dog-woods, which can reach 20 feet to 30 feet in height and branch out to 25 feet, are not easy to grow. Most are downright picky about their surroundings. Worse, native species are susceptible to anthracnose, a devastating fungal disease, and to several pests, including borers.

Another alluring feature is their fall color. In some seasons, depending upon weather conditions, they shed leaves early. But in a mild, extended fall, their leaves turn a beautiful scarlet. Their red berries then last from four to six weeks.

New types are hardier, although they require different growing conditions. Cherokee Sunset has variegated foliage in bright yellow and green. It features purplish–red blooms and distinctive pinkish–red tips on new growth. In fall, leaves turn red to purple. Another is

Cherokee Daybreak, a white flowering tree with variegated leaves of green and white. In fall, leaves turn pink to deep red.

Another hardy relative is the Chinese dogwood introduced by the National Arboretum in Washington, D.C. It is called *Cornus kousa chinensis* National and has large, creamy-white star-shaped blooms with dark-green foliage. This Asian counterpart was introduced to the area by the late Fred Heutte. It blooms a month later than the American species and has pointed bracts. But it is more tolerant of drought and has fewer problems with borers and canker.

The legend

Easter is an appropriate time to tell the legend of the American dogwood. The cross on which Christ was hung supposedly was dogwood. Before that, the tree was tall and erect; thereafter, it was destined to grow crooked and grizzly, but loved and admired.

Today, if you'll inspect its blooms, they will appear cross-shaped. The flower pistil in the center is symbolic of the nails in the cross. The lower center of each petal carries a brown stain, which legend says is blood from the cross.

Planting

Spring is the recommended time to plant because dogwoods seem to do better if they don't have to survive winter in their infancy. Specialists at North Carolina State University say that no matter the color of its flowers, the dogwood is always a good choice in the home landscape. When grown as a lawn tree, it only reaches 12 to 15 feet, with a low, broad head and tiers of horizontal branches. It can be trained to have several trunks, making it a distinct landscape accent, somewhat like clump birch. You'll often find dogwoods growing that way in the woods.

The dogwood is adaptable, but the most favorable soil condition is a moist, fertile loam. Soil should be slightly acid to neutral. To im-

prove it, mix peat moss or leaf mold into the planting hole. The trees also like a mulch of leaves or other coarse organic material, which helps keep the soil moist near the surface, where the tree's shallow root system is most active.

Plant shallow in partial shade. Young trees don't like full sunshine. A dogwood doesn't bloom until it's 5 to 7 years old. As it grows, it will need more sunlight to bloom.

They need maximum air circulation, so "limb up" surrounding large trees. Remove large limbs on other trees around your flowering dogwoods to maximize air flow and light. Don't use overhead sprinklers near them.

Be sure to protect the trunk from lawnmower and string-trimmer damage. Any wound in the bark allows borers to enter, which can kill the tree. And don't use weed killers near the tree or its roots, which extend far beyond the branches.

Experts suggest planting only nursery-grown dogwoods that have been root pruned and grown in full sunlight. They are superior to those transplanted from woods. Wild dogwoods also may be infected with the dogwood anthracnose, which is a problem in higher elevations but not in our coastal plain (Southeastern Virginia and Northeastern North Carolina). The disease has difficulty surviving high temperatures. Trees growing in well-drained soil that receive at least one-half day of sunshine daily are at low risk of infection.

If you need to move a dogwood, root prune it for at least a full season before moving. Spade just under the tips of the outer branches to cut the rangy roots. This makes the tree form a more compact root system. After moving, the tree is weak and borers often attack. Reduce damage by wrapping the trunk with burlap or heavy paper tree wrap.

If it doesn't rain weekly, soak the soil around the tree once a week. High winds quickly dry the soil, so keep that in mind when deciding to water. Fertilize once a year early in the spring with 1 pound of 8-8-8 per inch of trunk diameter. You also can use spike fertilizer, or make holes in the soil and drop in 1 pound of tree fertilizer for each inch of trunk diameter.

Improved white cultivars include White Cloud, Cherokee Princess and Gigantea. The pink dogwood is a natural mutation developed for ornamental use. Improved pinks in-clude Apple Blossom and Spring Song. Red cultivars are Sweetwater Red and Cherokee Chief.

Despite its difficulties, the dogwood deserves a place in the hearts of Southern gardeners. It truly is a tree for all seasons. Besides, who says love is easy?

Vines Worth Clinging To

Vines serve so many purposes, yet usually are overlooked by landscape architects, nurserymen and homeowners. They can be used for shade, to cover an unsightly structure, hide an unpleasant view, and to provide flowers, fall color or even fruit. Most importantly, they can be planted where there is too little space for trees and shrubs. Another advantage is that vines will provide shade within two or three years compared with five to 10 years needed by most trees. Here are some suggested vines and ways to use them:

Wisteria: Known by its fragrant lavender or white pendants of flowers in early spring, wisteria supports itself by twining and must be provided a trellis, wire or arbor. Be careful that it does not twine around a tree or any other plant, which will be strangled.

Actinidia (kiwi): You can grow edible fruit as well as colorful foliage with a kiwi vine. Also consider a grape vine. Both need an arbor or trellis on which to climb. These vines are fast growers, reaching 20 to 30 feet in length within three years.

Clematis: *Clematis paniculata* often is called sweet autumn clematis, with fragrant flowers. It would be ideal to cover a chain–link fence, but it can be invasive. Large–flowering, spring-blooming clematis that could be used include: Henryi, with creamy–white, 8–inch flowers; Nelly Moser with pale–mauve blooms; and Jackmanii, a popular variety with

large purple flowers. Another to consider is Duchess of Edinburgh, with white double blooms. It vines prolifically and provides a lush green cover.

The secret to successful clematis growing is to keep them alive through their first season. Their roots want to be cool, but the vine needs full sun to bloom. They like lime, so a regular application is usually necessary.

English ivy: There's plenty of this vine all over this area, so a friend or neighbor probably will be glad to give you some. It can be useful to hide unattractive architecture, and it will tone down stone or brick buildings that seem too overpowering. Several forms of euonymus also can be used for this purpose.

Hydrangea petiolaris: This vine is better known as climbing hydrangea. It's widely used in England, but I know of only a few plants growing in this area. I've tried and failed three times to grow it, but it's handsome if you want to give it a try.

Roses: Don't overlook climbing roses. America is a beautiful climbing rose but tends to die in severe winters. Varieties that won't let you down include Blaze, an old favorite in red. We have three on a fence at our house, and one is at least 15 years old. Pink Dawn is a good one, and Seafoam, a heavy-blooming white.

Carolina Yellow jasmine, or jessamine: This vine is native to Virginia and the Carolinas. You can see its yellow blooms in the woods and many home landscapes in mid-April. The flowers are fragrant, but the vine often does not support itself and usually needs to be tacked or tied where you want it. If used in a lawn area, the blooms can be a problem because they fall regularly and can turn a green lawn into a yellow-speckled carpet. Nearly every seed that drops germinates into a new vine that has to be pulled up.

Fruit Trees: A Feast For the Eyes

Despite their propensity for disease and pests, fruit trees have become a home-owner favorite in Southeastern Virginia and Northeastern North Carolina.

"You can grow fruit in your area," said Rich Marini, fruit specialist at Virginia Tech in Blacksburg, "but it's a lot of work. Too many people have the erroneous idea that it's easy to grow perfect fruit without pesticides."

Marini offered some cautionary statements about what will grow in Southeastern Virginia and Northeastern North Carolina:

➤ Peaches often get hit by a deadly late frost, he said. "That's why most peach-growing areas are in the mountains where they're planted on the foothills to avoid a frost. But if you can get a crop of peaches, they'll be good."

➤ "Apples, nectarines, cherries, plums and the other stone fruit all need cool nights at harvest. In Southeastern Virginia, there are not too many of those. That's why the mountains are better."

➤ Pears get fire blight. "That's why there are less than 100 acres (planted) in the state. Apples and other fruit get apple cedar rust from the native red cedar tree."

➤ "For the perfect apple, it (the tree) should

be sprayed 12 to 15 times per year with a combined fungicide and insecticide," Marini advised.

So, you still want to grow fruit?

Most of us don't expect perfect fruit, so we're willing to try. And if we spray pesticides, at least we're in control of the application and cleansing after harvest, which can't be said about store-bought fruit. Commercial growers use stronger, deadlier pesticides authorized for use only by certified pest-control operators.

Also, homeowners don't smother fruit with waxy preservatives to beautify their appearance, as do commercial growers. And don't forget that we have the bonus of enjoying spring blooms, plus the wonder of watching a flower bud grow into fruit.

But be prepared for disappointments and anger. You must have perseverance and gardening stamina.

Here are some recommendations for care and feeding:

Pollination: It takes two to tango in fruit growing. Usually you need two trees of a different variety to achieve cross-pollination. Apples, Japanese plums, sweet cherries and pears require mates. For instance, if you want to grow apples you should plant two different varieties, such as Criterion and Red Delicious They can be placed anywhere in your yard. Or, a neighbor's tree will work fine. Peaches and nectarines are self-fruitful and need no pollinator, as are sour cherries and European plums. But even self-fruitful trees produce more and better fruit if a pollinator tree is in the area.

Planting: Fruit trees should be planted anytime from October to April 15. Choose sunny, well-drained locations and avoid areas that are vulnerable to late-spring frosts.

When you plant, mix the soil taken out of the hole with compost or organic matter before replacing it. Set the tree in the hole at the same depth it grew in the nursery container.

Leave 10 feet between dwarf trees, about 35 feet for larger trees. Dwarf trees are the most practical for homeowners because they bear fruit within two to three years. Semidwarf take three to five years; standard, five years.

Finally, make a saucer of soil around your tree that will hold water. In dry weather, thoroughly water newly planted trees once a week.

Fertilizer: Most authorities agree that during their first year, fruit trees need no fertilizer. One horticulturist suggested using ammonium sulfate (21-0-0) in spring and fall.

Pruning: Fruit trees need annual pruning so that sun can reach the fruit and breezes can blow through the tree to help prevent disease. Pruning is best accomplished in late winter before new growth starts, usually February. There are some who believe a midsummer pruning is helpful, pruning less severely than in late winter. Prune to make your tree look like the cross-section of a bowl, with the center somewhat hollowed out so that light can enter. Always remove water sprouts, those limbs that grow straight up. Remove thin, weak, low-growing and shaded branches.

Thinning: You're glowing with pride at all the little fruit you see, but the truth is you should pinch off all fruit except one every 5 inches. Otherwise, you'll have small, less tasty fruit.

Spraying: Home fruit-tree sprays should consist of both a fungicide for disease prevention and an insecticide to combat bugs. There are many good products available in garden centers.

The spray schedule for apples and peaches is: Dormant spray, March 1 to 15; tight-in-cluster spray, April 4 to 12; buds separated in cluster, April 7 to 22; bloom spray, April 12 to May 5; 90 percent petal fall spray, April 20 to May 10; 10 days after petal fall spray, April 30 to May 20; three weeks after petal fall spray, May 21 to June 10; and two weeks after last spray, June 10 to June 24. Repeat the last spray in late June and again in mid-July. It can be applied once more if examination shows insect and disease problems.

Four to six sprays are recommended for plums, pears, nectarines and cherries.

Problems: Sooner or later, your peach trees will be consumed by borers. Try to delay that doom by placing mothballs in the soil around the tree as you plant. One organic control is to plant mint around the tree. Another possible remedy is to tie a cake of castile soap (containing lye) in the crotch of the tree so that rain slowly dissolves the soap, which runs down the trunk and deters borers. Virginia Tech's suggestion is to flood the trunk and soil around the tree with Thiodan. Lindane is another pesticide frequently recommended.

Also, fruit bandits include raccoons, birds and squirrels. Mostly, they are unstoppable. To attempt to deter them, try netting trees (tie the bottom around the trunk), or wind some shiny red and silver tape around the tree to frighten them. Inflatable snakes and a plastic owl perched on a branch also might help.

Recommended varieties: Apples include: Criterion, Jonared, Granny Smith, Lodi, Jerseymac, Paulared, Summer Rambo, Grimes Golden, Golden Delicious and Stayman; Pears include: Moonglow, Magness and Seckel; Plums include: Starkling, Methley and Shiro; Peaches include: Earlired, Sunhaven, Redhaven, Cresthaven and Georgia Bell.

Fussy Boxwood Sometimes Requires Extra Care

On the Eastern Shore, the number of boxwood you have shows how long you've been a First Family of Virginia. So popular are these shrubs, that you'd think they were native. But they're not. And no, they're not English either.

Boxwood is a native of East Asia, North Africa, Southern Europe, West India and Central America. We're all familiar with one variety called English boxwood (*Buxus sempervirens*, Suffruticosa). It traveled to England with the Romans and became a staple in stately gardens. According to historians, the first recorded introduction of boxwood to Colonial America was in 1652.

Today, as with many overused plants, boxwood is suffering. Following are a few answers to the many boxwood questions I receive in the mail.

Experts say discoloration of leaves may be caused by: (1) lack of nitrogen, which would be easy to correct in spring by applying cottonseed meal or any slow-release nitrogen to the soil; (2) leaf miner, which can be corrected by spraying regularly with Orthene; and (3) the sun shining brightly on frozen leaves, which happens to many plants with an eastern exposure after a harsh winter. Winter injury causes leaves to turn bronze, or they dry up and turn straw-colored. Prune out dead branches in April to discourage invasion by secondary disease organisms.

The U.S. Department of Agriculture recommends fertilizing with 10–6–4 fertilizer, applied at a rate of 1 to 2 pounds per 100 square feet of soil surface. Apply it in late fall just before the ground freezes or as soon as the ground thaws in the spring. Virginia Tech recommends spring feeding and says that large boxwood that look weak or starved will benefit from a deep feeding. Put fertilizer in a series of holes drilled to the root zone around the plant, about 1 foot apart and 1 foot from the trunk.

Virginia Tech warns that some boxwood may become so compact that very little light reaches the center of the crown. If that is true, interior shoots may die and the overall plant will be weakened. Pruning some inner branches will help open the plant, encouraging a green center where new leaves can grow all the way up the stem. If you fail to do annual thinning, you are asking for trouble.

Another problem may be boxwood root rot, according to Virginia Tech, but there is no known cure. Some landscapers create dry wells under new plants to ensure good drainage.

A different opinion is offered by spokesmen at the University of Maryland, who say that root rot is a result of magnesium starvation and acid-producing mulches. They recommend using Epsom salts to correct the deficiency and advise removing all mulch from around boxwood.

Virginia Tech doesn't agree with either the magnesium or mulch theory. Here are Tech's suggestions for care of English boxwood under conditions of decline:

➤ Prune out all dead or diseased stems where leaves have turned orange to red to bright yellow.

➤ Clean out and remove all dead leaves and stems from the center, or interior, of the plant.

➤ Maintain good soil moisture, especially during hot parts of the summer and into fall.

➤ Provide adequate fertilization in either early spring or late fall.

➤ Dig up and destroy all dead and dying plants. A plant may be considered dying when it does not respond to any of the above disease-prevention tactics.

I believe that using some liquid iron on each plant to check chlorosis can't hurt and might help. There's a woman on the Eastern Shore with handsome boxwood who always fertilizes them on Christmas Eve.

Lastly, if you're always having trouble with boxwood, why grow it? You might as well pull them out and plant something healthy. Dwarf yaupon holly, a native plant, is an excellent substitute.

But try to convince a longtime boxwood owner of that!

More About Boxwood

O ther than moles, probably no other garden problem has created so many questions as has boxwood. Back in March, 1983, Charles Bell, garden writer for The News and Record in Greensboro, N.C., wrote these words, which need to be heeded:

"If I had as much trouble trying to grow boxwood as some readers seem to have, I would dig them up and get rid of them. If you have to continually worry about, work on, ask about, and are dissatisfied with a shrub, why keep it around?

"Boxwoods are notoriously difficult to grow in many locations. The Plant Pest and Disease Clinic in Raleigh reports they get more inquiries about boxwoods than any other one species of plant.

"I recently received a letter from a reader which read: "Our English boxwoods are sick. They are pale, with yellow variegated leaves. Can you prescribe a cure?"

"Unfortunately, I can't. This condition can be caused by several things or a combination of them. Under the best circumstances, it might just be a temporary ailment due to a cloudy, wet, cold winter. But it could also be caused by root damage, resulting from excessive moisture in the root zone. The fungus Phytopthora cinnamomi is widespread in our soils and can be strongly activated when there is excess moisture in the root zone and soil is warm. The fungus invades the roots and starts killing them, though above-ground symptoms may not show up until months later.

"Roots can be damaged by excessive fertilizer. Too much fertilizer can "burn" roots – drawing moisture from roots so they can't function properly to supply water and nutrients to the plant top.

"Any type fertilizer may be used with boxwoods, but only a small amount at a time, thoroughly dissolved and washed into the root zone. When using a general–purpose garden fertilizer such as 8–8–8 or 10–10–10, use 1 tablespoon per foot of height in March, early May and late June. This light, frequent rate is less likely to cause damage than would one heavy application.

"Damaged roots can't function, so there is no way additional fertilizer can help. If roots have been damaged, perhaps a foliar application might be of benefit. Spray a soluble fertilizer on the leaves according to label directions.

"Nematodes can damage roots and cause tops to turn yellow or bronze. I don't know what to advise for nematode control in established plantings. Commercial producers may use Temik 20 G, but this is not available to home gardeners.

"Perhaps replanting, using these guidelines, might help. Truban and Subdue are supposed to be quite effective in root–rot control. When new spring growth begins, start spraying for psyllid control. About 30 days later, spray for leaf miner control.

"Substitute dwarf Yaupon holly as an evergreen shrub less susceptible to some of these ailments in your planting."

Fertilizer Basics

It's time to be thinking about fertilizer for spring, what kind or type to buy. Here's how Virginia Tech describes your choices:

Selecting a fertilizer: Base your choice of fertilizer on soil test recommendations. Soil tests often indicate high levels of phosphorus and potassium availability. When that is the case, a fertilizer supplying only nitrogen is needed. Use extreme caution, however, when applying such a nitrogen fertilizer. Make careful rate calculations based on fertilizer analysis and spreader calibration to avoid overapplication.

Slow-release fertilizer: Slow-release fertilizers release nitrogen over extended periods of time and are applied less frequently and at somewhat higher rates. In general, slow-release fertilizers are preferred as they lessen the chance of groundwater contamination through leaching.

Organic fertilizers: Examples of these include cottonseed, bone, blood, hoof and horn meals; fish emulsion, and all manures. Organic fertilizers usually contain relatively low concentrations of actual nutrients, but they perform other important functions, such as increasing organic content and providing micronutrients that synthetic formulations do not.

When you buy fertilizer, seed and soil additives, read the labels and know what they mean. Make sure you not only get the best buy, but also that you get what you want and need.

In spring there are many different and sometimes confusing advertisements about garden products. You'll see brands commonly listed as 8–8–8 or 5–10–5. How do you know which analysis is the best buy?

First, both of these analyses are good all-purpose fertilizers for gardens and flowers. The three numerals on a bag of 8–8–8 fertilizer mean 8 units of nitrogen, 8 of phosphorus and 8 of potash. In a bag of 8–8–8, there are 24 units of food. In a bag of 5–10–5, there are 20 units. Because nitrogen is by far the most expensive, 8–8–8 is the best buy. A better buy is usually 10–10–10.

Remember that grass needs nitrogen. Fertilizer for your lawn needs to be as high in nitrogen as 30–5–10 or 23–7–7. A common one is 21–7–14.

Neither 8–8–8 nor 5–10–5 is sufficient for lawns except at time of seeding. Tree food is typically sold as 16–8–8 or 12–6–6.

It's a good idea to use an organic fertilizer which lasts longer into the growing season. Organic sources of nitrogen include nitrate of soda, Milorganite sewage sludge and the Japanese formula of IDBU long-lasting nitrogen. Grass clippings also are high in nitrogen and make excellent fertilizer for your lawn.

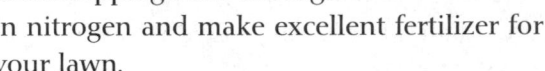

The Norfolk Department of Public Works recommends you use a slow-release fertilizer on your lawn because a fast-release food washes away quickly. Look for "W.I.N." on the package, which means Water–Insoluble Nitrogen. Do not overdo it. "Overfertilizing allows fertilizer to wash off your lawn onto sidewalks and into the storm drainage system," a department spokesman said. "The drainage system then carries it to the nearest body of water, where it eventually enters the Chesapeake Bay."

Most fertilizers on today's market derive their nitrogen from urea and/or ammonia. They do not contain long-lasting nitrogen.

Check three things when buying plant food: the analysis, weight and coverage in square feet. In a 50–pound bag of 8–8–8 fertilizer, there are 24 units of food, plus 26 units of filler (clay, sand, limestone) to provide the bulk you need to spread the food over the required area.

Gardening Reminders for April

Early month

Lawn care

➤ Check lawn mowers to see if they're working. Repair shops begin filling up this time of year, so try to beat the rush to have blades sharpened.

➤ You can apply a crabgrass-prevention product until the forsythia blooms fall. I prefer those NOT mixed with fertilizer. Any containing bensulide (Betasan), Dacthal or pendimethalin do a good job. Read the label carefully.

➤ Feed, aerate and water your lawn. Don't get discouraged. It takes three years to establish a good lawn around a new home. It's best to seed in the fall to establish strong roots. Seed again now and feed with an 8-8-8. In three weeks, feed again with a special turf food and water regularly and thoroughly.

➤ Get rid of wild onions in your lawn by digging them out or applying an herbicide.

Pest control

➤ Mild winters produce many insects, but don't use pesticides without good cause. Integrated Pest Management means you do nothing until you see damage caused by insects. Watch for stressed plants, which are vulnerable to bugs. Spray with horticultural oil, found in garden centers, which smothers some insects, such as scale, and their eggs. Spray before new growth begins. Do not apply oil when temperatures go below 45 degrees or when plants are suffering from lack of moisture. Dimethoate (Cygon) also can be used.

Apply at a rate of 2 teaspoons per gallon of water. Spray plants when new spring leaves are fully expanded, then apply again one month later. Inspect your plants and spray only if you find damage.

Planting

➤ Recycle packing peanuts by using them to provide drainage in the bottom of planting containers.

➤ Avoid repotting plants unless necessary because it can cause damage to tiny feeder roots. Most plants require several months of "post-op" care to get back to where they were before repotting. Instead, add nutrients to the soil to perk up plants.

➤ If you didn't do it in March, set out onion sets and plant cool-season crops such as radishes, Swiss chard, carrots, beets, turnips, lettuce and peas. Plant potatoes for early harvest, and transplant cabbage, cauliflower, Brussels sprouts, broccoli and kohlrabi plants into your garden. These all need an early growing season if you're to get a good crop before hot weather.

➤ Set out new shrubs and transplant old ones. Cool, wet weather is ideal for planting trees and shrubs, plus strawberries, as weather and soil conditions permit.

➤ Plant roses and remember to give them lime. Some people put oyster shells under their roses to ensure a plentiful supply of lime during the lifetime of the plant.

➤ Start tomato and pepper seeds, as well as many flowers, indoors where it's warm. All you need is some good potting soil and bright light (sun or ultraviolet lamps).

Pruning

➤ Prune crape myrtles before they leaf out. You can cut them back as severely as you want, even flush with the ground, and they'll come back. Be sure to cut away all dead wood. It's also a good time to fertilize them. Two cups of 8-8-8 or 10-10-10 per plant, or a good tree food, will suffice.

➤ To prune azaleas and forsythia properly,

wait until they've finished blooming. Reach down to the base of the plant and remove complete stalks. Then let the plant grow in the shape nature intended.

➤ Prune photinia severely if it looks shabby. Those afflicted with leaf spot should be sprayed with a fungicide once a week until the problem is under control, which could take all summer. It's easier to dig up the photinia and replace it with a more durable shrub, such as ligustrum or anise.

➤ Cut back liriope and mondo grass with shears or a lawn mower. Do it before inner buds start.

➤ Prune fall-blooming sasanqua camellias. Prune out small branches, as well as twigs, so air can get down to the center of the plant.

Midmonth

Lawn care

➤ Spring rains make grass green, but it still needs plant food to endure summer. Spring is the right time for the one light fertilization of fescue you should do. Use a high-nitrogen turf food that has a W.I.N. guarantee on the bag, ensuring plant food that will last into the summer. If you have zoysia, Bermuda or St. Augustine, fertilize monthly with a product that will provide 1 pound of nitrogen per 1,000 square feet.

➤ Pull up acorn sprouts in beds and lawns. It's easier after a rain, when the soil is wet.

➤ Remember that you'll get poor results from throwing grass seed onto an existing lawn without some cultivation. The surface soil must be raked, verticut or otherwise tilled, so seed can come into contact with loose soil. Only then will it have a chance to germinate and grow.

Miscellaneous

➤ Do not use a string trimmer or lawn mower near the trunks of dogwoods or other trees. The wounds can kill them.

➤ Pick up fallen camellia blooms promptly to prevent petal blight.

➤ To celebrate Arbor Day, plant a tree. Then feed and water it properly. And feed, water and spray existing trees in your yard now. They will become more disease-, insect - and drought-resistant.

➤ Make a list of where you're missing spring-flowering bulbs now, while they're in bloom. Then this fall, you'll know how many to buy and where to put them. Also mark bulbs that need to be divided in the fall.

➤ Clean gutters. Pine straw and leaves fill most of them now. You'll find young seedlings starting from the seeds off your trees, as well as a few unwanted insects.

Planting

➤ If you have trouble getting lettuce and other seed to germinate this month, some people say it helps to freeze them first. Put lettuce, spinach and herb seed in your freezer for two days. Then soak them in warm water several hours and plant. This supposedly ensures good germination, even in warm soil.

➤ Fences are ideal for growing vining vegetables, including cucumbers and cantaloupes. When cantaloupes begin to enlarge, tie them to the fence in a loose sling made of burlap or old pantyhose so they won't fall off the vine before they ripen. Vining lima beans or snap beans also can grow on a fence. And you can use it as a trellis for tomatoes.

➤ Grow bush-type cucumbers in hanging baskets, including Early Salad, Tumblin Tom and Basket King varieties.

➤ Remove all containers (metal, plastic, paper or pressed fibers) when putting a plant into the soil. Pressed-fiber pots will decay, but very slowly. Remove all twine tied around trunks.

➤ Plant your first row of gladiolus. Then replant every two to three weeks to have blooms all summer. Glads are one of the best bulbs to provide beautiful blooms for bouquets.

➤ Sow seed of alyssum, nasturtium and California poppies in the open ground. They germinate best in cool weather.

➤ Plant corn in blocks of at least four short

rows. That way, you ensure adequate pollination. One long row and you won't get good ear set. To prevent cross-pollination between yellow and white or ornamental types, separate your varieties of sweet corn by at least 10 feet.

Pruning

➤ Trim browned fern fronds. Some plants such as Christmas fern and holly fern stay green all winter. But by now their fronds are broken and brown. Prune them down to the ground to promote new shoots.

➤ Renovate old, overgrown shrubs with drastic cuts. If you have a tree, shrub or perennial that has moped and sulked the past couple of years, move it to a new site, if possible. It may simply need a sunnier, drier, less windy home.

➤ Prune hydrangeas, according to variety. Hydrangea grandiflora Hills of Snow, for instance, is low-growing and clumpy, seldom reaching more than 3 feet high. It blooms from late June to September. Prune by cutting it back each year to within a foot of the ground, and thin out the weakest canes. The tree or Pee Gee hydrangea grows about 25 feet high and spreads to 15 feet. Large blooms start out white but change to pink in mid-July. Prune it back to a few buds to promote new growth and control size. Cut out crowded stems and weak wood. The florists hydrangea (H. macrophylla hortensis) is the most recognizable with its pink and blue blooms. It is a smaller, rounded bush, usually 3 to 5 feet wide, with many unbranched thick stems. Flowers appear in July and August. If you want blue blooms, put aluminum sulfate around the bush; for pink, apply lime. To prune, remove the weak, crowded and dead branches at the base now. Do not cut off any of last year's flush of growth because that's where the flower buds form. In late summer, immediately after flowering, prune the flower heads. From now through early summer, nurseries and florists sell hydrangeas as house plants. After they've faded, set them outside and usually the plant will grow into a healthy outdoor shrub.

End of month

Disease control

➤ A wet spring means more plant diseases. Watch peonies for botrytis blight, whose symptoms are wilting of new shoots and brown or blackish rot of leaves and stems. A dark-brown blight also may show up on the flowers. One recommendation is to spray with a fungicide such as Funginex when the peony shoots are 3 inches to 6 inches high and again when they're 10 to 18 inches high.

Maintenance

➤ Feed fig trees now with bone meal or wood ashes. If your soil is very acidic, lime should be sprinkled on top of the soil around the bush each spring. Fertilize in early June, late July and again in late winter with a light application of 8-8-8 or 10-10-10. Use one-half pound per foot of height of the bush. Provide a large, continual supply of water throughout summer to produce a high yield. Mulch around the bush to conserve moisture.

Miscellaneous

➤ It's time to dust off your hummingbird feeders. The birds will soon show up in your yards.

Pest control

➤ Tree pests are beginning to crawl up tree trunks. Here's a roundup:

Orange-striped oakworm. Found mostly on oak trees in Norfolk. Wrap trunks with a band of duct tape smeared with petroleum jelly. Leave it up for a month, or until worms are gone.

Bagworm. Nests look like a crusty ice-cream cone on tree branches of mostly cedars, Leyland cypress and arborvitae. Pick off the nests and destroy them. Or, spray in May or June when worms emerge. Spray twice, 10 days apart, with Orthene. Trichogramma (small parasitic wasps) are a natural control.

Forest tent caterpillar. Nests look like spider webs spun in the crotches of branches. Attacks wild cherry, crab apple and fruit trees. Pick them off and destroy. Spray now during the day, when caterpillars are moving, with Sevin or Orthene. Or, use Bacillus thuringiensis (Bt), a non-toxic bacteria.

Galls. Lumps look like small, crusty potatoes and usually appear in clusters of two or three on tree branches. They're caused by an insect and are harmless. You don't need to spray. Eventually, they fall off. Found mostly on oak trees and sometimes on azaleas and native bay trees. Pick them off if they bother you.

Planting

➤ Plant lily-of-the-valley now that the plants are ready to leaf out. Or, wait until dormancy in fall. They need shade and must be moist but well-drained to survive. Take note that they are poisonous to pets and small children.

➤ Pick off the blooms on strawberry plants the first year so they won't form berries. You shouldn't allow fruit to form until the second year.

➤ Plant blueberries. Why not have a hedge that makes good eating? If you already have blueberries, an application of aluminum sulfate, plus some fertilizer, will help them grow healthy and strong. You can buy blueberries in containers at local nurseries or bare-root by mail. If you plant a dozen, get at least two or three different varieties that ripen at different times.

M A Y

Earthly Plot: The Summer Vegetable Garden

Show me your summer vegetable garden and I'll tell you what you are, wrote a gardener from the last century. How true, even today. Earthly plots come in as many shapes and sizes as their gardeners, proving that you are what you sow.

A 100–by–100–foot plot will produce all the vegetables a family of five needs for the year, while a plot half that size will serve the growing season. A 10–by–20–foot garden can feed two or more on a suburban lot, or in the back yard of a town house. People whose time is short may be satisfied with a 4–by–4 square-foot garden, or just a few containers.

First, a few tips.

Draw a rough plan of what goes where. A week or more before planting, churn up the soil. To create a loamy consistency, add lots of organic matter, such as compost, which provides nutrients and aids drainage. Dedicated veggie gardeners start this process in the fall. The better prepared the soil, the stronger your plants will grow and the fewer problems they'll have. Healthy plants greatly reduce the need for pesticides.

It's important to rotate your plants in a garden every year. Planting the same vegetable in the same place every year causes disease and insect problems. Avoid planting potatoes after tomatoes because they're in the same family and susceptible to the same maladies.

If you wish to sow early from seed, you can begin in April with lettuce, radishes, peas and beets. To simplify things, however, it's perfectly acceptable – and much quicker – to buy young plants from garden centers for your summer crop.

Warm–season vegetable seeds – squash, cucumber, melon, okra, eggplant, peppers, bush or pole beans, and tomatoes – are best started this month; but even then, you may have cold nights, causing germination failure. If it's been more than two weeks since you planted, you probably should plant again – or buy some healthy seedlings. It's best not to rush summer veggies because they grow faster and produce more fruit when the soil is warm, usually by mid–May.

Cover seeds to the recommended depth, following instructions on the seed packet. Thin and space plants as directed.

Take care that no trees are within 10 feet of your plot. Trees shade the soil and rob your garden of water and plant food. And keep grass from invading the territory. The garden should receive sunlight at least half the day. Sun is especially vital during spring and fall, when temperatures are cool.

Keep soil uniformly moist. Provide mulch to retain moisture. Vegetables grown in containers need careful watering because the soil dries faster. Provide good drainage in pots by placing small stones or gravel at the bottom before adding soil and compost.

Feed plants occasionally, adding compost or special fertilizers. Use insect controls when and if necessary, but sparingly. Organic products are widely available.

Whatever size the plot, make sure the soil has proper drainage. Ridge up the rows and plant on top of them. Old timers say that you should run rows in your garden from east to west so the plants will get more sun. Plant tall-growing vegetables together but on the north side of the garden so they don't shade the sun from the shorter ones.

It's best to leave 10 to 24 inches between rows, but for intensive gardening, leave only 10 inches. Give vining crops plenty of room to crawl. Don't plant small vegetables nearby or they will be swallowed by floppy foliage.

As the summer weeks go by, you'll want to replant and/or replace some vegetables. For instance, plant bush beans every two weeks to provide continuous summer harvest. Sweet corn also should be planted every two weeks until July.

After all your hard work, you will enjoy a bounty of delicious vegetables.

Save Money Growing Your Own Vegetables

In the vegetable garden featured, the total seed cost is around $10, capable of yielding over $100 worth of fresh vegetables. For the beginner, fertilizer and tools may be an extra expense, but clearly the potential savings are worthwhile. Time spent in the garden can be written off as healthy exercise.

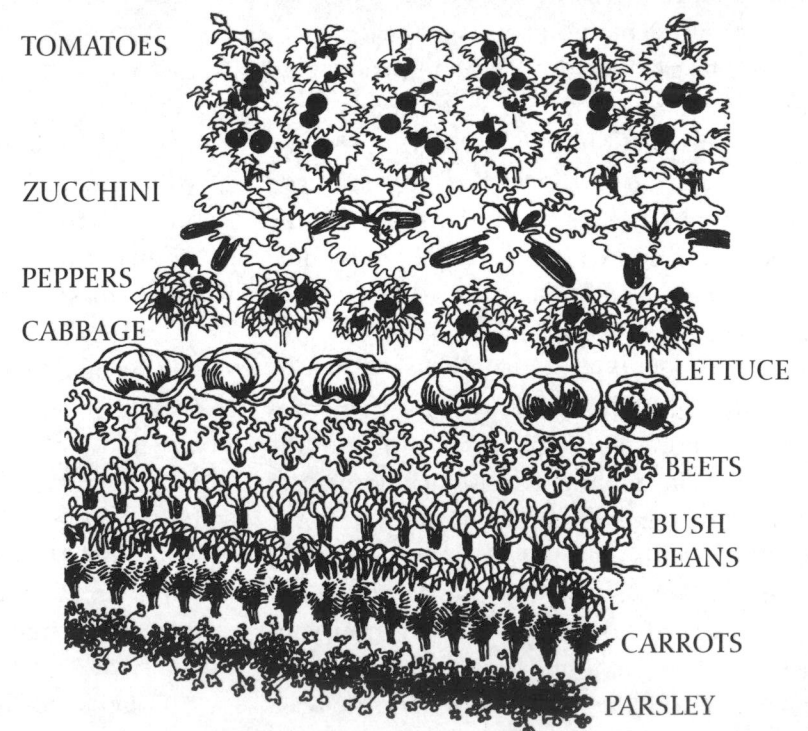

TOMATOES

ZUCCHINI

PEPPERS

CABBAGE

LETTUCE

BEETS

BUSH BEANS

CARROTS

PARSLEY

Weeds and Vegetables Don't Mix

The average 770-square-foot garden in the U. S. can easily gross 50 cents per square foot in produce, says the National Garden Bureau. Experienced gardeners, using intensive gardening techniques – especially in long-season areas like Southeastern Virginia and Northeastern North Carolina – can realize $1 per square foot in produce at retail prices. The return is clear profit, all tax free.

But weeds can murder a vegetable garden. An acre of land may contain as much as 1 1/2 tons of weed seeds. Even after 70 years, mullein, curly dock and primrose seeds have germinated. Wild mustard, pigweed, ragweed, peppergrass and plantain have germinated after being buried for 40 years in 18 inches of soil.

You hear all sorts of excuses for letting weeds grow among vegetables. They all boil down to "a few weeds won't hurt." But even a few weeds are bushy. A few more begin shading and strangling vegetables. When your vegetable garden starts looking really weedy, you are watching murder take place.

Evidence for this is in Cornell University Bulletin 521. New York state scientists planted 12 plots of vegetables. Two plots each of six kinds of vegetables were planted at the same time, side by side. Each plot was given the same care except that one set of six was regularly scraped clean with a hoe. Weeds were permitted to grow in the adjoining comparison plots. Here are the results:

Vegetable	Pounds harvested No weeds.	Pounds harvested. With weeds.
Carrots	503 lbs.	28 lbs.
Beets	240 lbs.	46 lbs.
Cabbage	234 lbs.	129 lbs.
Onions	68 lbs.	4 lbs.
Tomatoes	164 lbs.	23 lbs.
Potatoes	148 lbs.	53 lbs.

The results are clear. If you want to get the most from your garden, get rid of the weeds.

Square-Foot Vegetable Gardening

Gardeners can overcome just about any soil problem by using raised beds framed in boards or landscape timbers, which are filled with a healthy mixture of soil and compost. These plots save space by accommodating more plants per square foot than conventional gardens. And often the soil is warmer earlier in the season, so summer vegetables can be planted early.

Square-foot gardening features raised beds divided into 12-inch squares. Usually, each bed is no larger than 4 feet square so that gardeners can simply bend over them to do maintenance without trampling the soil.

Beds can be built anywhere from a foot high to waist high, making them accessible to wheelchair gardeners and people with back problems.

Give beds some fertilizer before planting. Plant seeds or plants in each square foot. Water more frequently than regular gardens because the soil dries faster in a raised bed.

Herbs Add Flavor to Home Gardens

Whether you pronounce it "urb" or "hurb," you'll love how easy it is to grow herbs. You can start them indoors or out, and most aren't picky about placement.

Herbs are non–woody annual, biennial or perennial plants that die back each year after flowering. In flavor usage, there is a distinction between herbs and spices. Herbs generally are leaves of low–growing shrubs and herbaceous plants. Spices are primarily derived from bark, flower buds, fruit or roots of perennial tropical plants.

Annual herbs that can be grown for cooking include anise, basil, borage, chervil, cress, coriander, cumin, dill, marjoram, nasturtium and summer savory. Among the biennials are caraway, celery, fennel and parsley. The perennials include angelica, burnet, chives, dittany, garlic, horseradish, lemon balm, lovage, mints, oregano, rosemary, rue, sage, sorrel, sweet cicely, tarragon, thyme and winter savory.

Herbs are not difficult to grow and seem to thrive when neglected. They can be grown in a small area of the garden, in shrub borders, or in containers. Some will tolerate indoor conditions, but sun–grown plants have more distinct flavor and fragrance. Those that can easily be grown in pots indoors include dill, savory, parsley, thyme, borage, sage, marjoram and basil. You can start them indoors in fall and plant them outdoors in spring.

A dry, loose, well–drained soil is best, but they'll grow in almost any kind of soil. They require little fertilizer. Too much produces poor flavor and fragrance. Those that do better in moist soils are mints, parsley, cress, chervil, lovage, angelica and celery. Sage, rosemary and thyme like slightly moist soils.

Keep weeds under control and conserve moisture by applying mulch. Very few diseases or insects attack herbs. Rust infects mints, however. In hot, dry weather, red spider mites may be found on low–growing plants such as sage and lemon balm.

Most herbs, particularly the annuals, can be grown from seed. Check the seed packet for germination times. Rosemary, with a long germination time, can be planted directly in the ground in fall. Lemon balm, rosemary, sage and winter savory will grow from cuttings. Chives, garlic, mints and horseradish are increased by division of the clumps as new spring growth develops.

If you want instant gratification, many herbs can be started from plants available in garden centers.

Fresh leaves should be picked as soon as the plant has enough foliage to maintain growth. To ensure good oil content, pick leaves or seeds after dew has disappeared but before the sun becomes too hot.

To dry for winter, harvest leaves before flower buds open. Pick seed heads as color changes from green to brown or gray. Wash dirty leaves and seed heads in cold water and drain thoroughly before drying. After allowing them to dry for one or two hours, make them into small bouquets and tie at the bottom with a string. Hang each bouquet out of direct sunlight and let dry thoroughly. Drying

will take about a week, depending on humidity. When the bouquet is dry, strip the leaves from the stems, crumble them and store in covered jars.

Jeanne Pettersen of the Tidewater Unit of the Herb Society of America grows myriad herbs around her Virginia Beach home. She's the author of "Growing Herbs in Hampton Roads – A Basic Guide," an excellent booklet full of tips and plant choices.

Following is a planting and care guide suggested by Pettersen for some easy–to–grow herbs:

Soil preparation: For most herbs, garden soil should be prepared to a depth of 9 inches to a foot. Work in a little compost, manure and sand to build a humus layer and good texture. Some herbs can be planted in the same bed, but make sure growing conditions are compatible. "Parsley and chives like a more moist soil than rosemary or thyme," Pettersen said.

Containers: For indoor potting, Pettersen recommends using a soil–less mixture, which is devoid of disease organisms and lightweight. For most herbs, let the planting mix get slightly dry between waterings. "I actually put my containers outside in the summer and spray them with a hose once a day." Overwatering is the No. 1 cause of death among herbs, she cautioned.

Fertilizing: Do not overfertilize. For house plants, use one–quarter to one–half the normal strength of fertilizer and apply once a week.

Outdoors is another matter. "I don't fertilize outside that often. It's not critical. I do put some manure or compost around the plants about once a year. Or, you can put some dry or liquid fertilizer on when you're watering. If it's liquid, apply it every couple of months."

Pests: Mealybugs are common in rosemary and some of the other herbs. Wash plants in soapy water, she advised, and spray with an organic herbal solution.

Pettersen prefers the natural approach. "Herbal pesticides is my hobby. If you buy any kind of chemicals and spray them in your yard, you could be polluting the groundwater or poisoning yourself because the chemical stays in the plant for a long time."

She recommended garlic and red pepper for mealybugs, whitefly and aphids. Crush three or four garlic cloves per quart of water, or use two or three red peppers per quart (a blender is helpful). Allow the mixture to sit for 24 hours, then strain. Fill a spray bottle and apply directly to plants.

"Also, some herbal fungicides keep mold down." To control black spot on roses, Pettersen applies a solution of chamomile and horsetail herbs. To make your own, brew a tea from dry or fresh herbs and allow it to soak for about 24 hours. Strain, and use the concoction as a spray.

"It's not quite as effective (as chemicals), but it does work somewhat. It also doesn't kill all your beneficial insects or butterflies. I can stand a few holes in leaves or black spot just to keep the butterflies around."

Parsley: This biennial plant has a clean, fresh flavor that perks up many foods. The curly leaf type looks pretty on a plate, while the flat–leaf variety is a tad zestier. It will grow in full sun or part shade and likes rich soil that's normal to slightly moist. It grows about 8 inches tall.

If you choose to plant seeds, soak them first for a few hours. Plants should be placed 9 inches deep, or more. "It has a very deep tap root that shouldn't be transplanted. You can plant it in your vegetable garden. It's supposed to be perfect to plant in your asparagus bed. They benefit each other in their growth pattern. Or, you can plant it next to some of your shrubs. It really will grow almost anywhere." After two years, it will go to seed but may live a third year if you remove the seeds.

The biggest enemy of parsley (and fennel) is the black swallowtail butterfly caterpillar. "I always plant extras so they can eat all they want," Pettersen said. "If you kill all the caterpillars, you won't have any butterflies."

Chives: Grow these from seeds or by division in your vegetable garden. They like full sun or partial shade. When mature, chives are about a foot to 14 inches tall. Regular chives have a pinkish flower that can be dried and used in floral decoration or for herbal vinegar. Remove flower heads before they go to seed, and divide plants every year or two.

Mint: It likes rich soil and grows best in part or full shade. Depending on the variety, a mature plant can reach 1 foot to 18 inches high in bloom. Colors and sizes of flowers vary.

Thyme: Pettersen recommends upright thyme (grows up to 1 foot) or lemon thyme (about 8 inches tall). All varieties like full sun and average growing conditions with soil "a little dry." If you grow it from seed, it takes about six weeks to two months to mature. Or, you can buy a plant or root a cutting and harvest them in about a month, depending on the size. "Try to keep them clipped so they get bushy."

An Ounce of Prevention Produces Pounds of Tomatoes

Homegrown tomatoes are one of the blessings of summer. Taking a few precautions now will ensure that you have plenty all season.

When buying tomato plants, look for disease-resistant varieties. You will find the letters V, F, N or T after the variety name. V means resistant to verticillium wilt: F to fusarium wilt (FF covers two strains); N to nematodes; and T to tobacco mosaic. These plants include Celebrity, Quick Pick, Floramerica and Mamma Mia.

Plants fall into three categories:

➤ Determinate tomatoes are bush plants that stop growing at a certain height. All the fruit tends to ripen at the same time. Examples are Super Bush, Celebrity, Roma and Tiny Tim.

➤ Indeterminate plants continue to grow until killed by frost. Most popular are Beefmaster, Better Boy, Whopper and Early Girl.

➤ A new class, indeterminate short-internode, combines the bushiness of determinate with the fruiting qualities of indeterminate. Better Bush variety is one, a compact, stocky plant with fruits the size of larger tomatoes.

Also check plant labels for the number of days to maturity. Usually, the earlier the fruit, the smaller it is. Early Girl, Sweet 100 and Champion are among the earliest.

Perhaps you want to grow cherry or large beefsteak tomatoes. Sweet 100, a cherry type, is one of the sweetest and best. For a beefsteak, Beefmaster, Whopper or Champion are recommended. The pear- or plum-shaped Roma and Mamma Mia are the choices for pasta, sauces and salsa.

To be different, try Pink Girl, Golden Boy or Lemon Boy. You may have to start with seeds because plants are difficult to find.

Here are some tips on planting:

➤ If you transplanted seedlings to your garden in April, be sure to have cold-weather protection devices handy. Uncover plants when the sun comes out so they don't bake. Wait to transplant a seedling until it has at least five leaves to ensure a sturdy plant. But plant it with only a couple of leaves showing, so that it can develop deep roots, providing a strong base of support.

➤ Buy only fresh, healthy transplants. Size isn't important. If the plant has blooms or buds on it, pinch them off so all energy goes into the plant and root system.

➤ The planting area should be well-drained and have good exposure to the sun. If you don't have a vegetable garden, plant tomatoes in open spots among foundation shrubs. Or, put a plant or two in pots with room for root growth, and keep them watered.

➤ Plant tomatoes in a different spot in your garden each year to help prevent disease.

➤ Also work 1 to 2 inches of compost, peat moss or other organic matter into the soil. It helps to let the mixture rest for a week or so before planting.

➤ Experts recommend you apply two large handfuls of agricultural lime and one handful of 8–8–8 fertilizer around each plant. Work it into the soil to a depth of 12 inches. About once a month, add small amounts of fertilizer, perhaps half a cup of 8–8–8, or a special tomato food. Be sure to water it in. Fertilizer spikes work well. Or, use organic fertilizers.

➤ Add a tablespoon of Epsom salts (to provide calcium and magnesium) to a gallon of water and pour it around each plant early in the season.

➤ Plant tomatoes no closer than 36 inches apart; then they should be staked or grown in cages to produce better yields. Anchor a cage securely by tying it to stakes driven in the ground on each side or to a wire stretched over the top of a row of cages so they can't blow over in strong winds. I use a wire coat hanger, cut into two "V" sections, using each "V" to anchor the bottom of each cage.

Some experts don't like cages because they cramp the plant and provide breeding grounds for whiteflies. This is true, but using cages is a much easier way to grow tomatoes than staking. If you use stakes, make them about 6 feet tall so the vine can spread. Tie branches to stakes using a soft material, such as old hosiery. Mulch immediately after planting, using straw, leaves, grass clippings, newspapers or plastic.

Check the cages every day or two and push protruding ends back inside. The growing ends of tomato vines are less brittle in the afternoon or evening than in the morning. A healthy plant should fill the cage by midsummer. Let it grow over the top of the cage and hang down toward the ground.

Blossom–end rot is a common malady usually caused by a lack of calcium in the soil or stress from too little or too much water. You'll notice a big black or brown spot on the bottom of a tomato, and it usually rots up into the center of the fruit. Calcium moves through the plant in water, so a constant moisture supply is vital. Tomatoes need an inch of water per week. You can reduce the problem by spraying leaves with a calcium chloride solution, available at garden centers. Spraying should start when the fruit is the size of a silver dollar and should be repeated weekly for a month. You can test your soil in the fall, and add lime if necessary to help prevent a calcium shortage next season.

Tomatoes set fruit according to temperature. Most require nighttime temperatures of 55 to 65 degrees and daytime temperatures of 60 to 90 degrees. If blossoms drop, the cause may be nights that are too cool or too warm. Other causes are an excessive amount of nitrogen, insects or too much shade.

It's important to begin a spraying program (chemical fungicide and insecticide, or organic sprays) to control disease and insects soon after setting out plants. Early blight greatly reduces the yield and length of the harvest season unless it is stopped. Spray the plants from all sides every seven to 10 days and be sure to cover both the top and bottom of the leaves.

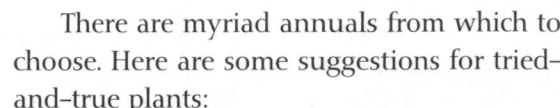

Summer Annuals Give Your Garden a Splash of Color

It's time to put out bedding plants, those marvelous, colorful annuals that brighten your life all summer.

Buy only healthy plants. Look for diseased or dead plants in the packs or containers before buying. Check the soil. It should be moist. Inspect the roots, if possible. They should be white or straw–colored, not brown. If roots are protruding from containers, they may have been there too long and will be injured when the plant is removed. Also check for stem injury at soil level.

The best plants to buy are those not in bud or bloom at planting time. If your plants are in bloom, pinch off flowers so the plant will bush out and be stronger.

To provide the most impact in your garden, group plants in beds or borders. Beds should be small areas with a regular shape, while a border implies a larger area that may be regular or irregular in outline.

Arrange groups of annuals so each group functions visually as a floral mass, rather than as straight rows of individual plants. Use smaller plants in much greater numbers than large plants. Vary heights.

Think of color combinations, too. A single color scheme may dominate the whole border, or you may want to place groups of different–colored annuals next to one another for contrast.

There are myriad annuals from which to choose. Here are some suggestions for tried-and–true plants:

For sunshine: Geraniums (in a variety of colors), sweet alyssum (white is great combined with geraniums), ageratum (bears blue button blooms), begonias, marigolds, petunias, snapdragons, verbena, vinca major (periwinkle) and zinnias.

Shade: Impatiens, coleus and caladiums.

As with any plants, prepare your bed so the soil is loamy, enriched and has good drainage. Evening is the preferred time to put your plants into the garden. The plant then has the cool of the night before it has to face the heat of the day. Bury the plant slightly deeper than it was in the pot. If your plant is in a peat pot and you're planting the pot, always bury the pot much deeper. If its edge remains above the surface, it has a wick effect and the roots will dry out.

Water plants well after planting. Protect small plants from wind and cold–weather damage with collars you can make from tin cans, foam cups or plastic bottles with the tops removed. If slugs and snails are around, use some bait to deter them. Fertilize every few weeks.

Early month

Lawn care

➤ Mow grass often so clippings will be short and will filter through the grass to the soil. Don't remove more than 30 to 40 percent of the growth. You also can save clippings for compost.

➤ Spray weeds in your lawn, if you must, as they are getting thick now. Make sure it's not going to rain for 24 hours after application. Fertilize warm–season grasses. Fescue should not be fertilized until mid–May , and then only lightly. Avoid weed–and–feeds, which can do more harm than good if used recklessly.

➤ If you're fed up with watering, fertilizing and baby-sitting your grass, the easiest to grow in this area is Centipede. You can start it from seed now. Buy a bag of seed in a garden center, and it can grow into a thick green turf that requires little care. Some readers have called it "retirement grass" because it needs so little care. Just remember that it turns brown every winter but usually stays green longer into fall than Bermuda.

Maintenance

➤ Now that spring bulbs have finished blooming, cut the flower stem, but do not braid or cut off leaves.

➤ Place house plants on outdoor porches or beneath large shade trees now. Sink pots in beds to conserve moisture. Do not place in full sun, or scorching will result.

➤ Divide large, old clumps of chrysanthe-mums. Failure to divide plants may result in weak, spindly growth with few flowers. Save the smaller plants at the edges of clumps. They will be your strongest plants. Discard old, woody portions. Fertilize chrysanthemums monthly until they bloom. Pinch tall–growing varieties until about July 4, so you will have a low, compact mass.

Pest control

➤ Check hosta leaves for holes, which indicate slug or snail damage. The pests feed at night, stripping leaves and stems from low-growing plants. A product called Deadline is the best chemical control. For organic, use wood ashes or sand sprinkled around the plants.

➤ Regularly spray peaches, plums, apples and pears to prevent insects and disease from taking their toll. Seven sprays are required in Southeastern Virginia–Northeastern North Carolina to produce healthy fruit each year. Any good multipurpose spray will do.

➤ Put a net or some other distraction over your strawberries, which may be ready to ripen. It's a battle to get them before the birds or possums do.

➤Ticks have been a greater problem than usual the last few years. Remember that they need brush or tall grass to crawl up on and drop on to their hosts. Remove as much of that kind of vegetation as possible around your home. The Bio–Integral Resource Center points out that ticks prefer humid environments. Trim tree branches so sunlight can reach the ground to dry it out. Water your lawn deeply but infrequently so it can dry out thoroughly between waterings. Ticks feed on birds and deer, and then move onto people and dogs. They recommend you NOT feed birds on your property because a couple of pregnant female ticks falling off a bird can send the tick population soaring. As for me, I'm going to continue to feed the birds, check myself carefully for ticks, and prune up shrubs that I normally brush against.

Planting

➤ Put out warm–season vegetable crops, including sweet potatoes and watermelon, if the soil temperature is warm enough for germination (60 to 70 degrees F).

Pruning

➤ Prune forsythia and other spring–blooming shrubs after they've finished blooming. Cut some forsythia branches back to the ground, and they'll grow back as long, arching fountains of color next spring.

Midmonth

Lawn care

➤ Don't fertilize fescue in the spring until mid–May and then only lightly. Virginia Beach extension horticulturist Randy Jackson says 90 percent of fertilizer on fescue should be applied in the fall. Fertilize only lightly now with an analysis like 25–5–10. Warm–season grasses such as zoysia, Centipede and St. Augustine should be fertilized monthly with a high-nitrogen fertilizer that will provide 1 pound of nitrogen per 1,000 square feet.

Maintenance

➤ Increase cucumber yields by growing them on a trellis. Give them some help getting attached. Fertilize cucumbers, squash, watermelons and cantaloupes with 1 pint of ammonium nitrate per 200 feet of row when vines begin to run.

Miscellaneous:

➤ Please don't kill honey bees. Eighty per-cent of our food production depends on them for pollination. If you have a bee problem, call a local beekeeper to remove them.

➤ If you grow spinach, endive or lettuce, be sure to pinch out the tops before the plants bolt and go to seed.

Planting

➤ Rhododendrons are in bloom or have just finished blooming, depending upon variety. They're sometimes difficult to grow here. Give them special attention. They are cool, moisture–loving plants and need sheltered high shade in a soil that is moist, well–drained, rich and acidic, with a pH of 4.5 to 5.5. If planted near a lawn, be sure to maintain that pH. Plant them on top of the ground with 10 inches of mulch, perhaps combined with a bit of soil, around the root ball for good drainage. When blooms are finished, fertilize them.

Late month

Maintenance

➤ Water hanging baskets frequently and use fertilizer at least once a week.

Pest control

➤ Eliminate aphids with pesticides to prevent sooty mold from covering camellia, holly and gardenia leaves. Or, use an insecticidal soap.

Planting

➤ Plant caladium bulbs if the soil is warm enough (70–75F).

J U N E

Preparing Your Garden For Summer

June begins the swelter season, meaning hard times for plants. Nurturing your garden now will prepare it for the onslaught of heat and humidity during the next few months. Watering, pruning, weeding and disease control should be your priorities.

After spring blooms fade, most plants and trees put all their energy into producing buds, or "fruiting," for next year's flowers. Unless there has been an unusually wet spring, now is a critical time to provide ample moisture. Supply all plants with at least 1 inch of water per week, or until the soil is wet one–half inch deep. Damaged plants, such as those stressed by a severe winter, probably will need water every other day. Newly planted shrubs and trees need water daily, especially during parched periods. Trees need 2 inches per week.

Early summer months are ideal for pruning the accelerated growth of evergreens. The purpose is not to decrease size but to increase density, or thickness. Density is related to the number of branches formed at the trunk by the end of each growing season. Proper pruning controls how far a new hub is from a previous one. The closer they are, the denser the shrub. Pruning too deeply robs the tree of its hardest working component, outer foliage.

Timing is important. Pruning should be done when new, pale–green foliage starts to turn dark. This change occurs when the "candle" of new growth begins to open. To stimulate growth, trim one–third of new growth. To contain a tree or shrub's size, prune 90 percent of new growth. New buds will form behind the cut to hide it, and new branches will increase thickness.

Indoors or out, a variety of plants are candidates for powdery mildew, especially if they grow where sunlight or air movement are restricted. The most obvious sign of the disease is a white to gray powder or webby coating on leaves, stems or buds. Infected plants become stunted with distorted leaves, buds and growing tips and eventually die. Wind carries spores from plant to plant.

Powdery mildew is most likely to occur when days are warm and humid and nights are cool. Among vegetables, melon, squash and cucumbers are most often afflicted. In the flower garden, chrysanthemum, zinnia, roses, phlox, monarda (bee balm) and verbena are popular victims. Others are lilac, crape myrtle, azalea, viburnum, English oak and dogwood. House plants include jade, African violet, begonia and grape ivy.

To prevent mildew, plant mildew–resistant varieties. Spray affected plants with fungicides such as Daconil 2787, Funginex, Phaltan or Flotox, a sulfur spray. Always clean up infected leaves when they fall. Place susceptible plants in areas with plenty of sunlight, well–drained soil and good air circulation. Prune trees and shrubs to improve air circulation and sunlight. Avoid overhead irrigation because it helps spread the disease.

Fragrance Makes a Scents-ible Garden

It's important to have color in your garden, but equally satisfying to have it smell good. Plant breeders have discovered that folks like fragrance in their flowers, shrubs and vines. A bloom is twice as nice when its scent lingers in the summer garden.

Many of the new hybrid lilies blooming this month have elegant floral essence. A single stem will perfume an entire room. Ginger lily, which is not a lily but a member of the ginger family, is one of the most sought-after plants for its delicate fragrance in late summer.

One evening blooming flower known for its sweet scent is *Nicotiana alata*, an annual that is hardy and may last through a mild winter; if not, it will reseed. It's superior to its hybrid dwarf cousins, which have no fragrance. Other fragrant plants include heliotrope, lemon thyme, rosemary, sweet alyssum, moon flowers, petunias, four o'clocks and carnations.

An easy-to-grow perennial and surely one of the most fragrant is tuberose (*Polianthes tuberosa*). There is both a single and double form, with the double said to be the most fragrant. Bulbs should not be planted until the soil is warm, around mid-to late May. Be sure to plant in well-drained soil.

Gardeners in Hampton Roads always have had a soft spot for gardenias, even though keeping them alive through severe winters is almost impossible. People are still planting them, though, because they like that sweet Southern scent.

There are more and more choices today among fragrant shrubs and vines. Many of these plants were bred in California, so care must be taken for them to grow in this area. Some suggestions:

• **Jasmine** (*J. sambac*) is an elegant vine on the West Coast, but in three attempts, those I've planted have not made it through the winter. A better choice is Carolina yellow jessamine, a native plant with spring blooms.

• **Mock orange** (*Philadelphus*) is an old favorite that's often overlooked. It's easy to grow and very fragrant.

• **Butterfly bush** (*D. Buddleia*) also grows easily and is available in pink, white or blue. It attracts butterflies and bees and is quite fragrant. It might die out in a bad winter but will come back from the roots in spring. It is attacked early in the season by spider mites, so be on guard.

• **Carolina allspice** (*Calycanthus floridus*) is another shrub native to the area that's simple to sustain.

• *Clerodendrum bungei* will grow 6 to 15 feet high with large, heart-shaped leaves as much as a foot long. It often dies back in winter but returns in spring and bears fragrant, rose-red flowers in dense clusters about 8 inches wide that butterflies love.

Day by Day, Enjoy the Glory of Daylilies

Mention daylilies and many people still conjure up images of those tall "orange things" that grow along roads.

But a wide range of colors, easy cultivation and outstanding performance have made daylilies the most popular perennial of the decade. Visit a daylily garden in June or early July, and you'll soon be won over. These dazzlers of summer are beautiful, aristocratic and easy to grow.

"This often overlooked perennial is now available in colors and forms that boggle the mind – glorious shades of rose and pink, sultry purples and blacks, and subtle shades of melon, along with sunshine yellows and golds," said Stephen Baldwin, past president of the Piedmont Daylily Club and an artist for the American Hemerocallis Society.

Actually, the rusty-colored "tawny" daylilies that line many older highways are descendants of the plantings of early American settlers, who were inspired by the plant's self-sufficiency. No daylily is native to the Americas. But from 16 species native to Eurasia, more than 35,000 varieties have been registered. At least 12,000 varieties are on the market today.

The name daylily is a source of confusion. The plant is not related to lilies, although its flowers bear a superficial resemblance. The botanical name *Hemerocallis* means "beautiful for a day" in Greek. Blooms last one day, but many flowers are formed on each stem throughout the blooming period. Once established, a clump of daylilies sends up many stems. They grow quickly and propagate readily. In a few years, clumps are so large that weeds are not a problem. It's been said that a daylily display is the closest most of us will come to a plant-it-and-forget-it garden.

You can plant from spring through Oct. 15, to establish daylilies before a heavy frost. Daylilies are categorized as evergreen, semi-evergreen and dormant. Evergreen refers to varieties whose foliage remains green until a heavy freeze; semi-evergreen foliage recedes partially, though sometimes not at all in a mild winter; dormant means deciduous, where the foliage dies back to the ground each winter. The first two usually out-perform dormant varieties.

The selections are nearly limitless. New miniature varieties, bred for small gardens, containers or mixed borders, are popular. More than 65 night-blooming varieties are available.

Early varieties bloom with peonies and iris and, carefully selected, will continue blooming long after other perennials have quit. Many repeat in fall.

Some daylilies, such as Stella D'Oro, will bloom repeatedly, sometimes all summer. Others, such as Bitsy and Green Glitter, bloom almost continuously through the season and are ideal covers for weedy banks or hillsides.

New hybrids are not invasive like their naturalized cousins.

A new daylily I started growing in 1995 is Forsyth Lemon Drop from Sterrett Gardens on the Eastern Shore. It is a golden yellow of medium height and blooms all summer long. I recommend it for every garden where you want summer–long color.

You can mass daylilies to create a riot of color. The largest selection of long–bloomers is in yellows and golds. For visual impact, choose hot colors such as coral, flamingo–pink or cerise.

The plants are sold by bare-root divisions called fans. When you plant, keep them shallow. Allow the soil to cover the top of the roots by one half inch and space them 12 to 24 inches apart, depending on mature size. After 30 days, scatter fertilizer around the plants and keep them watered. Quantity and quality of blooms are related to moisture in the soil. They grow well in almost any soil that is not consistently soggy or swampy. Sandy, heavy clay, alkaline and acidic soils are all fine. Extra organic matter, such as old leaves or peat moss, provides better growing conditions.

With a little care, daylilies even tolerate drought, weed competition or salt. They are one of the few perennials that thrive near the seashore.

Daylilies love sunshine, the more the better. But they also will grow and bloom with half a day of shade. A little afternoon shade protects sensitive varieties from sun bleaching.

For best performance, lift and divide daylilies every three to five years. Use a spade to dig and separate a mature clump into individual fans, or wash them apart with water and a hose. Newly divided plants often will bloom within a few months of replanting.

Once a freeze kills the tops, set your mower high, and mow them down. In early spring, fertilize with 10–10–10.

(Some growing data for this article was used with permission from Daylily Discounters Catalog, which quoted with permission from "Gourmet Gardening" by Anne Mayer Halpin, Rodale Press.)

The Essence of Organic Gardening

Organic gardening advocates have reason to celebrate because a swelling number of home gardeners have joined the move toward natural practices. Gradually, the chemical fervor of the '50s, '60s and '70s has ebbed.

"There are now more gardeners using primarily organic gardening techniques than primarily chemical techniques," according to results of a 1995 survey conducted for "Organic Gardening" magazine by National Family Opinion Research.

"Concern among homeowners for the environment has caused them to seek more effective, ecologically safer products for gardening and landscaping needs," said Gregory Gill, president of Harmony Products in Chesapeake. "Demand for natural organic products continues to grow, and the organic philosophy is being embraced by a whole new generation of gardeners."

The first step toward successful organic gardening is getting the soil right, experts say.

"Always emphasize enriching your soil," says Jeff Restuccio, a Memphis–based organic gardener and writer. "The main goal is creating an environment where the soil is very healthy – rich, porous soil."

In other words, strive to produce soil with the consistency of chocolate cake, and just as rich.

The best enrichment comes from your own compost heap, made from wastes such as chopped leaves, grass cuttings, vegetable matter and manure. But first–timers who lack a seasoned compost heap have myriad commercial options. Soil blends, peat, manure, or ganic fertilizers and even organic pesticides are widely available at gardening centers today. Some cities also sell compost, wood chips and treated sewage sludge for garden use.

The organic movement has been around a long time, led by J.I. Rodale, who founded "Organic Farming and Gardening" magazine in 1942 from his Emmaus, Pa., headquarters. That publication soon shortened its name to "Organic Gardening" and remains the communications backbone of the movement.

The growing list of alternative fertilizers include green manure (also called cover crops), seaweed, fish emulsion, bat guano, cow and horse manure, bone meal, blood meal, dolomitic limestone, granite dust and green sand.

Conditions must be right for the breakdown of natural plant foods, including proper soil temperature, soil moisture and microbial activity. Advocates say that organic products make for a healthier soil environment by increasing activity of soil beneficial microbes and earthworms, reducing thatch build–up, preventing and reversing fungal diseases and improving the physical structure of the soil.

In addition to soil enrichment, there are natural products and approaches to combat harmful pests. The place to start is with plant selection, choosing hardy, appropriate plants for the site, preferably native to our area. Healthy plants are more resistant to harmful insects and diseases because weak plants are attacked first.

Natural approaches to insect and disease control sometimes are not as quick or effective as chemical means, so organic suppliers remind gardeners to check plants frequently and learn when sprays and products are needed. Many visible pests can be picked off and destroyed by hand. Mechanical controls for pests include traps, barriers, cages, row covers and other devices that capture or exclude pests. Strong water sprays also can dislodge some insects, according to "Taylors Master Guide to Gardening."

Biological pest controls, also known as natural enemies or beneficial organisms, include: predators, which feed on other organisms; parasitoids, which kill the hosts they live on; and pathogens, which are micro–organisms that release toxins into insects that ingest them. Encouraging natural predators, such as birds and beneficial insects, aids pest control.

Bill Wolf, president of Organic Pioneer, his own company in New Castle, Va., recommends providing food and water for birds to encourage cardinals, hummingbirds and swallows to stick around and eat bugs. He suggests a T–perch on a pole to give birds a place to sit and search for bugs.

Organic substitutes for chemical pesticides include rotenone, which helps control aphids, cabbage worms, caterpillars, mealybugs, leaf miners, white flies and thrips, among others. Pyrethrum is used as a contact spray or dust to kill aphids, leaf miners, mealybugs, thrips, leafhoppers , spider mites and white flies. Bacillus thuringiensis (Bt) is a toxin–producing bacteria that kills caterpillars and insect larvae. All are derived from plants and break down quickly in the soil. Many organic gardening books also recommend a wide range of naturally occurring or naturally derived materials or organisms that can be sprayed or dusted on plants to control pests and diseases. These include insecticidal soaps, horticultural oils, sulfur dusts and other minerals and pesticidal compounds derived from plants.

Gardeners may have to spray organic products more often but only if pests are prevalent enough to require treatment. Insecticidal soap, for example, is effective against most soft-bodied indoor and outdoor insect pests, including aphids, squash bugs, flea beetles, leafhoppers, mites, mealy bugs, scale and white flies, but must be used more often than a chemical spray.

Early month

Lawn care

➤ Make sure the lawn mower blade is sharp so it doesn't mutilate your grass.

➤ Colorite, a company that makes a drinking water–safe lawn hose, recommends the following watering program: Water each section of lawn for about 20 minutes, early in the day, preferably on less windy days, on an average of three days per week. Token watering (less than 20 minutes) will only encourage shallow root growth.

Grass under trees may require extra watering because of the amount of water absorbed by roots. New sod requires a morning and afternoon watering for the first few days, after which morning watering will be sufficient. Too much watering, apart from being wasteful, will increase the lawn's susceptibility to fungus disease.

Maintenance

➤ Resist the urge to trim daffodil foliage. Tops should be left alone until they turn brown. Do not fold down the leaves and secure them with a rubber band, and do not braid them. Leaves are the plant's factory, necessary to produce blooms for next season. Daffodils also like some bulb food after they've bloomed. Some folks use bone meal.

➤ Hydrangea colors can be altered by changing the soil. A neutral soil produces white flowers. If the soil is acid, the flowers will be blue; if it is alkaline, flowers are pink. Flowers can be kept blue by applying aluminum sulfate to the soil, or you can make them pink by adding lime. You can even take one bush and add lime to one side, aluminum sulfate to the other and produce pink and blue flowers on the same bush. Aluminum sulfate, however, can burn a plant, so be careful. Use no more than 1 teaspoon on a square foot of soil. Apply to a damp soil and then soak it in.

Miscellaneous

➤ Be patient with flowering plants and trees. Some plants, such as dogwood, alternate flowering by blooming heavily one year, then failing to flower for the next year or two. Excessive pruning at the wrong time of year also can cause failure to flower. Another cause is too much nitrogen in the soil. This problem often occurs when trees are in a heavily fertilized lawn area. Finally, most plants undergo a juvenile stage when they're not old enough to flower. Southern magnolia, dogwood and wisteria, for example, may not bloom before age 10.

➤ If you use cut flowers in your home, you've probably noticed that the water gives off an offensive odor, even before the flowers are dead. The Dawes Arboretum Newsletter recommends adding three or four cloves to the vase water to keep the water smelling better.

Pest control

➤ Suggestions for natural pest control: Slugs are stopped by a ring of crushed egg shells. Be careful using Safer's Insecticidal Soap on ferns because they are susceptible to foliage burn. Set mealybug–infested house plants outside where birds can eat the insects.

➤ If yellow jackets spoiled your picnic, here's a natural way to control them. James Duke, an economic botanist for the U. S. Department of Agriculture, says to first find the nest. (They usually live in the ground.) After dusk, place a handful of molasses–flavored horse food on the ground within an inch of the nest opening. In the middle of the night, some critter (probably a raccoon or possum) will come in, eat the horse food, excavate the nest and eat them up. "They did a thorough job that was well worth that little bit of molasses and horse feed," said Duke, adding that his approach has worked more than once for him. To discourage yellow jackets, always keep garbage cans tightly covered.

Planting

➤ There's still time to plant warm–soil vegetables, such as melons, cucumbers, squash, peppers, eggplant and okra. Also plant flower seed, or put out new plants. Water daily if rain is sparse.

➤ Fancy–leaf caladiums can be planted now. Place them in a warm, well–drained, shady location, about 2 inches deep and 8 inches apart. After leaves appear, water them freely. Or you can buy them already started in pots.

Pruning

➤ Prune wisteria if it did not bloom this year. Get rid of long, straggling canes and all dead wood. If that fails to produce blooms next spring, try root pruning.

➤ Fertilize and prune azaleas by the first week if you haven't already done so. They soon start forming next year's buds.

Weeding

Inspect beds, driveways and walkways for grass and weeds. Warm days and frequent showers are ideal for all kinds of pest grass to germinate. Just squat down and yank them out by the roots, especially if they're near plants that would be hurt by herbicides. The hands–on method uses more calories and is safer than spraying.

Midmonth

Insect control

➤ Use leftover wood ashes to control pests in your vegetable garden. Spread them around cauliflower, onions and cabbage to repel snails and maggots. Ashes also help control red spider mites, bean beetles and scab on beets and turnips and supposedly discourage aphids from eating peas and lettuce.

➤ Check tomatoes for the nasty tomato hornworm. It can defoliate a plant in a hurry. Picking them off by hand and destroying them is the best control.

➤ Go after Japanese beetles. If you prefer pesticides, use Sevin dust or spray or malathion. Another method is to use a beetle trap, which offers both a sex attractant and a perfume that draws beetles. Place the trap at least 30 feet away from your beloved plants and you'll catch beetles by the hundreds before they do any damage. A long–term solution is to use milky spore, which can be sprayed or sprinkled on your entire lot. It gives the beetles a disease, which they spread to one another. It takes two to three years to become effective but supposedly lasts for 20 years. It's sometimes hard to find.

➤ Spray for scale. Among 150 or so varieties, oyster scale and cottony scale are two types that are easy to identify because they look like their names suggest. They can be found on the undersides of leaves of holly, magnolia, gardenia, azaleas (sometimes), camellias and others. Spray controls include malathion, diazinon or Orthene. Use them this month two or three times, at weekly intervals. An effective, less toxic alternative is dormant oil spray.

➤ Pick the bagworms off your evergreens lest they defoliate and kill the bushes.

Lawn care

➤ Raise the height on your mower blade to 3 to 3-1/2 inches. The taller the grass blade, the more it shades the soil, which means less evaporation of ground moisture.

Miscellaneous

➤ Pinch back chrysanthemums now through July 4 to keep them bushy instead of leggy.

Planting

➤ Pull pea vines which have stopped producing by now and replant with either lima or snap beans for a second crop. Do the same with radishes. It's time to buy waterlilies.

Pruning

➤ Prune Japanese black pine by cutting the new growth "candles" back about three-fourths of their length. New growth will sprout. A June pruning of these and similar pines should be an annual practice.

Late month

Maintenance

➤ Renovate strawberry beds. The berries need abundant water to fully recover after renovating or replanting.

Pest control

➤ Prevent the squash borer by dusting or spraying with Sevin, getting under the leaves and at the base of the plant, once a week from now until fall. Do it at dusk, after bees have quit flying.

Planting

➤ Put out sweet potato plants if you want to harvest them this fall. You also can pull lettuce and replace it with tomatoes (until July 15), peppers, eggplant or okra.

J U L Y

Saving Water By Xeriscaping

Our gardens may be soggy or parched this month, depending on rainfall. But even if we're blessed with daily showers one season, we could be cursed with drought the next. Parched summers of past should not be forgotten.

As temperatures rise globally and water supplies dwindle, conserving water is a growing concern among gardeners. More are turning to "xeriscaping" (zeer-i-scaping), a landscaping method that features drought-tolerant plants and efficient irrigation.

Xeriscape comes from the Greek word zeros, meaning dry. The term was coined in Denver in 1978 to describe a project that demonstrated how water could be conserved through creative landscaping. Since then, thousands of water-thrifty projects have been undertaken in the nation's arid states. Today's landscapes often require about 50 percent of home water use. But xeriscaping can reduce that amount by 30 to 80 percent.

Because of adverse growing conditions, drought-conscious planting has become the norm among beach gardens in Southeastern Virginia and Northeastern North Carolina. Sand, wind and salt spray are ever-present. Plants recommended by professional landscapers include Indian hawthorn (*Rhaphiolepis*), Japanese black pine (*Pinus thunbergiana*), perennials and ornamental grasses.

For inland homeowners, who invariably prefer carpets of green grass and lush borders, saving water may be a frightening concept. City-enforced water restrictions already are common in Southeastern Virginia. Homeowners are increasingly tapping their wells to feed sprinkler systems.

And here's a shocker that turf lovers will have to take sitting down: Someday, probably sooner than we think, there simply isn't going to be enough water to sustain those pretty lawns. Fertilizing may be taboo.

As was written in Poor Richard's Almanac in 1738: "When the well's dry, we know the worth of water."

Tips to make your garden drought–tolerant

Every homeowner can design his or her yard to conserve water. The best time to establish new plants is before a crisis occurs. Those who have planted wisely will be the envy of the block when the wells run dry.

Here are some guidelines provided by horticulturists and landscape architects:

➤ **Limit turf areas:** Lawns are water guzzlers. Keep grassy areas small and near other plants that need lots of water. Alternatives to lawns are wood decking, patios and naturally mulched walkways. What grass you do grow should be cut less often. Use a mowing height of no less than 3 inches to encourage deep root growth.

➤ **Use only water–saving plants:** Group plants according to water requirements and their need for shade or sun. For instance, cover a planting bed with a thick carpet of pine needles to make it a moist oasis for ferns and other shade ground covers. Convert lawn areas to deeply mulched azalea beds in the shade of tall pines and live oaks. At least one area should be dependent only on rain. Another zone should contain plants that need occasional watering.

➤ **Mulch heavily:** Two to three inches of mulch, whether it be pine needles, shredded oak leaves, bark or stone, becomes even more important. Organic mulch helps hold water and reduces evaporation.

➤ **Irrigate efficiently:** Overhead sprinklers are outdated because they waste water. In their place are drip irrigation systems and "leaky" hoses, which allow water to drip slowly into the soil at the base of each plant. Both systems water plants much more deeply than sprinklers. They also can be connected to private wells.

Oasis and turf areas can use spray or mist systems. Drip emitters or bubblers are best for vegetable and flower borders, shrubs and trees.

Probably the most important thing about watering is that it be done thoroughly so that the water penetrates deeply. A light sprinkling with a hand–held hose can do more harm than good because it draws roots to the surface.

Homeowners who have automatic irrigation systems should put them on manual control. Then the automatic sprinklers can be turned off when it rains.

➤ **Practice proper maintenance:** "Less work" is a key phrase in xeriscaping. You spend less time watering, weeding and mowing. Resist the urge to overwater or overfertilize. Let nature manage things.

➤ **Improve the soil:** One drawback to drought–tolerant plants is that they don't like to have wet feet; therefore, soil preparation is important. Clay and sandy soils hold water poorly, but amendments can boost water retention. Add organic matter such as compost, manure and topsoil to planting beds. Do this regularly because heat and humidity break down organic matter.

In times of crisis

In case of a water shortage, figure out your plants' priorities. Newly installed shrubs should be watered first, followed by old shrubs under stress, young trees, vegetable crops, container plants and perennial flowers. Annual flowers and lawns are at the end of the list. Home turfs will suffer very little serious damage from a temporary lack of water. Above all, don't worry about appearances.

Here are several ways to use water efficiently:

➤ Recycle "gray water," the waste water from shower, bathtub, sink and laundry. Unless polluted with detergents or other chemicals, it can be used on landscapes.

➤ Collect rainwater in a barrel at the downspout. If you don't have gutters, install them.

➤ Keep all weeds pulled because they hog moisture.

➤ Experts sometimes recommend spraying newly planted hollies and similar shrubs with an anti–transpirant (Wilt–Pruf or Cloud Cover) at planting time.

➤ Space plants closer together so their foliage shades the soil, as long as it doesn't create problems in pest control.

➤ Don't jump to conclusions when plants wilt. It's natural during the heat of the day, as long as plants recover by early evening. If they're still wilted the next morning, then it's time to water. Don't wait for the leaves to curl; otherwise, permanent damage is done.

➤ If no city restrictions are in place, the best time to water is in the early morning or evening when there will be less evaporation. Otherwise, follow your city's ordinance to avoid peak water-use times.

Drought-resistant choices

Contrary to popular belief, not all drought-tolerant plants are cacti. There are myriad colorful shrubs, blooming plants and trees that can get by with little water and lots of heat.

Herbaceous evergreen perennials do well also. The low-growing blue Pacific juniper is hardy, as well as Helleri holly, a Japanese shrub that grows 2 1/2 to 3 feet tall and 4 feet wide. Each requires excellent drainage. Perhaps the No.1 choice is yaupon holly, available in a dwarf form. Flower favorites include *Rudbeck-ia* (black-eyed Susan), iris and daylilies.

Many sun lovers are gray, such as artemisia, known as "silver mound." Ajuga, with its blue flowers, is a perky ground cover for dry shade.

Ornamental shrubs: Redbud (*Cercis*); the hawthorns (*Rhaphiolepis*); loquat (*Japonica*); American, Chinese, Japanese, Mahonia and yaupon hollies (*Ilex*); crape myrtle (*Lagerstroemia*); wax myrtle; red bay; pittosporum; beautyberry (*Callicarpa*); Japanese privet (*ligustrum*); yew; podocarpus; hackberry; euonymus; photinia; broom; autumn olive; cactus; yucca; nandina; mugho pine; black-haw viburnum; cotoneaster; pyracantha; and oleander.

Trees: Chaste tree (*Vitex*); Japanese Zelkova; lacebark elm; Leyland cypress; Virginia pine; water oak; live oak; bald cypress; hardy rubber tree; Chinese pistache; and Southern magnolia.

Salt-tolerant trees: Australian pine; seagrape; chinaberry; live oak; cabbage palm; and Japanese black pine.

Ground covers: St. John's wort (*Hypericum*); sedum; liriope; Virginia creeper; ajuga; Lamb's ear; rosemary; vinca; and low-growing junipers.

Summer Savior: The Crape Myrtle

From July through September, green patches of this area burst with shades of pink, red, lavender, purple and white. That's when *Lagerstroemia* (Latin for crape myrtle) converts neighborhoods and city streets into colorful spectacles.

So pervasive is their cheer that some leading horticulturists and veteran gardeners believe that our area should be the crape myrtle capital of the nation. Not only is this shrub/tree among the showiest, it's also the easiest to grow. For its long blooming season, it is known as the "tree of 100 days."

The late Fred Heutte is considered the father of crape myrtles in Southeastern Virginia. In the 1940s, he coaxed the City of Norfolk, as well as many garden clubs, into lining streets with the hardy shrubs. Today, about one-third of Norfolk's city trees are crape myrtle.

It can be either a shrub or tree, depending on how you prune it (homeowners are encouraged to prune those planted by the city). There are varied sizes. Dwarf varieties grow up to 9 feet tall, semidwarf up to 15 feet and the standard up to 30 feet. Some have weeping foliage, while others are upright.

During fall, some trees have yellow or orange foliage. Their twisted limbs and trunks are interesting during winter, when the bark peels.

There has long been an argument on how this shrub should spell its name. Fundamentalists insist it is "crepe." In the past, I have been chastised by more than one gardener for writing "crape." Interestingly, however, North Carolina State University spells it c–r–e–p–e, while Virginia Tech spells it c–r–a–p–e. I think I'll stick with the Virginia preference.

The crape myrtle was introduced into the United States in 1747 from China by early English colonists. Charleston, S.C., claims to have had the first planting at Middleton Plantation, where original plants still thrive.

The tree has only two known enemies: aphids, which usually are not much of a problem because there is so much more that's better eating in the garden; and mildew, which was a severe problem until mildew–resistant varieties were introduced in the 1970s. Mildew creates a musty gray shadow on the leaves and inhibits the plant's growth and beauty.

Overall, it's a hardy shrub that fares well in our sultry summer heat.

Care and feeding

Ideal planting sites for crape myrtles have well–drained soil and full sun. But they will grow well in heavy loam or clay, of which there are considerable quantities in Southeastern Virginia and Northeastern North Carolina. In Richmond and other slightly cooler climates where winters can be harsh, crape myrtle trees tend to die back in winter and return in spring as low shrubs.

Best pruning time is between late fall and early spring. It's the last shrub to leaf out in the spring.

Prune suckers at base of plant to keep trees looking trim and to discourage mildew.

To increase flowering, prune seed heads as soon as blooms fall. You'll get a second round of blooms in September.

Blooms are produced on new growth. If the plant is old, it can be pruned down to a stump, which will promote long shoots and arching flower trusses. But if you want a shrub, cut it off at ground level and it will rejuvenate in spring.

To form a tree (most are multistemmed), prune lower, weaker branches in the early stages of growth.

Don't plant them over a pool or driveway because they drop flowers, seed pods and leaves throughout the season. This makes them "messy" around a pool, deck or patio.

Fertilize annually before the end of May. Do not apply fertilizer, however, unless you can water it in. Also, a good mulch of well–decayed organic matter around the base will help hold moisture. To help boost flowering well into fall, feed in August with 2 or 3 cups of a complete fertilizer such as 8–8–8 or 10–10–10 around the base.

PLANTING TREES AND SHRUBS

If roots are densely matted, use a sharp knife to slice outside of the root mass vertically to help separate the roots.

Remove girdling roots, which are large roots that grow across or around other roots. If left intact, they can choke off tissues in the tree.

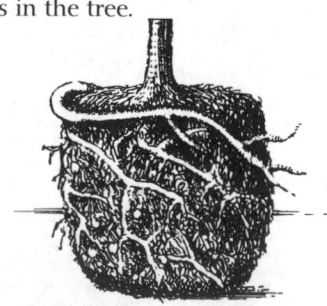

Illustrations printed with permission from The Davey Tree Company

20 *Lagerstroemia (indica X fauriei)* Cultivars Introduced by the US National Arboretum (Mildew–Resistant)

Cultivar	Flower Color	Trunk Color (on mature, exfoliating trees)	Fall Foliage Color
Semidwarf (Up to 9 ft.)			
'Acoma'	Pure white	Light gray	Red-purple
'Caddo'	Bright pink	Light cinnamon brown	Orange-red
'Hopi'	Clear light pink	Gray-brown	Orange-red
'Pecos'	Clear medium pink	Dark brown	Maroon
'Tonto'	Fuchsia	Cream to taupe	Maroon
'Zuni'	Medium lavender	Light brown-gray	Dark red
Intermediate (Up to 15 ft.)			
'Apalachee'	Light lavender	Cinnamon to chestnut brown	Orange-russet
'Comanche'	Dark coral pink	Light sandalwood	Purple-red
'Lipan'	Medium lavender	Near white to beige	Orange-russet
'Osage'	Clear light pink	Chestnut brown	Red
'Sioux'	Dark pink	Medium gray brown	Red-purple
'Yuma'	Bicolored lavender	Light gray	Yellow-Orange
Tree-type (Up to 30 ft.)			
'Biloxi'	Pale pink	Dark brown	Orange-red
'Choctaw'	Clear bright pink	Light to darker cinnamon brown	Bronze-maroon
'Miami'	Dark coral pink	Dark chestnut brown	Red-orange
'Muskogee'	Light lavender	Light gray-brown	Red
'Natchez'	White	Cinnamon brown	Orange to red
'Tuscarora'	Dark coral pink	Light brown	Red-orange
'Tuskegee'	Dark pink to red	Light gray-tan	Orange-red
'Wichita'	Light magenta	Russet brown to mahogany	Russet to mahogany

Options Abound For Seaside Gardening

Salty winds, sand and tides are problems for many gardeners in Southeastern Virginia and Northeastern North Carolina. If you live near the ocean, storms from the East cover trees and shrubs with salt spray. Those who live along inland waterways are bothered by high tides.

No plant, even a hardy one, likes to be battered by constant winds. If your garden faces the ocean, it would help to build a windbreak, such as a wall, thick hedge or fence. High dunes sometimes provide a natural barrier. A protected area will provide a microclimate for a variety of plants.

Sandy soil should be enriched with plenty of organic matter such as compost and peat moss. Raised beds are ideal for providing deep, fertile soil. Mulch will help retain ground moisture.

Protect trees and shrubs from storm damage by keeping them healthy and trimmed of weak branches. When storms hit, bringing high winds and salt spray, the first step is to prune any broken branches and tidy up the garden. Thoroughly hose down plants to remove harmful salt. Then apply an anti-transpirant such as Wilt-Pruf to broad-leaved evergreens to help them save what little moisture they have left. After a particularly bad storm, such as a lingering northeaster, it might be a good idea to do a soil test to determine the effect of salt and sand buildup.

Perennials that generally do well along the shore include: daylilies, dianthus, yarrow, artemisia, Butterfly weed (*Asclepias Tuberosa*) chrysanthemum, lantana, Gaillardia, Dustymiller, plumbago, Japanese iris, phlox, Hawaiian hibiscus (*Hibiscus Rosa-sinensis*) and liriope.

Popular grasses are dune grass, American beach grass (*Ammonphila breviligulata*) and sea oats.

Flowering vines include trumpet vine, climbing hydrangea and honeysuckles.

Many trees and shrubs are suitable for sandy soils that lack nutrients and water-holding capacity. If planted where ocean winds will buffet them, trees do best when placed in clumps of three. One lonely tree is less likely to withstand harsh winds. Here are some suggestions:

Live oak (*Quercus virginiana*): This wide-branching evergreen is especially hardy and can grow to 70 feet in height.

Juniper: For a low ground cover, use creeping juniper or shore juniper. The common juniper is a hardy shrub or a tall, upright tree growing to 10 feet high. All junipers are slow growing and require full sun.

Hydrangea macrophllya: This shrub develops globes of pink or blue in midsummer. They need lots of water their first year, however.

Yaupon holly (*ilex vomitoria*): Another evergreen shrub that can be grown as a small tree, from 15 to 25 feet high.

Bayberry or wax myrtle (*Myrica pennsylvanica*): This plant, native to Southeastern Virginia, is an upright, rounded shrub of 6 to 8 feet that grows in full sun or partial shade. You'll find it on many wooded lots. No serious disease or insect problems affect it. It's good for a rambling kind of natural hedge and will grow in clay or sand.

Russian olive (*Eleagnus augustifolia*): For a different color effect, use this

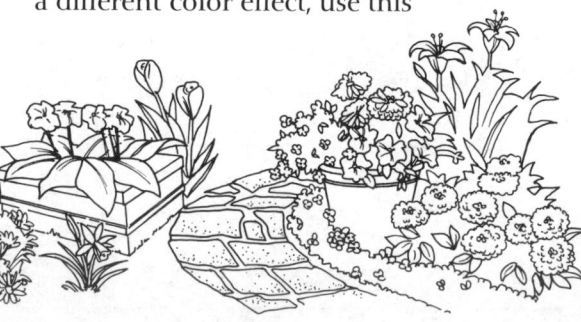

plant on sandy sites. The 3-inch leaves of the 14-foot shrubby tree are silver-green. It prefers full sun.

Staghorn sumac (*Rhus typhina*): This fast grower is a large, open shrub that can reach 15 to 25 feet high with an equal spread. Its upright clusters of fuzzy red berries and red-orange fall foliage are very showy in late summer and fall. The seed berries fall in spring. Be careful, or you can have a yard full of sumac.

Birch: The river birch, as well as most pine trees, will grow in sandy soil, but they must be fertilized and watered well when they are young. Good care during the first few years is crucial for their survival. White birch is especially difficult to grow in our area, but if you start with a very small tree, sometimes it will survive.

Bearberry (*Cotoneaster dammeri*):This slow-growing evergreen ground cover never gets more than 12 inches high and is native to the sand dunes of the Great Lakes. But it is grown from coast to coast. It does well in containers and has no serious disease or insect problems.

Yucca: The good ol' yucca is effective with modern architecture. Its flower stalk grows 3 to 5 feet tall. Long, straplike leaves grow in a low clump and spread out 3 to 5 feet. Hardy and pest resistant, it needs full sun. It will keep away children, pets and probably you with its knife-like leaves.

Tamarisk (*Tamaricaceae pentandra*): This shrub can grow up to 15 feet and has delicate, drooping branches with pink flowers. It needs pruning to keep it compact.

For stabilizing sand dunes: Japanese black pine (*Pinus thunbergiana*) is effective, as is Canadian hemlock. Scotch pine, another choice, likes full sun and sandy soil. And don't overlook Scotch broom. It grows up to 10 feet tall with slender green branches that stand erect.

Alternatives: If you're tired of taking care of plants, you can always landscape sandy areas with decorative walls, railroad ties or rock gardens. Then fill in with juniper, bearberry and other low-growing plants to visually soften the large rocks and walls.

A Look Inside 7 Private Beach Gardens

Seven seaside homes opened their private gardens for the annual "Gardeners in Their Gardens Tour" in May 1995 to benefit the Norfolk Botanical Garden. All were located at the North End in Virginia Beach. The sites varied from small native-plant collections to woodsy areas and a formal garden.

Here are brief descriptions of the gardens, which contain excellent suggestions for those wanting fresh ideas.

In the Gibbs garden on 69th Street, Ethel Gibbs celebrated her 90th birthday the week of the tour, proving that gardening is an enduring hobby. Her garden is a mature one, rich with memories dating back to 1959, when she and her late husband, Albert, moved into this home. Seven flats of Dusty-miller and pink dianthus fill a border flanking the front lawn. Simplicity and Fairy roses are behind them. Farther back are some of the largest and most beautiful live oaks in the area. There are many beautiful hollies. Under the old-fashioned arbor are hanging baskets of New Guinea impatiens, with a climbing hydrangea on a lattice nearby. In the back is a miniature vegetable garden, plus nectarine, pear and fig trees.

The Campbell garden, also on 69th Street, is tended by William T. and Meg Campbell. They are writers and artists who applied their creativity to design much of their own garden, though they credit Jack Campbell, formerly a landscape designer with McDonald Garden Center. Much of the yard is shaded by huge live oaks, but the primary feature is an elevated boardwalk through the garden. Lamium covers the shaded area, while blue pansies and pink carnations highlight sunny areas. They also have a vegetable garden and like to experiment with perennials.

The Addington garden on Ocean Front Avenue offers a good view of the ocean. Joe and Anne Addington planted masses of hydrangeas and Japanese black pine at the entrance. They also have a tamarisk, a seldom used but excellent flowering shrub for salt and sea locations. Along the pathway of walking stones are Powis Castle artemisia, lythrum, plumbago, daylilies, yaupon holly and vitex. In a protected spot on the southwest side are more than two dozen vigorous tea roses.

Dr. Alan L. and Jody Wagner have a terraced garden on Ocean Front Avenue, with an 8–foot drop from the dunes to the driveway. The gardens were planned and planted by Bill Pinkham of Smithfield Gardens. Their front patio is surrounded with pink Meidiland roses and white Indian hawthorne and offers a wonderful view of the Atlantic. Surrounding a playground for their children are Fatsia, holly ferns and eleagnus, all tough plants. Featured on the lower terrace are Gold Flame, a yellow–foliaged spirea, plus vitex, wax myrtle and a fig. Most of the plants are native varieties, best for surviving winter winds.

A small, private garden planted by Eleanor Marshall and her late husband, John, on Ocean Front Avenue is one of the most inviting. Eleanor is a devotee of native woodland plants. Fish in a pool with a fountain are shaded by a small Japanese red maple. A slate walk guides you through this peaceful garden, with native columbine, clematis and other woodland plants. Butterfly bushes and blue salvia lure butterflies and hummingbirds, and a purple martin house has attracted residents for 15 years. Unfortunately, rabbits devour native plants, so the Marshalls erected a low fence to protect their garden. Who would have thought rabbits would be a problem amidst sand dunes?

Betty and Josh Darden, also on Ocean Front Avenue, have a new garden designed by Smithfield Gardens. It was planted so that as it matures, it will be in the bold style popularized by Oehme and van Sweden at the U.S. National Arboretum in Washington, D.C. It features shades of lavender and purple with Homestead verbena and Baths Pink dianthus. A stone walk leads through a perennial bed of ornamental grasses, Russian sage, sedum 'Autumn Joy', Stella D'Oro daylilies and Moonbeam coreopsis. Creeping herbs such as prostrate rosemary, thyme and Herrenhausen oregano, provide a fragrant edge to paths and tumble over a low retaining wall. High winds ravaged an oleander but did not kill it. Rugosa roses provide color at the garden's perimeter.

Nearby is an impressive formal garden kept jointly by Vincent and Catherine Mastracco and Catherine and Preston White, whose homes are back to back. The homes, pool, black iron fencing and gates are done in the Mediterranean style. Single pink climbing roses cover the wall with overhanging lavender wisteria as you enter the garden from the Mastracco side. In front are masses of white daisies. Large clay planters filled with flowers of many varieties border the front patio. Catherine White says she's found that vining geraniums do best near the ocean. Boston ivy climbs the side of the home on the White's side, which is dominated by a swimming pool. On the ocean side of the homes are three floors of planter boxes filled with flowers. The garden contains many ocean–resistant perennials such as daylilies, veronica, yarrow, santolina and Joe Pye weed. Giant crimson hibiscus, rugosa roses and vitex provide a riot of color in summer.

Flowers Made to Last

Many flowers can be dried now so you can enjoy the ones you grew all winter long. Select fresh flowers and cut them at lengths from 12 to 16 inches. Strip away most or all the foliage. Tie them into bunches of half a dozen stems and hang upside down in a dark, dry room.

Virginia Tech's Diane Relf says that stems will remain in the same position when dried as they were when you hung them up. If you want a curved stem, bend it before drying. Florist wire can be wrapped carefully around thick, woody stems to hold their curves while drying.

Avoid drying in the direct sun because that will fade the color. Basements may be too damp for good drying. Good air circulation is necessary.

After two weeks, your flowers should be dried. Check, and if flowers are stiff and the stems snap, they're ready to use. Cones, pods, twigs and ornamental grasses can be dried without hanging.

Store dried flowers in roomy boxes of dust-free containers. A smart way is to stand them in an upright container and cover with plastic.

Easy – to – dry flowers

Amaranth	Dock	Mullein
Baby's Breath	Eucalyptus	Pussy Willow
Bachelor's Button	Ferns	Okra pods
Bittersweet	Goldenrod	Queen Anne's Lace
Butterfly Weed	Grains	Salvia
Cattail	Grasses	Statice
Celosia	Honesty Plant	Strawflower
Chinese Lantern	Hydrangea	Sumac
Corn	Lavender	Yarrow

Tips for Gardeners With Arthritis

Many "seasoned" gardeners do have difficulty with daily tasks because of arthritis. But there are myriad ways to help ease the pain and still have fun in the garden.

Here are some suggestions from the Arthritis Foundation compiled by North Carolina State University.

➤ If you have a large vegetable garden, it would help to have the soil mounded into raised beds or plowed into terraces that are about knee high. This will allow you to harvest and weed with less bending. A technique called Square-Foot Gardening uses raised beds that are boxed and divided into square-foot sections. A 4-foot-square box, for instance, would hold four different types of plants with one type per section. Beds even can be raised high enough for wheelchair accessibility.

➤ Foam-rubber pads can help protect your knee joints when you kneel in the garden. Look for them in sporting goods stores, discount stores, hardware stores or garden centers.

➤ Use a lightweight wheelbarrow or garden cart to move tools, seeds, soil and fertilizer around the garden without excessive lifting or carrying.

➤ Make tools easier to grip by adding foam-rubber padding to the handles. The "toy" utensils made for children to play with may be quite useful in the garden because they are smaller, lighter and easier to manipulate than their counterparts. To keep trowels, seeds and other supplies handy, wear a carpenter's apron.

➤ To avoid handling seeds, buy young plants from a garden center. Some seed companies offer pre-packaged seed tapes for some plants, mostly vegetables.

➤ Some perennials and bulbs do not require a lot of care, yet come back every year. Among those needing the least care are daylilies, daffodils, yucca, hardy cyclamen, butterfly weed (*Asclepias tuberosa*), various sedums, green-and-gold, coreopsis, purple coneflower, gaura, gaillardia, Lenten rose, black-eyed Susan and grape hyacinth.

➤ Use a soaker hose or sprinkler and leave it in place for the season. This will eliminate pulling out the garden hose or toting watering cans. It is also a more efficient way to water.

➤ Some plant lovers are limited either by space or ability to gardening in pots on balconies, decks or in windows. Ask your favorite garden center for suggestions about plants to grow in the conditions you have. Vegetables are not out of the question because there are many space-saving varieties.

➤ Wear a whistle around your neck, especially if you are gardening alone. That way you can signal for help if needed.

➤ If your hands and wrists are affected by arthritis, wear a pair of cotton or canvas gloves to help protect your joints from bruising. For hands that are especially sensitive, buy gloves one to two sizes too large and place foam padding in them. This extra layer will reduce pressure on painful joints.

➤ If you are unable to lift a large bag of potting soil or bird seed, take small bags or containers with you to the garden center and have someone there pour the soil or seed into bags you can handle.

➤ Stay in touch with other gardeners. Many gladly would provide emotional and physical support.

➤ Pace yourself and don't overdo. Remember, what is true for the garden is true for the gardener: Proper care brings rewards, neglect brings ruin.

Gardening Reminders for July

Fertilize

➤ Fertilize lackluster vegetable gardens. If your plants look like they're fading, North Carolina State University horticultural specialists suggest applying a "side dressing" of plant food. They recommend 8–8–8 or 10–10–10, or a special vegetable fertilizer. Use three or four cups of 8–8–8 per 100 feet of row, or one cup of ammonium nitrate or two cups of natural nitrate of soda. Place the fertilizer no closer than 6 inches from the plant stem. Water in thoroughly after the application.

Lawn care

➤ Set lawn mower blades higher.

➤ Watch for brown patch in fescue lawns if there's been a lot of heat and humidity. It's nearly impossible to control, so consider it a fact of life. Spraying weekly with a fungicide might help. If you must water, do it in early morning and only once a week.

➤ Continue to fertilize warm-season grasses (zoysia, Bermuda and St. Augustine) monthly through September. They seldom need weed killers because they grow tightly enough to choke intruders.

House plants

➤ Attend to house plants that have been moved outside for the summer. They need twice as much water as they did inside because of heat and wind.

➤ Give poinsettia plants some attention if you want them to rebloom for Christmas. Place them in a sunny spot in a flower border or near the edge of the patio. When new growth starts, pinch back long stems to develop a low, bushy plant. Don't forget to take them back inside before the weather turns cool.

Maintenance

➤ Check peppers, tomatoes, cucumbers, melons and squash, which grow fast with lots of rain. Harvest daily before they get overgrown.

➤ Prune deadheads (dried blooms and seed heads) from roses so that energy can be channeled into the plant. Prune down to the first five-leaved stem. Feed monthly and spray weekly if there's been a lot of rain.

➤ Keep spent blooms off perennials and annuals so energy won't be wasted making seeds. Sheer them severely to keep blooms coming through late summer and early fall.

➤ Use dry foliage from daffodils as mulch for tomato plants, or toss it on the compost pile. Mulching tomatoes helps prevent blossom end rot.

➤ Move or divide irises. Throw away the center rhizome but replant the outer ones. Most growers prefer to do it a month or six weeks after blooming. Replant rhizomes in well-drained, sunny beds and cover them with about 1 inch of soil. In heavy clay soil, leave the tops of the rhizomes uncovered.

➤ Give cucumber vines some help in the beginning to climb a trellis or fence. Once they take hold, they'll keep going. Watch for cucumber beetles and eliminate them with pesticides.

➤ Check foliage of gardenias, hollies, azaleas and camellias to see if they're anemic (yellow leaves, or not quite as green as usual). There might be a lack of iron in the soil. Apply chelated iron to improve health and color. It's available as a dry powder, liquid concentrate or ready-to-use liquid.

➤ Until July 15, pinch or prune your chrysanthemums so they'll bush up and throw out more blooms.

➤ Keep geraniums looking tidy by picking off yellow and brown leaves. Don't overwater, or their stems will rot. Give them a small amount of fertilizer monthly and they should bloom until fall.

Miscellaneous

➤ Enjoy the heavy fragrance of gardenias, a lusty symbol of the South.

➤ Cut flowers for the house early in the morning when their moisture content is highest. Use a sharp knife for cutting and plunge the cuts stems immediately into a bucket of lukewarm water. Recut the stems under water before arranging.

Pest control

➤ Spray apple trees regularly with a solution that includes both an insecticide and fungicide (if the weather is wet).

➤ Control spider mites. If you've noticed a shrub or evergreen slowly dying, or a large limb on an evergreen that turned brown last year, the problem could be mites. First try hosing the plant thoroughly. Chemical sprays are kelthane and Orthene.

➤ Scare birds and squirrels away from fruit by placing rubber snakes or owls in your garden. Move them every few days or so to keep the birds guessing.

Planting

➤ Water newly set plants every day, or they'll die. Established plants can wait a few days.

➤ Set tomato plants in the garden if you want a fall crop. You can produce your own plants by pruning out suckers (those shoots that grow between the main stem and a limb) and rooting them in a soil mix; or, buy plants at a garden center.

➤ Plant seed for fall crops of cabbage, cauliflower, broccoli and others in that family. The secret is to keep the seed damp until it germinates.

➤ Grow your own. Many deciduous shrubs can be propagated now. Cut 7–inch tips of new growth, remove leaves from the lower half, dip into Rootone and plant in a moist, clean rooting medium such as perlite, vermiculite or sterilized sand in clean pots. Cover the pots with a plastic bag and seal with a rubber band. Place pots in the shade indoors or out. In two weeks, check to see if your cuttings are rooted. If not, keep longer in the covered pot. If rooted, plant in the ground or pot it up in good soil in partial shade.

Prune

➤ Prune overgrown trees and shrubs so they have time to throw out new growth and harden off before fall.

A U G U S T

Feeling At Home in a Native Garden

It's time to go native. That doesn't mean you should dress like an American Indian, but you may want to plant some of the flowers, shrubs and trees that are native to this area, plants that may have grown in Colonial times.

Native plants are hardy because they grow naturally in Southeastern Virginia and North-eastern North Carolina. They require less water, less fertilizer, less total care. Most are pest–free and disease–resistant.

If those virtues appeal to you, then convert your garden. Pull out those fussy shrubs that continually have to be pruned and watered. Or, if you have an area not yet landscaped, plan to use some indigenous favorites.

Native flowers often are called wildflowers. The Vermont Wildflower Farm, a large purveyor of seeds, begins its video on how to build a wildflower meadow with the following instructions:

"Do not use fertilizer.

"Do not use lime.

"Do not use peat moss."

You can't beat that for low–cost gardening.

Let's look at a variety of tried–and–true plants that grow well in this area. We'll begin at ground level with ground covers and work up to the top with trees. Note that many plants go by more than one name.

Ground Covers

Galax aphylla: A shade–loving plant, often found in woods around Virginia Beach. Blooms are 5–inch white spikes in late spring.

Asarum, **arum** or **wild ginger:** Heart-shaped, glossy leaves stay green all winter.

Partridge berry, or *Mitchella repens:* A small, rapidly spreading evergreen with white blooms in late spring, followed by red berries.

Marsh marigold, or *Caltha palustris:* Shiny green leaves disappear when hot weather arrives but revive in fall, followed by many yellow buttercup–type blooms. It often has the first blooms of spring. Its seeds spread, so the plant may appear in different places in the garden from year to year.

Pachysandra terminalis, or **Japanese spurge:** The best ground cover for shade, this easy-to–grow plant stays green year around. White blooms in spring are insignificant. It does not like sunshine.

Ferns: There are many woodland ferns: Christmas, Cinnamon, Royal Fern and Bracken, to name a few, and they're all native. They prefer shade. One outstanding native that few people grow is the Japanese climbing fern.

With beautiful delicate foliage, it is a winner, but is sometimes hard to find.

Flowers

Shade Lovers

Wild red columbine, or *Aquilegia canadensis:* Red and yellow nodding blooms in early spring are beguiling. The seeds will blow around and germinate in other parts of your garden. This is the best columbine to grow, unless you want to replant every two years. The colorful hybrids are beautiful, but they won't come back after a couple of years in our hot, humid summers.

Jack-in-the-Pulpit, Indian turnip, or *Arisaema triphyllum:* Anyone who has ever walked in the woods is familiar with this wildflower. It grows 6 to 8 inches tall and has an unusual hood over its greenish-brown bloom. Children are fascinated by it. Birds like the seeds.

Dwarf iris, *Iris cristata* or crested iris: Only 6 inches tall, this blue iris prefers full shade and blooms in early spring. Also available in white and lavender.

Celandine, woods poppy or *Stylophorum diphyllum:* Yellow to orange blooms emerge in early spring. It prefers full shade but may not come back the second year.

Sun Lovers

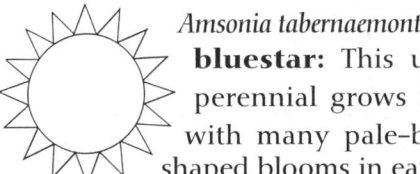

Amsonia tabernaemontana, Texas bluestar: This underused perennial grows 2 feet tall with many pale-blue, star-shaped blooms in early spring.

Asclepias tuberosa or Butterfly weed: Grows 30 inches tall in full sun. Orange-yellow to red, flat-topped cluster blooms provide a perfect landing strip for butterflies.

Baptisia alba, or white wild-indigo: This plant grows 2 to 3 feet tall in full sun with white pea-like flowers. Both blooms and foliage are beautiful. A blue version also is available.

Coreopsis or tickseed: Usually 2 feet tall, coreopsis is covered with 1-inch yellow blooms all spring. Butterflies like it, and songbirds eat the seed.

Echinacea purpurea, or purple coneflower: In full sun, this plant has oversized daisy-shaped blooms, pink to rose in color. It grows 3 feet tall, flowering in late spring and early summer. Available in other colors too.

Monarda didyma, bee balm or red bergamot: This native plant grows up to 4 feet tall in full sun with barn-red 4-inch clusters of blooms. There also is a purple version.

Oenothera tetragona, or Sundrops: A yellow-blooming plant that grows only 1 foot tall, providing lots of color in sun or half shade.

Phlox carolina: Old-fashioned tall purple phlox is a native. It is much easier to grow in this area than any other phlox.

Crinum lily or southern swamp lily: A white, flushed-with-pink, true native lily. Very large bulbs are easy to grow. But it's not much good as a cut flower.

Joe-pye weed, *Eupatorium fistulosum,* queen-of-the-meadow, or trumpet weed: Perhaps the easiest of all native plants to grow. Found along roadsides, it often grows 6 feet tall. Wants full sun. In late summer, it features soft, violet-purple blooms.

Seashore mallow, or *Kosteletzkya virginica:* This plant is abundant in the Cape Hatteras area, where it grows in ditches along the road. It will grow in your back yard if you have full sun, sandy soil and a wet spot. It doesn't mind being flooded, so it can be planted along the seaside. Pink blooms appear from summer to early fall.

Liatris graminifolia, gayfeather, or blazing star: This tough plant grows about 3 feet high and bears purplish-pink bloom spikes between June and October. It prefers poor but moist soil. Excellent for cutting. Also in white.

Rudbeckia, or black-eyed Susan: There are several Rudbeckias, all identifiable by their large yellow blooms and darker centers. It requires full sun and blooms in late summer.

This plant will move around because birds and wind carry the seed.

Boltonia asteroides: Blue green foliage grows 3 feet high or more, covered with small white daisy-like flowers. It's a good filler for bouquets, taking the place of baby's breath.

Wild ageratum or *Eupatorium coelestinum:* This plant grows 24 inches tall in sun or shade. Each stalk is covered with lavender-blue fuzzy flowers in late summer to midfall, creating a sea of blue. But it is very invasive, so be prepared to cope.

Helianthus augustifolius, or **swamp sunflower:** This dwarf sunflower grows only 3 feet tall and has small gold blooms 3 inches across. It blooms in fall and is easy to grow.

Goldenrod, or *Solidago juncea:* This is a love-it-or-hate-it plant. Once it moves onto your property, it never departs. Often seen along country roadsides, it grows as a 5-foot spike with a fireworks-like burst of yellow blooms at the top. There are new varieties that are shorter and brighter yellow. All are good for drying. It prefers full sun and wet feet.

Sun or shade lovers

Virginia spiderwort or *Tradescantia:* This flowering plant features grass-like leaves with blue to lavender blooms in early summer. It will bloom in sun or shade and spreads quickly to engulf a bed. It could be used as a ground cover because it's only 10 to 12 inches tall. Also available in white or magenta.

Cardinal flower, or *Lobelia cardinalis:* Bright-red flowers appear on 8-inch spikes atop 3-foot plants in late summer, just in time for hummingbirds. It's easy to grow but must have lots of water. White, pink and purple flowers also are available. Will grow in sun or shade.

Stokesia: This flower is so sophisticated looking, you'd never guess it's native. Grows 28 inches tall in sun or shade with blooms of blue, lavender or white. Attractive foliage usually stays green all winter.

Physostegia, or **obedient plant:** A fine plant for cutting, it has 2- to 4-foot stalks topped by lavender, rose or white blooms. It does best in sun but will grow in shade. This one spreads by roots, so it can be invasive.

Remember that most of these native flowers have been around a long time, so they're dependable. Animals found them edible in Colonial times and still do. Rabbits will devour Cardinal flower, liatris and black-eyed Susan overnight. You will have to protect young plants.

Vines

Carolina jessamine (*Gelsemium sempervirens*): A popular vine with yellow, early spring blooms. It must have sunshine to bloom. Every seed that falls makes a new seedling in your yard.

Climbing hydrangea (*Hydrangea petiolaris*): This plant is classified as native but is sometimes difficult to grow and more difficult to get to bloom. But everyone wants a challenge, so a lot of gardeners try it.

Coral honeysuckle (*Lonicera sempervirens*): Don't confuse this beauty with the horrible Japanese honeysuckle that takes over your back yard if you're near woods. Coral honeysuckle is bright orange-red and a desirable plant.

Passion flower or **maypop** (*Passiflora edulis*): Large, lacy lavender blooms will keep on coming all summer. It can be invasive.

Wisteria (*Wisteria floribunda*): Fragrant lavender blooms appear in spring. A tough plant, it has been known to climb trees and eventually strangle them.

Shrubs

Inkberry (*Ilex glabra*): A member of the holly family, this evergreen shrub will grow in wet spots.

Mountain laurel (*Kalmia latifolia*): It is one of the most beautiful native plants in this area. But it is nearly impossible to move, and plants purchased in nurseries almost always die. They simply do not want to grow anywhere except where birds or wind have dropped their seeds. Consider yourself lucky if you have one.

American beauty (*Callicarpa*): Blooms are insignificant but are followed by showy purple berries. Prefers full sun.

Sweetshrub (*Calycanthus*), or **Carolina allspice:** Dark red blooms in spring smell like ripe fruit.

Sweet pepperbush (*Clethra*): It features blooms of white or pink on 8–inch spikes and is fragrant in summer.

Strawberry bush (*Euonymus americanus*), hearts–a–burstin' or Wahoo: It grows wild in woods around Suffolk. Blooms are followed by large 1–inch strawberry–like seed pods that open to show scarlet seeds in fall.

Oak–leaf hydrangea (*Hydrangea quercifolia*): Blooms are huge white clusters, often 12 inches across. It prefers a rich, acid soil.

Silky camellia (*Virginia stewartia*): An underused shrub that grows to 15 feet tall with large, single, white blooms in late spring.

Yucca (*Yucca filamentosa*): You may not love it, but it is native to sandy soils from here to Louisiana and may grow where nothing else will. It grows 5 to 10 feet tall with evergreen leaves and requires no maintenance, rewarding you with 2–foot spikes of white blooms in midsummer.

Virginia sweetspire (*Itea*): A slow–growing, small shrub that blooms in spring with 4–inch white spires.

Sweet mock–orange (*Philadelphus coronarius*). A sweet–scented bush covered with white flowers from May to early June.

Double kerria (*Kerria japonica 'Pleniflor'*): Festive pom–poms of yellow–orange appear in late March and April. It grows 3 to 6 feet wide and tall and performs best in partial shade but tolerates full shade.

Trees

Evergreens over 40 feet

Loblolly bay (*Gordonia lasianthus*): Grows in sun or shade and likes wet soil. Gordonia

blooms are white, opening one at a time from May to September, providing a bloom period of two to three months.

American holly (*Ilex opaca*): Many thrive throughout this area. Fragrant blooms in spring are small and insignificant, followed by red berries if it's a female tree. It is one of the South's most versatile evergreens.

Longleaf pine (*Pinus palustris*) and Loblolly pine (Pinus taeda): These pines are tall and good for this area. Longleaf has just what the name implies: long needles and very large cones. The loblolly, which is slightly shorter and has shorter needles, is prevalent throughout the area and provides just the kind of shade that camellias and azaleas prefer.

Live oak (*Quercus virginiana*): This wonderful tree, sculpted by winds along the coast, is the pride of the South. Very slow–growing, but if your lot is large enough, this is a tree that will capture your admiration.

Deciduous over 40 feet

Most homeowners prefer evergreen trees, but if you want a tall tree that sheds its leaves each fall, try these:

River birch (*Betula nigra*): It has light–green leaves that turn yellow in fall, but it is grown mainly for its trunk, which is salmon to peach and peels to silver. Its brown catkins in summer can stain a patio or walkway.

Blackgum (*Nyssa sylvatica*): Greenish new leaves turn brilliant red in fall. It has shiny, dark–blue fruit and, best of all, doesn't have gumballs.

White, or **Willow oak** (*Quercus alba*): Grows wider than tall but reaches up to 100 feet tall when uncrowded. In fall, leaves turn an orange–red, and it has large acorns. It has whitish bark and is a tough tree.

Trees 15 to 40 feet

Witch hazel (*Hamamelis x intermedia*), snapping hazelnut or spotted alder: A sturdy little tree with starlike yellow flowers, blooming from late September to mid–December. It grows to about 12 feet tall with a smooth, gray bark.

Yaupon holly (*Ilex vomitoria*): An easy-to-grow native with small red berries that birds like. It grows in sun or shade, in wet or dry soil.

Wax myrtle or **southern bayberry** (*Myrica cerifera*): Easy to grow, with a floppy, natural look. Often used for informal hedges and kept to 6-foot height.

Wild olive (*Osmanthus*): Small white blooms that are very fragrant appear in mid-winter.

Serviceberry or **shadbush** (*Amelanchier*): This tree grows in woods throughout the area and has beautiful white blooms in spring. It thrives in sun or shade.

Eastern redbud (*Cercis canadensis*): Rosy purple blooms in spring always attract attention in a garden.

Fringetree (*Chionanthus virginicus*): Here's a beautiful, showy tree with drooping white clusters of blooms in spring.

Flowering dogwood (*Cornus florida*): This is the native dogwood that brightens every landscape. It prefers some shade but must have well-drained soil.

There are many more, including silverbell (*Halesia*) and sourwood (*Oxydendrum*, or sorrel tree), each planted for attractive blooms.

Native plants can be found at garden centers and in catalogs. If you want to see a variety of them before shopping, visit one of the several native plant gardens in the area.

Be good to yourself – and your garden – by making gardening easier with native plants.

Proper Pruning of Hydrangea Types

There are many different types of hydrangeas. Many require different methods of pruning. First, be sure you know the identity of the hydrangea in the landscape, so the proper pruning procedure can be used. Here are some good tips from the Long Island Gardening newsletter:

Hills-of-snow hydrangea (*Hydrangea arborescens 'Grandiflora'*): Prune to the ground line each winter or early spring because it flowers abundantly on new growth and is frequently killed back during winter. If a larger shrub is desired (3 feet or more) and/or it is not killed back over the winter, prune less severely. Remove certain branches to the ground. Cut others back at varying heights from 1 to 3 feet.

Peegee (Hydrangea paniculata 'Grandiflora'): This is the most common hydrangea because of its massive displays of large white flowers in mid- to late summer. They gradually turn to pink and remain on the plant in a semidried condition long after the leaves have fallen. Pruning involves the removal of dead flowers, if unattractive, and annual corrective pruning of vigorous shoots. Thin and/or cut back the previous season's growth in late winter or early spring because flower clusters occur on newly developing branches. Without regular pruning, this hydrangea can rapidly become quite overgrown and out of scale in the landscape. It can, however, be developed into a single or multistemmed tree.

Florist, or **Hortensia** (*Hydrangea macrophylla*): This is a commonly grown hydrangea with large globe-shaped flowers. It is frequently forced by florists and sold as an indoor pot plant during the spring season. Once moved outdoors, flower color is dependent on the pH of the soil in which it is grown. blue if acid; pink if alkaline. There are also several white-flowered cultivars. Pruning can be accomplished at two different times. Late summer is more desirable because most hortensia types flower only from the end buds of upright or lateral shoots produced during late summer and fall of the previous season. Prune as soon as the flowers have faded and strong shoots are developing from the lower parts of the stems and crown. Remove at the base some of the weaker shoots that are both old and new. Always try to keep several stems of old productive wood, with a sufficient number of stout new stems that will flower the following season. Early spring pruning, although acceptable, will result in the sacrificing of blooms for that growing season.

Pruning this species too late in the fall (after September) is harmful. New growth, both vegetative and reproductive, will not develop proper maturity. As a good seaside shrub, flowering is more profuse in an open, sunny location. This however, increases its vulnerability to bud killing. Winter protection of the plant should be initiated in December to preserve buds for next year's flowering. Tie the shoots together and wrap with burlap. If left unprotected, delay any spring pruning until the buds swell in order to determine which wood needs to be removed, and then cut back to below the point of injury.

Oakleaf hydrangea (*Hydrangea quercifolia*): This plant is grown primarily for its handsome oak leaf–shaped foliage, excellent fall color, attractive flowers and interesting winter bark. It is ideally suited to a lightly shaded or protected location, and if grown in an exposed site, it is subject to some winter dieback. Prune back in early spring to remove dead wood. Cut back to below the point of injury and remove old wood to the base.

Climbing hydrangea (*Hydrangea anomala petiolaris*): A desirable mid–summer flowering woody vine that attaches itself by aerial roots to brick, masonry or wood. It requires little or no pruning. If certain shoots have grown out of bounds, reduce their length in summer. Frequently, concern is expressed about climbing vines that may be inundating a tree and causing irreparable damage. But there has never been a proven case of damage resulting from climbing hydrangea.

Cooperative Extension Service, Cornell University

Webworms, Caterpillars Make a Mess of Trees

The time is just about right for homeowners to start seeing large webs on the end of tree branches. The culprit is the fall webworm. But even though their work is ugly, the insects usually don't constitute a serious problem.

Fall webworms often are confused with the tent caterpillar. The distinction is that webworms form large webbed areas that cover the ends of branches, while tent caterpillars operate in spring and form webs in the crotch of tree limbs.

Webworms attack the foliage of at least 120 varieties of trees, say Virginia Tech horticultural authorities; however, most evergreens escape. Some of their favorites are pecan, hickory, persimmon, sweet gum, ash, cherry, willow and apple. Often you'll know the pests are back when you see webs in wild cherry trees growing along roadways.

Webworms are most active at night and feed in colonies within the webs. As the food is devoured, the caterpillars spin webs farther up the branch or will take in a new branch.

Unfortunately, their large webs seriously detract from the beauty of shade trees. And defoliation caused by their feeding on pecan leaves can reduce the quality of this season's nuts. If defoliation is extensive, crop yields will be reduced next season, according to experts at Louisiana State University.

Massive defoliation of trees is uncommon, but if that should occur over a period of several years, it may weaken a tree, making it susceptible to damage by other insects and diseases.

Folks who spray regularly, such as in fruit orchards, seldom are bothered because the early spraying keeps insects under control. Most homeowners, however, don't have the equipment to adequately cover a large pecan tree. If only a few webs are involved on small trees, it is more economical and environmentally prudent to prune them from the trees and destroy the webs. If you choose to spray (Sevin, diazinon or organic Bacillus thuringiensis), be sure to penetrate the web, or treatment is useless. Choose a still day so spray won't drift into your neighbors' yards. For large trees, contact an arborist or commercial spray company.

The best prevention is to check your trees regularly so you can remove the webs before they become large and numerous.

Other tree pests are common this time of year, too.

Bagworms are a perennial pest of evergreens and many deciduous trees. They form a silken bag over their body and weave leaves and needles into the bag. To control them, you must find them in spring when they are small and the protective bag is not quite formed. Then, Orthene will control them. For now, pick off and destroy them. Do it again in winter because they overwinter in their bags.

You'll sometimes see the orange-striped oakworm on oaks. They have two hornlike projections close to their black heads. These pests feed together and strip foliage from one branch before moving on to others. In severe cases, once they have consumed all the leaves on a tree, they'll crawl down the trunk and head for other trees.

Green-striped mapleworms feed on silver maples but seldom are severe in this area. They look like the orange-striped oakworm, but their stripes are green and their heads are red.

Poplar tentmakers, once obscure pests, are making a comeback on fast-growing hybrid poplar trees. They are black caterpillars with yellow stripes. In severe cases, they can defoliate an entire tree.

Other late-summer defoliators include the azalea caterpillar, yellow-necked caterpillar and red-humped caterpillar.

Some leaf miners also are defoliators. Browning and leaf loss on locusts can be caused by the locust leaf miner. Oaks can have similar problems with oak leaf miners.

Preparing a Fall Vegetable Garden

Summer is nearly over, and while it may have been devastating to your vegetable garden, you can start fresh for fall. In this area, fall gardens often do as well or better than spring crops because of cool weather and clear, sunny days. The proximity of the Atlantic Ocean also helps keep the climate mild, allowing many vegetables to remain in the ground until a hard freeze in December or January.

Frost enhances the flavor of greens such as collards and turnips. With the cooler nights, cabbage, cauliflower, broccoli and turnips develop a sweet or sometimes nutty flavor associated with high quality.

One drawback, however, is that lingering hot, dry weather sometimes hinders seed germination. Seeds must have moist soil to germinate. A cool soil mixture should be maintained until enough roots are established for plant survival.

First, clear your garden of dead or dying

summer vegetables, and destroy them so they don't contaminate the new crop. Check the soil for any diseases or insects, especially cut worms and wire worms, that attacked your spring garden. Applying diazinon granules before planting will eliminate lingering pests.

Fertilize the soil with 6 to 8 pounds of 8-8-8 or 10-10-10 fertilizer over each 100 square feet of your garden. Apply mulch and wet the soil thoroughly to a depth of 10 inches 24 hours before planting. Do not fertilize plants as soon as they come up or you may burn them, resulting in death. After the days cool off, you can feed growing plants.

Rotate planting sites every season so that you don't encourage insect and disease problems by growing one crop in the same spot each time. Also, plant cool-season vegetables (broccoli) away from frost-tender plants (lettuce), so you can till the soil and prepare it for spring after your frost-tender plants have given out.

Planting at the right time is important. Compare the maturity date of the vegetables you want to plant with the first frost date. Planting dates will vary, depending on how close you live to the ocean. But expect a killing frost anytime between Nov. 1 and 15. Check the seed package to learn how many days are needed for that particular vegetable to mature. Then pick a variety that gives you enough growing time.

To prevent the problem of dry, crusted soil, cover seeds with vermiculite or compost material rather than soil; that way, no crust will form and seedlings will germinate quickly. For extra protection from the elements, lay an old sheet or curtain over the garden until the plants come up. Then remove it. Continue frequent waterings, using 1 inch of water a week as your guide.

Protection from the western sun is vital. Use a board, cloth, chicken wire or anything else suitable as shade material to keep plants from getting too hot. But be sure to check soil moisture daily.

If you use transplants, set them out late in the day when temperatures are cooler.

Be ready to use fungicides or insecticides because fall gardens are prone to problems. Here's a look at some fall favorites:

Spinach: It will produce a crop in fall, grow all winter and produce even more leaves next spring. Water daily to keep seeds damp for at least two weeks to germinate. After spinach plants appear, check them daily for aphid or slug damage. Thin spinach to 3 inches between plants. You can cut plants with only five leaves, to just below the bottom leaf. New leaves will shoot up. In severe cold, cover with Reemay, a spun-rayon blanket.

Broccoli: Sow seeds 10 to 12 weeks before the first frost, usually in early September. Thin seedlings to 18 inches apart. Harvest the central head while florets are tightly closed and the heads are 6 inches across. Cut with a 4-inch stem, and side shoots will continue to develop for several weeks.

Brussels sprouts: This vegetable is easy to grow, but it's best to buy plants instead of seed in fall. Tall stalks emerge slowly, sporting an umbrella of large leaves on top. Little sprouts form gradually, from the base of the stalk to the top. Harvest when they're the size of Ping-Pong balls.

Cabbage: Choose slow-maturing varieties that are bred for fall. Space seedlings 24 inches apart. Cabbage resents too much water and fertilizer. If heads begin to crack, give the plants a sharp twist to break some of the roots and slow up growth.

Chinese cabbage: This easy-to-grow vegetable has a sweet, peppery flavor. Sow seed by mid-September, then thin to 24 inches apart. Apply fertilizer every two weeks.

Collards and kale: Both produce large blue-green leaves and are loaded with vitamins. Sow seed now, and thin to 24 inches apart. Pick leaves when ready, or cut out the entire rosette.

Other vegetables that can be grown in fall include beets, carrots, Swiss chard, kohlrabi and leeks.

Gardening Reminders for August

Early month
Fertilize

➤ Give flower and vegetable gardens a "side dressing." This feeding should be applied around the sides of the plants, but not touching them. Use 8–8–8 or 10–10–10, and water thoroughly afterward.

➤ Water hanging baskets, containers and newly planted shrubs daily. Use a soluble fertilizer once a week to produce more blooms on impatiens and begonias.

Lawn care

➤ Follow these precautions from Virginia Tech to help prevent brown patch in fescue lawns: Do not water improved fescues, such as Rebel II and Shenandoah, which are drought tolerant. Too much water helps launch brown patch. Raise the mower blade. Never mow closer than 2 1/2 inches; Remember that Kentucky 31 fescue is the most brown–patch resistant variety. If you spray, you must start whenever night temperatures soar over 70 degrees. That's when brown patch, as well as pythium blight, begins. Daconil is the best control but has to be applied every seven to 10 days. Granular Bayleton also helps but may not be as effective as a liquid. Fertilize only twice in fall, on Oct. 1 and Nov. 1, contrary to previous advice for three fertilizations. Fescues in good health should be light blue in August, not the dark green most homeowners want. Overseed every fall, but use only 4 to 5 pounds of seed per thousand square feet instead of the 12 to 15 pounds most homeowners apply.

➤ Feed warm–season grasses (such as Bermuda, zoysia, St. Augustine and Centipede) for the last time this year. Use a high–nitrogen fertilizer that provides 1 pound of nitrogen per thousand square feet. Then leave the lawn alone to harden off before winter.

Midmonth
Maintenance

➤ Rake up and destroy fallen leaves from diseased trees. Discard sick plants, especially in the vegetable garden and around fruit trees. Tidiness around the garden goes a long way in preventing diseases from spreading.

➤ Cut dead bloom stalks off daylilies as soon as the last bud blooms. Don't let the plant's energy go into the worthless stalk or seedbud.

Pest control

➤ Use snail and slug bait around precious plants. Hot, rainy days bring the pests out in force at night. Another problem now is mildew, so spray with a fungicide. Moss on sidewalks can be obliterated with household bleach.

➤ Use Sevin around your squash and tomato plants if you suspect stink bugs. If your tomatoes are distorted and dimpled, with corky or spongy inner tissue, as well as light yellow or white cloudy spots on the ripening fruit, stink bugs probably are the cause. Damaged tomatoes are edible, but you'll find pithy portions under the skin.

➤ Watch squash plants for borers. These white, grublike caterpillars bore into the bottom portions of the vine. Borers can be cut out with a sharp knife. Sometimes you can throw a shovelful of good soil on the vine, outward from borer damage, and it will re-root. Heavily infested plants should be pulled out. Large plantings may need spraying with malathion or rotenone. Experts recommend applying either product liberally at the base of the plant early in the season.

➤ Check eggplant for black beetles jumping like fleas when disturbed. They're flea beetles, and they scrape the upper layer off the fruit, leaving a brown scar. Virginia Tech recommends spraying with Sevin or rotenone when damage becomes severe.

➤ Look for the cucumber beetle on squash, pumpkin, cucumbers, cantaloupes, gourds and watermelons. One is pale green with black spots on its wings. The other is pale green with black stripes. Both transmit bacterial wilt, which kills plants. If you find one beetle per 100 feet of row, Virginia Tech recommends using a foliage spray. Ohio State University experts suggest Sevin or rotenone.

Lawn care

➤ Resist using weed killer on your lawn until fall. High temperatures increase the chance of volatilization, which causes vapors that can move to nearby sensitive plants. Directions on most weed killers say, "Do not use when temperatures are above 90 degrees F."

Disease control

➤ Spray roses with a fungicide weekly during rainy weather, or black spot will run rampant. For a non–toxic spray, mix 1 tablespoon of household baking soda per gallon of water, adding 1 teaspoon Sunspray horticultural oil and 1 tablespoon liquid soap. Also watch out for powdery mildew on crape myrtles and zinnias. Spraying Funginex or Daconil will help control it.

Fertilize

➤ Fertilize mallow hibiscus and butterfly bush (*Buddleia*) and remove dead blooms to encourge blooming from now into fall.

Miscellaneous

➤ Feed the birds. Cardinals, chickadees, nuthatches, titmice and others enjoy black sunflower seed year–round, according to the National Bird–Feeding Society. Niger (thistle), cracked sunflower and both red and white proso millet seeds attract finches. Beef suet appeals to woodpeckers and nuthatches. Use rendered suet, which has been melted and re-cooled, to avoid a melted mess. As for feeders, finches prefer tube feeders. Cardinals like platforms. Juncos and doves eat on or near the ground.

➤ Propagate new plants from your favorites. Take cuttings from holly, viburnum, pittosporum, azalea, camellia, and yellow jasmine. Cut about 5 to 6 inches new tip growth, leaving two to four leaves on each cutting. Cover the base of each cutting with Rootone. Place cutting in moist sand, vermiculite or a mixture of both. Keep the bed damp, and humidity as high as possible by covering the planting box with plastic and putting it in the shade. In six to eight weeks, your cuttings should be rooted. You can remove the plastic in October and put the new plants in the ground. I keep the plastic on all winter, remove it in spring and then put the plants in the ground.

➤ Flying insects such as hornets and yellow jackets like hot, dry weather. If you have a problem with bees, a local group will remove them for free. There's a charge for other critters. For information, call Tidewater Beekeepers at 481–0706 or Bee and Wasp Eradicators at 429–3134.

Pest control

➤ A lack of moisture or plant pests may affect next year's blooms on camellias and azaleas. Water all you can and check regularly for insects. Spray if you find damage.

Planting

➤ Although heat and drought are discouraging, you can still have garden color with summer tub plantings. Consider begonia, geranium, marigold, croton, Dusty Miller, verbena, vinca and plumbago. Or allamanda, cypress vine, passion flower, lantana and hibiscus. All should bloom until a November frost.

Pruning

➤ If you want large rose blooms in fall, some experts recommend pruning roses now to condition them. This pruning should not be as severe as early winter pruning. Cut canes back to 24 to 30 inches from the ground. Also thin out some of the canes. Continue to spray roses at least every 10 days and fertilize them monthly through mid–September.

➤ Cut back dahlias to about half their growth now that the first crop of blooms is finished. Stake them. Plants will branch out and produce a good crop of fall blooms in October. A light application of fertilizer is helpful.

Late month

Maintenance

➤ The dog days of August have arrived, and there is plenty to do in your garden. Pulling weeds and laying mulch are the most important tasks, as well as watering. Water once a week if there is no rain. But make sure you penetrate the soil to a depth of 6 to 8 inches.

➤ Pick green tomatoes off vines that may be drying now. Let fruit ripen in a cool place out of the sun in your house. If you leave them on the vine, insects will attack them.

➤ Divide and replant iris now to help them settle before winter. Cut leaves back to about 8 inches. Dig with a pointed shovel around all sides of the plant and lift the entire clump out of the ground. Wash away soil. With a sharp knife, cut off the short side branches with a cluster of leaves at the end. Throw away any soft rhizomes (roots). Replant new divisions and cover the rhizomes (the fleshy parts) with not more than 1 inch of soil. Water thoroughly.

Planting

➤ Fall is the best time to plant many herbs. Planting in the fall helps develop sturdy root systems in cooler weather and ensures the herb will be well established before next summer's heat. Jeanne Pettersen, founder of the Tidewater unit of the Herb Society of America, says hardy annuals and biennials that thrive when planted in the fall include coriander (also known as cilantro), parsley, chervil and German chamomile. Hardy perennials include lavender, oregano, chives, sorrel, thyme, sage, mints and tansy, all of which benefit from fall planting. Continue planting up to mid–October. Parsley seeds should soak for two hours before planting. Prepare soil by digging to a depth of 18 to 24 inches and adding compost, coarse sand, well rotted manure or other organic materials. This advice comes from Pettersen's booklet "Basic Herb Growing in Hampton Roads." For a copy, mail $4.50 to Plants With a Purpose, P.O. Box 2884, Chesapeake, Va. 23327–1686.

Pruning

➤ If heavy rains cause your trees and shrubs to grow like kudzu, resist the urge to prune severely. It could cause extreme winter kill because pruning prompts new growth. Tender leaves will not have time to harden off before a freeze, which could kill the plant. Wait until late February.

SEPTEMBER

Caring For Your Cherished Lawn

The time has arrived to give your fescue lawn the spa treatment. For healthy good looks next spring, it needs attention now.

In Southeastern Virginia and Northeastern North Carolina, reseed your fescue lawn between Aug. 15 and Sept. 15. Labor Day weekend is ideal.

Whether you're planting a new lawn or renewing an old one, fescue is the recommended grass for Northeastern North Carolina and Southeastern Virginia. Virginia Tech no longer recommends Kentucky 31 seed. Instead, experts advise using one of several improved fescues.

To decide whether to renovate or renew, follow this simple rule: If half of your lawn has desirable grass, all you need do is renew. If more than half is unacceptable, then you probably need to plow it up and start over.

Warm–season grasses

If you grow warm–season grasses (Zoysia, Bermuda, Centipede or St. Augustine) you need do nothing now. These grasses should be planted in spring because they won't germinate until the weather is hot. Some can be started easier with "plugs" rather than seed. Turf specialists recommend that the first fertilizer for these grasses have little or no nitrogen but lots of potash to help develop a good root system. Beginning in May, fertilize monthly through August with a product high in nitrogen such as 25–5–10. Many weed killers used on fescue are harmful to warm–season grasses, so be sure to buy the appropriate product.

Warm–season grasses turn brown with the first heavy frost and remain dormant all winter. Overseeding with rye grass is a waste of time and money. If you have a thick stand of Bermuda, you'll have a weak stand of rye and vice versa.

Instant lawn

If you're starting from scratch this fall and want an instant lawn, you may want to install sod or use plugs. Sod comes in rolls or squares and is laid like tile with pieces fitting neatly together. Several varieties of fescue grass are available. It can cost from up to around $5 per square yard, depending on the amount of soil preparation required, while seeding costs about half that per square yard.

Out with the old

For those who want to plant fescue seed, the first thing to do is rake out the old, dead grass, particularly where brown patch or other diseases ravaged it. Then mow the lawn short and collect clippings.

You would be smart to go over the entire lawn with an aerator to punch holes in hard soil. This gives seed a place to rest and develop roots. Don't seed by hand; instead, use a rotary or drop–type spreader so the seed is evenly applied.

Next, fertilize with 8-8-8, 10-10-10 or a special starter fertilizer. Now you're ready to seed. But which kind?

New fescues survive summer heat down through the "transition zone," which is the unpredictable area between regions ideal for growing northern and southern grasses. We are in the transition zone.

According to most authorities, these six fescue varieties always produce good results in our area: Shenandoah, Clemfine, Crossfire, Rebel II and Southern Belle. They have finer leaf blades, better sod–forming characteristics and develop root systems that make better use of available soil moisture and mineral nutrients (fertilizer) than any other lawn grass. Also, they are more resistant to diseases and insects, are more tolerant of mowing than older types and will grow in a soil whose pH ranges from 5.5 to 6.5.

Plugs and "sprigs" are available for Zoysia, St. Augustine or Bermuda. Sprigging, which costs about as much as seeding, is the process of cutting mature grass into short sprigs. Sprigs are then inserted into the soil about 6 to 10 inches apart and partially covered with soil. Allow a full season or more for it to spread into thick turf.

Add to this list the Titan variety, with an endophyte fungus to ward off insects and disease. And Shenandoah, which has a narrow leaf that looks almost like bluegrass, is also reported to be insect and disease tolerant and requires less fertilizer and water.

The Lawn Institute recommends seeding a single tall fescue to produce the most uniform turf. Locally, Rebel II and Shenandoah seem to be the most popular seeds, retailers report, because they are slightly darker green than their rivals.

Blends of two or more of the new fescues are popular and available in local garden centers. Do not, however, use a mix of Kentucky 31 and one of the new fescues. The 31 is so much more aggressive, it will crowd out the new variety.

But if you plan to overseed an established Kentucky 31 fescue lawn, you probably should stick to that variety. I haven't had any luck trying to introduce one of the new varieties in its midst.

Don't expect great results from seed that has been stored away in your garage. Like vegetable seed, grass seed loses about 20 percent a year in germination ability. After three years, it would be best to throw it away or feed it to the birds.

Starting a new lawn

Those who have Kentucky 31 – or any other grass – and want to switch to another variety, should first obliterate existing grass with a glyphosate (Roundup, Kleenup, Blot Out, etc.) Make sure no rain is forecast for about 24 hours. Reseed in 10 days with the grass of your choice.

For a new lawn, use 7 to 10 pounds of seed per 1,000 square feet (50 feet by 20 feet) and 6 pounds to cover the same area in an established lawn. Once you've seeded, water immediately and keep the seed damp by watering every day if there's no rain.

Many people mulch newly seeded areas with straw to keep the seed damp. Use one to two bales per 1,000 square feet.

In 18 days or less, the seed will germinate. Then you can fertilize a second time with a high-nitrogen turf food, such as Scotts Pro Lawn 37-3-3 or an organic such as Espoma 18-8-6. There are other good analyses high in nitrogen, but for fall application, I prefer those containing more than 30 units of nitrogen.

Wait until the grass reaches a height of 3 inches before mowing. Do not scalp it. Then keep it at that height until your last mowing in December, when you should mow short for winter.

If you have not applied lime to your lawn in three years, you can bet it needs some. If in doubt, take a soil sample to your local agricultural extension office. Allow from two weeks to a month to get the results. Several local nurseries also offer this service and can do it quicker.

Lime can be applied after the grass germinates and starts growing, about three weeks after seeding. Remember that it often takes six months before lime becomes effective.

Opinions vary on whether lime applied just before planting burns seed. To be safe, you should apply it at least two weeks before seeding so that it soaks into the ground. If there is no rain, water it into the turf.

When to fertilize

Apply high-nitrogen fertilizer in mid-October and once more in mid-November, for a total of three times this fall. If your lawn is iron-deficient, you also may need to add iron (chelated or ferrous sulfate) to one of the fall feedings. It's effective on fescues as well as warm-season grasses, in which case it should be applied during a spring feeding.

In late fall, fescue grass doesn't have the sunlight to grow leaf tissue, so it pours energy into roots. Fertilizing in November and December provides nitrogen to hungry roots.

Iron-deficiency symptoms include yellowing of the grass. The result could be iron chlorosis, a condition caused by a high pH, which enables other elements to block the absorption of iron. In extreme conditions, a powdery mildew disease develops, turning leaves solid yellow. The problem also may be caused by excessive soil moisture, poor aeration, high soil phosphate levels, high levels of nitrate nitrogen, low or high soil temperatures, overwatering or poor drainage.

Lawns need an inch of water per week. Use sprinklers or an irrigation system if rainfall does not do it for you.

Keep enough of your favorite high-nitrogen fertilizer to feed one more time very lightly in April or May. That's all the spring attention a fescue lawn needs. If you use a professional lawn-care company, warn the workers that you do not want any fertilizer applied after spring. Summer fertilization is one cause of brown patch, a disease that ruins fescue lawns.

If you have lots of weeds and believe you must spray to eliminate them, it's better to do it this fall rather than next spring. But wait until your new grass is up and growing. Otherwise, spray in May or June.

Easy Does It: Low-Care Plants Replace Old Favorites

It's not that families don't want attractive yards, but dad is on the road, mom works full time and the kids are in school. Who has time to care for the landscape?

Many plants care for themselves and create a beautiful landscape without requiring endless hours of attention. The problem is that some of the plants we've all relied on for years are high–maintenance plants. They became popular when fathers worked 40–hour weeks or less and mothers usually were at home. Those conditions rarely exist these days.

It's time to let go of old–fashioned gardening ideas and unearth some easier ways of landscaping. We asked prominent Hampton Roads horticulturists to name high–maintenance plants and practices that are best avoided. And we also wanted to know what works well in most gardens. Our panel consisted of: Brian O'Neil, owner of Southern Meadows Landscapes, Virginia Beach; Jay Mears, owner of Virginia Landscapes, Chesapeake; Bill Kidd of McDonald Garden Center in four locations; Linda Pinkham of Smithfield Gardens Inc; and Bonnie Appleton, horticulturist at the Hampton Roads Agricultural Experiment Station in Virginia Beach.

Problem plants

Without exception, these experts named the rose as the No. 1 high–maintenance plant because it must be sprayed, pruned and fussed over weekly, if not daily. Easier to grow are old-fashioned roses, which are hardier, and disease–resistant English roses and miniature shrub roses such as Lady Banks and Fairy. Another new favorite is butterfly rose (*Rosa chinensis 'Mutabilis'*).

Second on the hit list are fruit trees, also requiring frequent spraying to combat insects and disease. Instead, stick to figs, persimmons or blueberries.

Other undesirables include wisteria, a fast-growing vine that often takes over a yard or house, and topiary and other formal shrubs that must be pruned meticulously four or five times a year. Just as bad are foundation shrubs that grow 12 to 15 feet tall, obscuring windows.

Not surprisingly, lawn grass also was high on the list. "I recommend to my clients that they reduce their lawn area," O'Neil said. "Expand ground covers or low shrubs, especially around and under trees where lawn grasses don't grow well."

The following are more plants to avoid: photinia, which must be pruned twice a year and has leaf–spot problems; fescue lawns, which require a strict fertilization and weeding schedule; purple–leaf plums, devoured by pests; crab apple trees, susceptible to diseases; azaleas, which are fussy in the sun and won't tolerate wet feet; boxwood, requiring careful pruning and good drainage, not to mention pest and disease control; leyland cypress and junipers, attacked by bagworms and spider mites; euonymus, which often gets scale; sweet gum tree, which drops prickly gum balls; English ivy, a persistent climber that is nearly impossible to kill; Carolina jasmine, which drops many seeds that make new plants; and trumpet vine, also a problem with numerous seeds.

Lastly, hanging baskets require a lot of

time. They must be watered daily and fed weekly during summer.

Easy plants

In addition to recommending plants that require little care, Pinkham offered the following tips for low maintenance:

➤ Create raised beds using good topsoil and compost so plants will thrive, rather than become stressed and disease prone.

➤ Mulch all beds once or twice a year to keep weed pulling to a minimum.

➤ Install an irrigation system such as a soaker hose or sprinklers.

➤ Plant shrubs that mature to the desired size, rather than buying the biggest for the money. This will save time and labor in pruning.

Here are the experts' plant recommendations:

Shrubs: Dwarf yaupon holly, a tough native plant; Nandina; forsythia; weigela; hydrangeas; witch hazel; any of the spireas; viburnum, many of which are fragrant; au-cuba; camellias; false yew (*Cephalotaxus*) with dark-green, needlelike foliage and tolerates sun or shade; barberry, which has beautiful red foliage (also in green or yellow) and is drought tolerant; and flowering quince, bearing white, red or orange blooms in spring.

Trees: Cornelian cherry (*Cornus mas*), an early blooming dogwood that is covered with small yellow blooms before the leaves come out; fringe tree; styrax; lacebark elm; Chinese pistache; Japanese cryptomeria; Chinese hollies; crape myrtles that are mildew resistant such as Tuscarora, Natchez, Tonto and Sioux; and Japanese maples.

Perennials: Daylilies, whose foliage nicely hides the dying leaves of spring daffodils planted amongst them; helianthus, similar to a small sunflower; hosta; ornamental grasses; sedum 'Autumn Joy'; and Rudbeckia 'Goldsturm'.

Ground covers: Liriope, a versatile plant for wet or dry locations; Pachysandra; periwinkle; and Asiatic jasmine.

Mums Extend the Season

To everything there is a season, and for garden mums, that season is from now until a heavy freeze. That usually means 10 to 12 weeks of vivid fall color from chrysanthemums purchased and planted now.

Care basically is the same for all garden mums. Yoder's, North America's leading mum breeder, offers the following tips, regardless of color, flower form or flowering time:

➤ Always plant mums in a sunny spot. At least half a day of sun is needed. Plant in fertile, well-drained soil. Loosen the soil to a depth of 6 to 8 inches and mix in peat moss or compost to condition the soil and improve drainage.

➤ Measuring from the center of each plant, space mums 15 to 20 inches apart, depending on size.

➤ Water thoroughly, adding 1 to 2 gallons of water to the soil around each plant. During times of sparse rainfall, continue to water as needed to prevent wilting. Keep soil moist as winter approaches.

➤ Never fertilize flowering garden mums planted in the fall. All the season's growing has been done by that time. Plants will not need fertilizer until the following spring.

➤ Nature doesn't prune back plants as winter approaches and neither should you. Let the brown foliage stand through the winter.

➤ Mulch plants after the ground begins to freeze – not before – with leaves, straw, peat moss or other organic materials.

➤ Spring is the time to prune away old stems and gradually remove mulch.

Growing Garlic

Now is a good time to plant garlic in home gardens. Garlic not only is good for humans, but it's also useful in repelling many insects if planted among flowers and vegetables.

Start with garlic bulbs purchased at any grocery, and separate them into individual cloves before planting. Louisiana State University horticulturists say several varieties are available, but a few may be difficult to find except by mail. Tahiti, or elephant garlic, is the largest and mildest. Italian and Creole varieties are smaller and have a stronger flavor.

Once you start growing your own, you'll have plenty of fresh cloves to plant. But be aware that growing garlic is a three-year process.

Plant cloves 1 inch deep and 1 to 6 inches apart in the row. Allow 8 inches between rows. Fertilize before planting with five pounds of 7–21–21 or 8–24–24 per 100 feet of row. Apply Dacthal after planting for good weed control. Side dress with ammonium nitrate or nitrate of soda after garlic is up and again in February and March. Good early plant growth is necessary for high yields of large bulbs.

The sultan of garlic in Virginia Beach is Charlie Ward, who provides this advice: "Nip flowers in the bud in spring, so all strength will go into growing the bulb," Ward says. "By the end of June, leaves start to turn brown. When leaves are totally brown, pull up the garlic, but be sure to catch all the little 'knobs' or bulblets around the main clove. Hang the large cloves up by their stems so energy from the stems can drain down into the clove. In three days, your garlic is ready to use.

"Take the bulblets, dry them in the garage and replant them in September. The next season, they'll be round, about the size of golf balls. Pull up and replant them in September. The following spring, repeat the process above, drying the useable-size cloves and holding the bulblets for replanting in the fall."

As you can see, growing your own garlic is a three-year cycle. The time to start is this month.

Plants For Wet Places

One of the questions gardeners frequently ask is, "What can I plant in a wet place in my yard?" They've usually learned the hard way that many plants cannot stand wet feet. They slowly die.

Most plants do best in rich, moist but well-drained soil. To correct a wet area, consider surface ditching or underground tiling to provide drainage. An alternative is to add soil to fill the low places.

It may be more practical to use plants suited for wet areas. The Dawes Arboretum in Ohio reports that there are many web-footed plants that will grow in soggy spots. Remember that we're referring to areas where fresh water accumulates. Most plants will not survive in brackish or saltwater.

Here is a list provided by Dawes:

Trees: Red maple (*Acer rubrum*), alder (*Alnus spp.*), serviceberry (*Amelanchier spp.*), river birch (*Betula nigra*), sugar hackberry (*Celtis lae-*

vigata), sweet gum (*Liquidambar styracifula*), sweetbay (*Magnolia virginiana*), London plane tree (*Platanus acerifolia*), sycamore (*Platanus occidentalis*), bald–cypress (*Taxodium distichum*) and all the willow trees (*Salix spp.*).

Shrubs: Chokeberry (*Aronia arbutifolia*), strawberry bush (*Calycanthus floridus*), fringe-tree (*Chionanthus virginicus*), summersweet (*Clethra alnifolia*), Siberian dogwood (*Cornus alba 'Sibirica'*), bloodtwig and redosier dogwood (*Cornus sanguinea* and *solifera*), inkberry (*Ilex glabra*), winterberry (*Ilex verticillata*), spice bush (*Lindera benzoin*), bayberry (*Myrica pensylvanica*), eastern arborvitea (*Thusa occidentalis*), blueberry (*Vaccinium spp.*), arrowwood (*Viburnum dentatum*), nannyberry (*Viburnum lentago*) and cranberry viburnum (*V. trilbobum*).

Perennials: Giant reed (*Arundo donax*), calico aster (*Aster lateriflorus*), astilbe (*Astilbe spp.*), marsh marigold (*Caltha palustris*), rose mallow (*Hibiscus moscheutos*), iris (*Iris spp.*), Canada lily (*Lilium canadense*), Turkscap lily (*L. superbum*), cardinal flower (*Lobelia cardinalis*), bee balm (*Monarda didyma*), true forget–me–not(*Myosotis corpioides*), sensitive fern (*Onoclea sensiblis*), cinnamon fern (*Osmunda cinnamomea*), royal fern (*Osmunda regalis*), Japanese primrose (*Primula japonica*), common arrowhead (*Sagittaria latifolia*), globeflower (*Trollius spp.*) and violets (*Viola spp.*).

Be Secure With Your Shrubs

Although most of us don't like to think about it, trees and shrubs can help or prevent would-be intruders. Here are suggestions from the American Association of Nurserymen.

Think visibility when you plant. It's nice to screen yourself from your neighbors, but sometimes it's the ability of these neighbors to see your front and back doors that prevents a thief from entering. Trim back any large shrubs that obscure a clear view of the would-be intruders.

Plant thorny shrubs around the foundations of your home and below any ground-floor windows. This makes entry through a window less desirable – and potentially hazardous.

Dan Milbocker at the Hampton Roads Agricultural Research Center recommends these as some of the most thorny:

Barberry: All varieties.

Eleagnus (Russian olive): It grows very large – 15 to 20 feet tall and wide and becomes almost impenetrable.

Pyracantha: Plant it thick, since it usually grows more tall than wide. It doesn't like to be moved, so plant it where it will remain forever. It sometimes winter kills in servere winters

Trifoliate orange: It has very long thorns and grows somewhat in the shape of pyracantha. It is slow–growing and often has small sour orange fruit.

Washington hawthorn: This is more a small tree than a shrub. It has showy red berries and long thorns.

All spiny hollies: Cornuta is the best variety for spiny leaves.

Finally, trim back tree limbs that could be used as a ladder. If you have lattice work running up the height of your home, plant it with a thorny or slippery vine that is difficult to climb.

Don't forget the outside flood lights, especially motion lights that light up when anything around your house moves. They help discourage intruders.

Early month

Fertilize

➤ If you didn't fertilize roses for the last time in August, do so now. Don't feed again until spring. Continue spraying for diseases and insects until freezing weather. In this area, roses usually are their best in October, so don't neglect them.

➤ If you're using organic fertilizer on your lawn this fall, apply it before you seed, and water it in thoroughly. Most organic fertilizers are dusty and smelly, compared with other types. Organics are apt to burn grass seed if you apply both at the same time.

Maintenance

➤ Fall is for weeding. Weeds rob your garden of necessary nutrients and moisture. Don't let them overwinter and create havoc in spring.

➤ If the weather's been dry, trees showing summertime stress are lacking water. Just let a hose trickle at the base of the tree for one to four hours, depending on size. With a large tree you can set a circular sprinkler with a low trajectory below the branches and soak the entire root zone for two to four hours.

➤ Camellias and azaleas need to be watered every five to seven days during dry weather, because this season is when their flower buds are forming.

➤ Mowers and string trimmers are mortal enemies of trees. Mowers compact soil over a period of time. Both mowers and trimmers easily damage bark, especially that of young trees, but also older trees, and particularly thin–barked ones such as beech. Mulch around the base of trees to deter weeds and provide a natural barrier to mowers.

Miscellaneous

➤ It's time to order spring bulbs for planting, which is best done between Oct. 15 and Dec. 15. Refrigerate tulips and hyacinths until you use them. All bulbs demand well–drained soil and will grow in full sun to part shade.

➤ One of this area's most prevalent wildflowers is often miscast as a villain that causes discomfort for thousands. Hayfever sufferers blame goldenrod for their late–summer sniffles and sneezes. The culprit, however, is ragweed (*Ambrosia artemisiifolia*).

➤ When buying or ordering bulbs, order jumbo or number one bulbs. Don't sacrifice quality for quantity.

➤ This is a good time of year to begin or add to your compost pile. Use leaves, lawn clippings and other organic materials. Apply about one–half pound or 1 cup of high–nitrogen fertilizer for each 10 square feet of material. Keep the pile moist but not soggy, and it's best keep it off the ground. Make a depression in the top to catch rain. Turn the contents every few weeks.

➤ Covering a compost pile with clear or black plastic will speed decomposition because of the increase in heat under the plastic. Keeping the pile moist and turning it every two to three weeks will also speed decomposition.

Pest and disease control

➤ If powdery mildew gets out of hand on plants, control it with a fungicide. Otherwise, maintain adequate air circulation around plants and give them sun. Don't water in the evening, when moisture encourages fungi.

➤ Spraying chrysanthemums weekly with a mixture of Maneb and malathion or diazinon may be necessary to control insects and diseases. Fertilize them at least once this month, using garden fertilizer. Mum flower size is greatly influenced by water supply. Keep plants well–watered during any dry period.

Planting

➤ Now is the time to plant a fall vegetable garden using transplants or seed for broccoli, Brussels sprouts, cabbage, Chinese cabbage and cauliflower. From seed, you can plant beets, endive, snow peas, kohlrabi, rutabaga, spinach, Swiss chard, turnips and kale. Remember that spinach seed is difficult to grow. The soil must be cool when you plant, and it must be kept damp every day until seedlings sprout. Slugs and cutworms often butcher young seedlings, so be alert.

Midmonth

House plants

➤ If you've a poinsettia you want to re-bloom, it should be kept in the dark for 14 hours a day from now until December. Water it very little.

Maintenance

➤ Dig iris if you didn't do it last month. They need dividing. Sort out the bad ones. Then re-plant the firm, good rhizomes. Iris borer gets into the plants regularly, so pick them out.

Pest control

➤ Check for azalea caterpillars, which may be on the prowl. Look for brownish-black and yellow caterpillars that strip off leaves and kill the plant. Prune limbs infested with the bugs. If they're covering the plant, spray with malathion or use Bt, an organic spray.

➤If you suspect borers in your peach or nec-tarine trees (and most every peach tree even-tually gets borers), this is the month to attack them. Virginia Tech recommends spraying with Thiodan now and again in 30 days. Be sure to use plenty around the trunk and on the soil. An organic control is Tanglefoot, wrapped around the tree trunk to prevent borers from getting in. If you're just now planting peach trees, keep in mind that garlic or mint planted around the tree is supposed to repel borers.

Planting

➤ You can start many perennials from seed now. Sow the seed thinly, and cover lightly with sand or sphagnum moss. Try pinks, baby's breath, columbine, shasta daisy, rud-beckia, coneflowers, foxglove and hollyhocks. Bedding plants such as larkspur, snapdragon, California poppies and alyssum can be plant-ed now, using the same method.

➤ If you crave a yard full of spring color but feel you don't have time to stop to plant the flowers, take heart. Plant Dutch bulbs. The Netherlands Flower Bulb Information Center says some of nature's most fabulous flowers are "'no-brainers," even for beginners. But when buying or ordering bulbs, order jumbo or No. 1 bulbs. Don't sacrifice quality for quan-tity. Dutch bulb experts say, the bigger the bulb, the bigger the flower.

Late month

Lawn care

➤ If you haven't reseeded your lawn with fescue yet, it should be done at once while the sun is warm and the mornings are wet with dew. Be sure to fertilize when you apply the grass seed. Use a low nitrogen, medium phos-phates, high-potash analysis such as 7-14-21.

➤ Remember that newly sown grass seed needs a constant supply of moisture to ger-minate.

Maintenance

➤ A long-handled dandelion digger is the most effective non-chemical way to eliminate dandelions. Try to get most of the root every time you dig one up, or else it will return.

➤ If you have hot peppers left in your gar-den, they should be picked before the first frost. Hang them up by their stems in a cool, dry place.

OCTOBER

Versatile Perennials Provide Months of Color

In a world of fast foods, fast cars, harried work schedules and children to pick up at school or drop off for soccer, when is there time to garden?

Perennials are the answer. These independent, nearly maintenance–free plants live at least two years, though most endure much longer. A garden full of perennials can be both a showpiece and work saver. With a little effort and a small investment, you can easily cultivate a dazzling array of flowers.

Fall or spring are the best times to plant or transplant most perennials. There are many plants for different uses. Helen Van Pelt Wilson included 500 in her 1975 book "Successful Gardening With Perennials." In 1989, more than 3,000 were listed in "Perennials For American Gardens," by Ruth Rogers Clausen and Nicolas H. Ekstrom. If you want a good book on perennials, "Perennials For American Gardens" is the one to buy.

How to grow

Versatility is a good description for perennials because different plants will grow in sun–baked sites, low–lying boggy areas, deepest shade or even in the most inhospitable soil. Most prefer full sun. Because the majority are deep rooted, they will occupy the same place in your garden for a long time. Most are grown in borders or beds, whichever suits one's space or taste.

You can have blooms from early spring to late fall, depending on the plant. Most bloom from two to six weeks, so it is important to have variety, if you expect never–ending color throughout summer.

In preparing a good home for your plants, be aware most need six hours of sun daily. Large trees not only block the sun but also become giant umbrellas, preventing moisture from getting to the plants beneath them.

"Shallow–rooted trees such as poplar, willow, beech and maple give too much root competition for most perennials to succeed under them," writes horticulturist and photographer Pamela Harper in her book "Designing with Perennials." It is a good book to have on your bookshelf.

Good drainage is important. Soil should be dug at least 1 foot deep. Incorporate humus, compost or peat moss into the bed.

Don't fret, however, because most perennials are adaptable.

Dividing

Another advantage is that perennials multiply. Most need to be divided every two or three years. There will be plenty of extras for friends.

Remember the old rule that if it blooms in fall, divide in spring (such as chrysanthemums); if it blooms in spring, divide in fall (peonies).

To divide, dig them up and cut the crown of each plant into several sections with a sharp knife. If the center portion of the old plant shows heavy, woodsy growth (iris is one example), discard and replant only younger outer portions of the clump.

Use quality plants

When planting in spring, you'll have better results if you start with plants growing in containers at garden centers. Although container plants may be a bit more expensive than dry-root plants available by mail, they're dependable. At a nursery you can see the plant, determine its health and decide whether you like it. Keep in mind that most of these plants look healthier in spring than fall because they go dormant as cold weather arrives. But planting in fall is acceptable, as long as it comes before freezing weather.

Quality is more important than quantity. If you're growing perennials for the first time, authorities recommend you build a bed no larger than 3 feet by 20 feet. Larger beds become discouraging because they're difficult to dig, expensive to fill and more work to maintain. So start small.

Rules of the road

A few rules suggested by Burpee Seed are:
➤ Mulch around your perennials with grass clippings, shredded leaves, compost, pine needles or bark. Mulch keeps soil moist and roots cool, and helps cut down on weeds.

➤ Stake taller perennials to prevent damage by wind. Tie plants up as they grow.

➤ After blooming, remove dead flower heads and stalks to prevent the plant from setting seed. Apply a slow-release fertilizer to keep foliage growing.

➤ Some plants (peonies are an example), die back to their roots in early fall. When that happens, cut stems back to 3 to 4 inches above their crowns.

➤ It's smart to mulch most perennial beds each fall with pine straw or shredded leaves to provide winter protection.

Say "no" to bugs

Perennials have few insect problems. If you spot a plant being chewed by bugs, a safe mixture of rotenone and pyrethrin usually will cure the problem.

Some perennials are prone to fungal diseases, such as powdery mildew on phlox and asters. That malady can be controlled by spraying with a chemical specific for mildew. Organic sprays include sulfur, bordeaux mixture or a copper fungicide.

Slugs and snails also can be a problem. If you notice holes in hosta leaves, most likely it's slug damage. Use a slug bait or sprinkle sand or wood ashes around the plants.

What to grow

In her book, Wilson says the most valuable "Big Four" are peonies, irises, daylilies and chrysanthemums. Those four alone can put on a show from March to late November in Southeastern Virginia and Northeastern North Carolina.

With a little planning, you can have a low-maintenance, inexpensive, pest-free border or bed that provides color from early spring to late fall – and have it return every year.

There are many ways to choose your plants: By sun or shade requirements, height; color; or blooming season. Following are suggestions by color:

White to silver foliage: Artemisia, Lamb's

Ears (*Stachys byzantia*), Snow-in-Summer (*Cerastium tomentosum*) and fleabane (*Erigeron*).

Yellow: Yarrow (*Achillea*), Coreopsis, daylilies (*Hemerocallis*) and Rudbeckia.

Blue to purple: Campanula, Statice (*Limonium*; hard to grow here), Salvia, Stokes aster (*Stokesia*), balloon flower (*Platycodon grandiflorus*) and Blue Lungwort (*Pulmonaria augustifolia*).

Pink to red: Dianthus, Geum, Mexican evening primrose (*Oenothera biennis*), Penstemon, Gaillardia, Bee balm (*Monarda*).

Sun lovers: Choose from Heliopsis, Aster Frikarti, Black-eyed Susan (*Rudbeckia*), Helenium, candytuft (*Iberis sempervirens*), Coral Bells (*Heuchera sanguinea*), Gaillardia, peony (*Paeonia*), Iris and Chrysanthemum.

Shade lovers: Choose from Liriope, mondo grass (*Ophiopogon japonicus*), Phlox subulata, Lamb's Ears, Hosta, vinca minor, Japanese anemones (*Anemone haroehenis*) ferns and foxglove (*Digitalis*; usually listed as a biennial but often seeds itself and repeats year af-ter year). Many daylilies will grow with half a day of sun.

Grasses

Not to be overlooked are ornamental grasses. The most popular are white and pink pampas grasses (*Cortadaria selloana*), fountain grass (*Pennisetum rupellii*) and Japanese blood grass (*Imperata cylindrica*, "Red Baron"). Some gardeners like to observe these plants when they brown down and arch gracefully in winter winds.

Growing 6 to 10 feet tall, pampas grasses make good hedges or screens. They can be 4 to 5 feet wide at maturity so should not be planted too close.

Fountain grass grows 3 to 4 feet tall and has flower spikes in shades of purple, coppery red or rose.

As its name implies, Japanese blood grass is red. It grows 24 inches high and prefers loose, well-drained soil.

Harvesting Broccoli and Cauliflower

Broccoli heads should be cut when they reach the size of your fist (3 inches in diameter) and individual flower buds are about the size of a match head, before they show any yellow. The yellow buds will open to be blooms, and you want to harvest before that. After the central or main head is cut off, small heads will develop on side branches. These "lateral" heads will continue to grow and provide more heads for you to cut later on.

The curd or edible part of cauliflower should be harvested when it is still compact and fairly smooth. Protect the curd from sunlight and frost by blanching or tying the leaves together over it when the curd is 10 to 12 inches across. Louisiana State University says the large bottom leaves can be snapped off and placed over the curds. Although strong winds may blow off the leaves, this method is easier and faster than tying. The head will then develop a good white color. But don't throw away off-colored heads, if yours end up that way, for they are edible and nutritious. A "ricey" or loose head indicates it is past maturity and low quality. Purple color in the head usually develops during warm weather, but it doesn't affect flavor.

Put Down Some Tree Roots

We need to plant more trees. The Society of American Foresters says that every year the average American uses the equivalent of one tree – 100 feet tall and 16 inches in diameter – for his or her wood and paper needs.

You might think you're doing your part if you use some of the 34 percent of paper annually recycled in the United States. But the foresters society says that even recycled paper consumes trees because it contains some new wood fiber for strength.

Still not persuaded?

Trees serve other purposes, too. Three mature, well-placed trees can cut a home's air-conditioning costs by 10 to 50 percent. An evergreen windbreak can reduce heating bills by about 23 percent. Real estate appraisers say trees can increase the value of your property by as much as 10 percent. Trees block out noise pollution, and can hide eyesores. Plus, they beautify the landscape and purify the air. One mature tree absorbs about 13 pounds of carbon dioxide a year, while adding back nearly 9 pounds of oxygen.

Oct. 15 through March 15 is the best time to plant trees in this area. If space allows, consider planting one tree per family member. Just don't plant all the same kind.

The Urban Horticulture Institute at Cornell University recommends at least 20 species in every urban area. "If you plant 10 trees, surely it would be wise to use at least five species with perhaps no more than three of one kind," says a Dawes Arboretum newsletter.

To plant a tree, choose a clean, open site with generous rooting area and good drainage.

Loosen and blend the soil in an area three to five times the width of the root ball and to a depth of 6 to 20 inches. In the center, dig a hole as wide as the root ball and slightly more shallow than the depth of the ball (or container).

Remove the tree from a burlap wrap or container and place it on solidly packed soil in the bottom of the hole. The root collar – where the tree's main stem meets the roots – should be slightly above the surrounding grade. Fill the hole with soil to half the depth of the root ball and settle the soil by watering. Fill the hole and water again.

Spread 2 to 3 inches of mulch over the area, about 6 to 8 inches from the trunk, to prevent rodent damage.

It is not necessary to stake your tree, but if you do, use a discarded rubber inner tube so the tree flexes in the wind. Remove staking at the end of six months. Water your tree deeply twice a week during dry periods.

If you don't know what kind of tree to plant, here are some good choices for Southeastern Virginia–Northeastern North Carolina: Pink dogwood (*Cornus florida*), False Cypress, Kentucky coffee tree, *Prunus* mume, red or white dogwood, oaks and pines.

More recommendations from Dr. Bonnie Appleton of the Hampton Roads Agricultural Research Center are:

Small and/or flowering trees: Kousa dogwood (*Cornus kousa*); cornellian cherry (*Cornus mas*); Chinese redbud (*Cercis chinensis*); Fringetree (*Chioanthus virginicus*); Smoketree (*Cotinus coggygria*); Carolina Silverbell (*Halesia carolina*); Japanese snowbell (*Styrax japonicus*); Sourwood (*Oxydendron arboreum*); Fernleaf or fullmoon maple (*Acer japonicum*); and Amur maple (*Acer ginnala*).

Shade or street trees: Lacebark (*Chinese*) elm (*Ulmus parvifolia*); Chinese pistache (*Pistachia chinensis*); Sourwood (*Nyssa sylvatica*); Yellowwood (*Cladrastis lutea*); and sugarberry (*Celtis occidentalis, C. laevigata*).

Evergreens: Japanese cryptomeria or cedar (*Cryptomeria japonica*).

Trees cost from $14.95 to $125 and more, depending on size and availability. Check around and see what suits your taste.

10 STEPS IN PROPER TREE PLANTING

1. Unpack a bare-root tree immediately and place in a bucket of water or thin mud. Do not plant with packing material attached to roots and do not allow roots to dry out.

2. Dig a hole, wider than seems necessary, so the roots can spread without crowding.

3. Cut off one-half inch of the end of the roots to expose live root tissue. Cut off about one-fourth of the length of the branches, or ask your nurseryman how much.

4. Plant tree the same depth that it stood in the nursery without crowding the roots. Partially fill hole and pack soil firmly around lower roots.

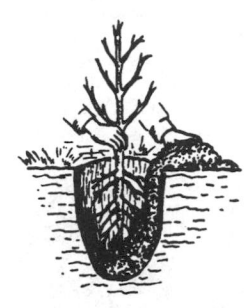

5. Shove in the remaining soil and pack firmly with the heel.

6. Give the tree plenty of water.

7. Pour protective mulch, such as pine bark or pine needles, around the base, after water has soaked in.

8. Wrap the trunk with burlap cloth, or strips of a commercial product available at nurseries to protect it from sunburn, rabbits, lawn mowers and other hazards. Don't use polyethylene plastic.

9. Fasten the tree to a stake to prevent movement of the root system.

10. Water the tree generously every week or 10 days the first year. Don't fertilize it the first year.

Art furnished by University of Nebraska

TREE GROWTH IN 10 YEARS

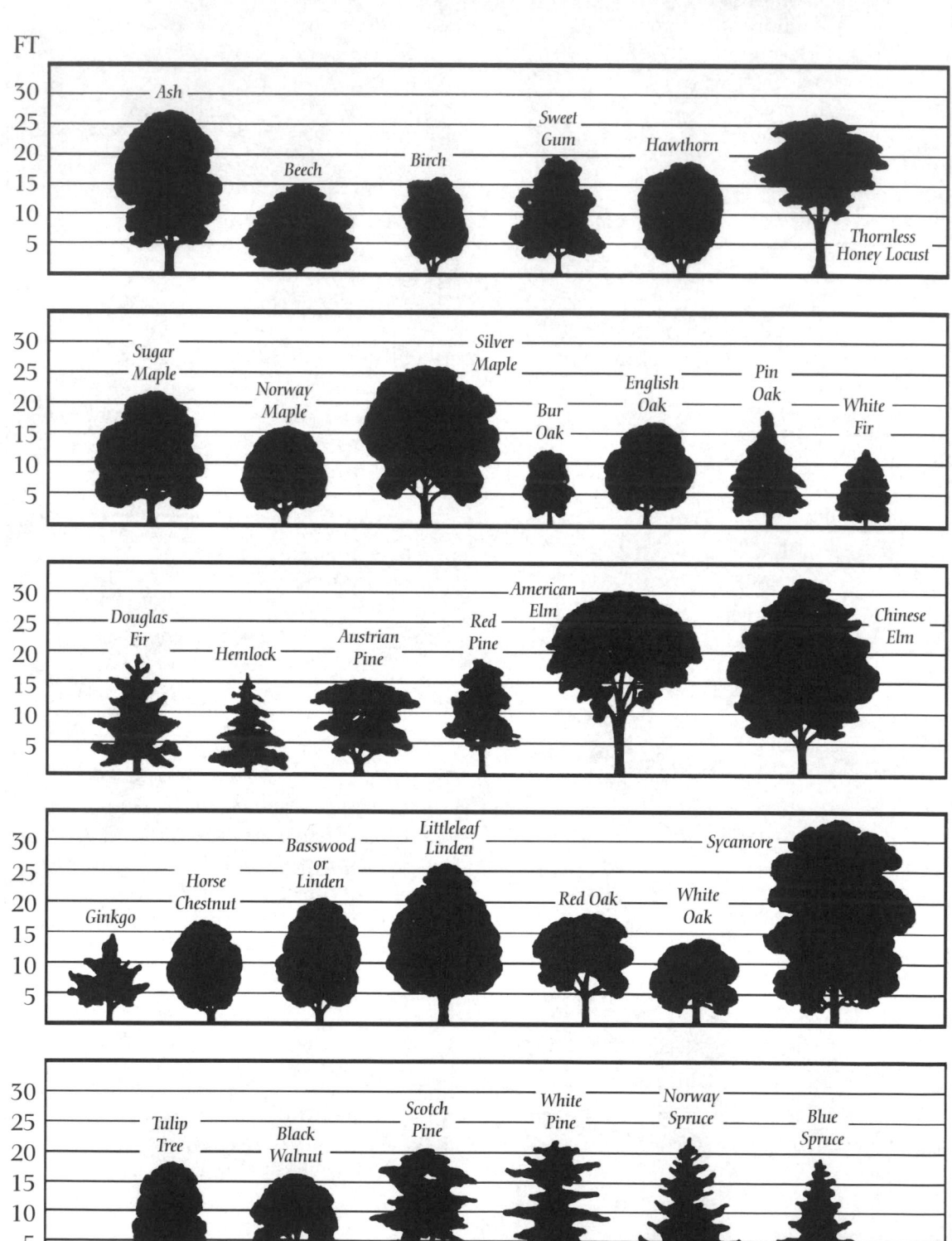

Illustrations reproduced with permission from the Bulletin of Popular Information, Volume 23, Number 3; published by the Morton Arboretum, Lisle, Illinois

Gardening Reminders for October

Early month

Lawn care

➤ Remember not to mow your lawn after reseeding until the grass is at least 2 to 3 inches tall.

➤ If the soil is compacted, aerate your lawn before reseeding.

➤ If you or your neighbor owns a dog, you probably have brown patches on your lawn where urine has killed the grass. Repair these spots by removing and discarding the top 2 inches of the highly acidic soil. Then spread a 2-inch layer of peat moss over the spot, topped with a thin layer of starter fertilizer. Use a trowel or shovel to work the mixture into the top 6 inches of soil. Then reseed the spot and rake the seed lightly into the soil so it is just barely covered. Keep the new seeds moist until you see they've germinated.

Maintenance

➤ Keep bird and grass seed in a mouse- and insect-proof container.

➤ Garden soils wear out from constant use, just like any natural resource, advises horticulture specialist Larry Bass of North Carolina State University. If you spend a little time now putting back what has been removed, your soil can remain productive. Adding organic matter is the solution. At least one-third of the soil in your garden should be organic matter. To have loam 6 to 9 inches deep, you should spread 2 to 3 inches of organic matter over the garden and mix it with the existing soil. You can add straw and leaves. But you must add extra nitrogen to feed the micro-organisms needed during decomposition. Usually 5 to 10 pounds of 10-10-10 per 1,000 square feet is recommended.

Planting

➤ Fall is the best time to plant trees and shrubs because the seasonal moisture helps roots develop before the heat of summer. Several, such as magnolia, dogwood, birch, tulip and golden rain tree are sometimes better when planted in spring because of their shallow root system.

➤ It's also a prime time to plant perennials. You'll have better results by using plants already started in pots.

➤ Gardeners who move to this area from the North complain about not being able to grow delphiniums. A good substitute is larkspur, which grows easily if you plant the seed outdoors early this month in a sunny spot. Cover lightly and by spring, you'll have nice plants. Often it reseeds itself so you'll have more every year in shades of blue, lavender, pink and white.

Midmonth

Fertilize

➤ Some researchers believe that a light fertilization in fall is good for camellias and azaleas by helping them develop stronger roots to get through winter. If you want to follow that advice, use a low-nitrogen food, such as 5-10-10 or 5-10-15.

➤ Yellowing of leaves on your Chinese holly can be caused by stress brought on by heavy fruiting. Fertilizing now with a special holly fertilizer usually cures the problem. Next season, begin fertilizing when the plant is in bloom and make a second application in early summer.

➤ It's a good idea to feed daylilies now. Experts say to use only half the recommended amount, and never use fertilizers high in nitrogen. Analyses such as 12-24-12 and 5-10-5 in fall and early spring are recommended. Daylilies also respond to bone meal or cottonseed meal.

House plants

➤ Bring house plants indoors and check for insects. Wash plants thoroughly with a forceful stream of water, including under the leaves. Sponge with a good insecticide, or spray one. Be careful not to break the foliage.

Lawn care

➤ Fescue and rye grass seed should be sown by mid-October in Southeastern Virginia-Northeastern North Carolina.

Maintenance

➤ Cover water gardens with netting, or skim daily, to keep out leaves and other debris. Feed fish extra food from the time the water temperature begins to fall until it drops below 45 degrees F.

➤ Compost leaves along with grass clippings instead of tossing them out with the garbage.

Miscellaneous

➤ It's called the "Narcissus myth." Most Americans know narcissi as daffodils, reports the Netherlands Flowerbulb Information Center. In the South, they traditionally are called jonquils. In fact, all daffodils and jonquils are narcissi, but only some narcissi are daffodils and only a few are jonquils. They are all beautiful, however, and this is the month to plant. Begin around the middle of October and continue until late November or even mid-December if bulbs are still dry and fresh.

➤ There is much confusion about the use of peat moss these days. Garden centers continue to sell it, but many universities' horticulturists don't recommend its use when planting. Virginia Tech extension specialist Bonnie Appleton suggests cultivating peat moss into the bed with a tiller if you're planting a new bed with shrubs, trees, bulbs or perennials. If you're digging a planting hole, refill only with the soil you take out of the hole. If you mix peat moss or bark with the fill dirt, roots often refuse to stretch beyond the hole. The roots also tend to stay too wet during rainy weather and too dry in drought.

➤ Leave hummingbird feeders up until mid-October to sustain birds that run late. Some birds hang around longer than they should and need to find food on their way to Central and South America for the winter.

Pest and disease control

➤ If you planted cabbage, cauliflower or broccoli, dust it regularly, about once a week, with Sevin or any natural control that works for you to combat insects. There are more bugs in the fall than in spring, and they love these cold-weather crops.

➤ For cricket control the natural way, animal nutritionist Lynn Christian recommends mixing 1 heaping teaspoon each of Borax, sugar and flour. Place the mixture on a sheet of aluminum foil wherever you find crickets. The next morning, you can dump plenty of dead ones. Keep mixture away from pets and children. If you're not a naturalist, spread granular Spectracide (diazinon) around the foundation of your house and at all entryways.

Planting

➤ October is best for planting camellias in this area. The late veteran camellia expert Zelma Crockett recommends placing two to three bricks in the bottom of the hole so the plant won't settle and be too deep. Light shade is a requirement. Pines that provide shade in summer and winter are best. Camellias grown in full sun often will have yellow leaves, according to authority Betty Hotchkiss in the American Camellia Journal. Camellia sasanqua will tolerate more sun than Camellia japonica. Protection from wind also is important.

Pruning

➤ Yoder, North America's largest grower of chrysanthemums, recommends cutting mums back to 5 or 6 inches above ground as soon as a freeze browns out the plant's foliage. Otherwise, the plant might grow throughout winter, becoming tall and leggy, with few blooms next year.

Late month

Lawn care

➤ Late October is an ideal time to control weeds. Many get their start in late summer and early fall. Usually they're so tiny you don't see them until spring. Herbicides are hard on grass, so be sure new grass is growing well before applying chemicals. The most efficient, inexpensive method is to spray an all-purpose herbicide, such as Weed-B-Gon, Weedone, 33 Plus, or any brand stocked by a garden store you trust. The next best control is a weed-and-feed product, if you haven't already fed your lawn for the second time this fall. For warm-season grasses, such as St. Augustine, check the label to make sure the spray is approved for your grass; otherwise, it might kill the entire lawn. The organic method is to thicken the grass so weeds can't get established. Provide the best soil bed possible, use organic fertilizer and mow tall (3 inches) to crowd out weeds.

Maintenance

➤ If you're growing gourds, it's time to harvest. Be sure the stem is dry and brown before picking. Let them dry before hollowing them out. Wash each gourd in 1 ounce of bleach mixed in 2 quarts of water, and dry with a soft cloth. Throw away bruised gourds, and place the good ones in an onion bag in a warm, well-ventilated area. Do not put them in the sun because they will fade. Curing takes one to six months. The outer skin hardens in two weeks, but internal drying requires another month. Turn them occasionally, and check for soft spots. Poke a small hole in the blossom end to quicken drying. When you can shake each one and hear seeds rattling, they're cured and ready for a coat of varnish.

Miscellaneous

➤ Whether red, blue, black or white, wild berries are among fall's showiest sight. But experts advise caution when picking them for home decoration because many are poisonous, such as baneberry and nightshade. Even berries from common ornamental plants such as dogwoods, hollies and mondo grass contain potentially harmful toxins.

Pest control

➤ If marigolds turned brown and died in August or September, check for small webs on foliage, which are signs of spider mites. They live on plant debris in the soil and attack many garden plants when temperatures are hot and humidity is low. Mites reproduce every two weeks during summer. By the time you see webbing, it's too late to save your plants. Spray twice a week with an insecticidal soap, making sure to cover leaf tops and bottoms. Spraying helps suffocate the insects. You also can spread diatomaceous earth around infected plants to help prevent mites from crawling onto other plants. For chemical control, use a spray containing kelthane. Clean up and destroy all affected plants in your garden this fall. Buy only healthy plants for replacements in spring.

➤ Bagworms, those little cone-shaped nests hanging from the bottoms of limbs on evergreen trees and shrubs, are full-grown now, and insecticides would be ineffective. Pruning and burning the bags provides better control. Bagworms defoliate and kill many shrubs and trees every year when allowed to spread.

Planting

➤ Cover crops add valuable organic matter to soil and help improve its structure in the vegetable garden. Bare soil is damaged by rainfall and erosion. Winter rye is one of the best cover crops, and it germinates rapidly. In the spring, when it's time to plant, plow under the cover crop to enrich the soil.

➤ Fall is an excellent time to start an asparagus bed. Allow two to three years before you can harvest. Garden centers have roots now, or they can be ordered by mail.

NOVEMBER

Spring Bulbs Bring Joy to Garden

You may not be thinking of it yet, but spring is as close as the nearest crocus bulb. Spring-blooming bulbs can be planted from Oct. 15 to Jan. 15 in Southeastern Virginia and Northeastern North Carolina. But experts recommend planting in November and early December.

Daffodils can be planted as late as December, but their spring blooms may appear later than normal the first year. Tulips need cold soil, so store them in your refrigerator until planting in late November or early December. It's best to get all bulbs into the ground before Christmas because they need time to take root and build energy for their debut.

By learning the bulb's blooming period, you can plan to enjoy flowers throughout the spring. Popular bulbs include crocus, hyacinth, daffodil and tulip. By planting some or all of them, you can enjoy a show from early March (crocus) to late April (tulip).

The problem with tulips in warm climates such as Hampton Roads is getting them to come up the second year. Mild winters often don't give the bulb a proper dormancy. Bulb authorities recommend planting them at least 10 inches deep, and be sure to cut off their blooms after they've peaked.

The following tulips are recommended as reliable repeaters by bulb authority Dr. A.A. De Hertogh of North Carolina State University:

- The orange Tulipa fosteriana and Orange Emperor, which bloom in March and April.
- Tulipa fosteriana Purissma, white, blooms in March and April.
- Tulipa Kees Nelis, blood red with an orange rim, blooms in April and May.
- Tulipa White Triumphator, white lily-flowering, blooms in April and May.
- Tulipa Apeldoorn, cherry red, blooms in April and May.
- Tulipa Apeldoorn's Elite, red and yellow, blooms in April and May.
- Tulipa Beauty of Apeldoorn, magenta with gold rim, blooms in April and May.
- Tulipa Golden Apeldoorn, golden yellow, blooms in April and May.
- Tulipa Oxford, scarlet flushed with purple-red, blooms in April and May.
- Tulipa Striped Apeldoorn, deep red with yellow stripes, blooms in April and May.

These tulips may be sold as Darwin hybrid or botanical tulips. One easy way to remember what to buy is that any with the name Apeldoorn should repeat.

Always purchase high-quality bulbs if you want healthy flowers. Large bulbs produce more flowers their first year in the ground. Small bulbs develop smaller blooms if they bloom at all.

Other early bloomers besides crocus are Snowdrop (*Galanthus*), winter Aconite (*Eranthus*) and Scilla sibirica. Scilla probably does best in Hampton Roads. More midseason bloomers include species tulips: Fosteriana and Kaufmanniana. Late–flowering tulips also include double–late peony, flowered, lily–flowered, Darwin, Cottage, Parrot and Breeder.

Spring–flowering bulbs must have well-drained soil to flourish. They need good moisture during their growing season but will rot if the ground stays wet for long.

Small bulbs need 3 inches between each bulb, while the larger ones should be at least 6 inches apart. Excavate to a depth of 5 to 10 inches, depending on the bulb. The general rule is to plant them so the bottom of the bulb is placed 2-1/2 times deeper than the width of the bulb. Loosen soil in the rooting area and fertilize with Bulb Booster, bone meal or 8–8–8 mixed in with the soil. Do not set bulbs directly on the fertilizer. Add bulbs and partially refill with soil and water. Make sure to set the bulbs with their pointed ends up. Finish refilling, and place mulch over the area.

When bulbs emerge in spring, fertilize again with Bulb Booster or 8–8–8. Spray if you observe the foliar disease Botrytis or aphids. Remove flowers as they fade so the plant's energy is directed back to the bulb. Allow the foliage to die naturally. This usually requires 10 to 12 weeks after flowering. Do not tie the foliage in bunches or trim it for aesthetic reasons because you'll only harm the bulb.

Daffodils are for all brown–thumb gardeners because they are the easiest to maintain. They will grow in shade but bloom best if they get some sunshine. Plant them 6 to 8 inches deep. Leave them alone, and they'll bring you joy for years.

Crocus also are easy, and they come in a variety of colors. But beware: Squirrels love them and will dig up and eat the bulbs. Plant a dozen or more in one small space for a bunch of color.

Daffodil bulbs are poisonous, so moles, voles, raccoons and squirrels leave them alone. That is not true for tulips, crocus, hyacinth or any other spring–blooming bulbs. Voles can devour them, while raccoons or squirrels will dig them up and carry them off. Methods to slow down this activity are to plant the bulbs with gravel all around them. That seems to keep voles away. Also, bulbs can be planted in small plastic baskets and although time-consuming, that seems to stop the damage. Finally, there are sprays and dusts in garden centers you can put on bulbs before planting that deters the varmints named above.

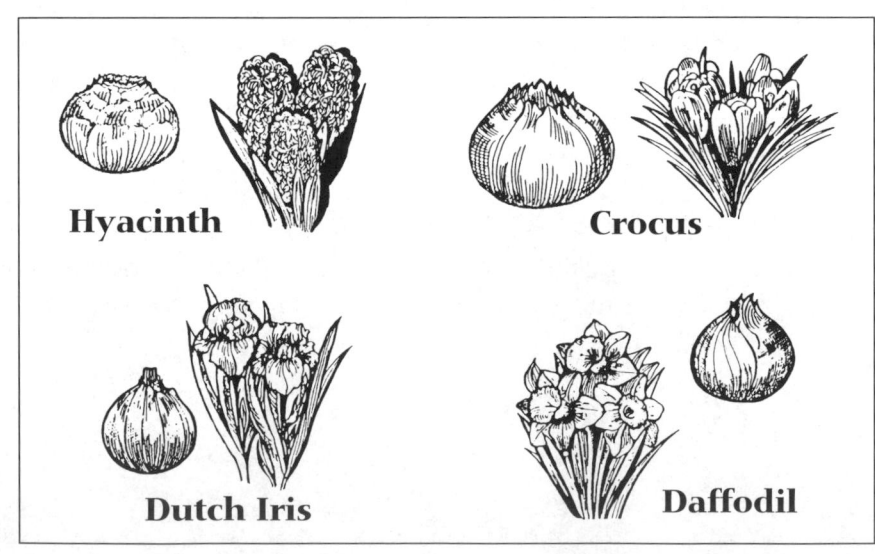

Popular Bulbs & Flowers

Hyacinth

Crocus

Dutch Iris

Daffodil

Colorful Trees and Shrubs Enliven Landscape

A winter garden need not be a dull sight. Granted, it can't compare with springtime. But there are trees and shrubs with elegant silhouettes that will add flair to your landscape. And a bit of color in January and February can lift spirits.

One suggestion from botanical experts at the University of North Carolina Botanical Garden is a red–stemmed dogwood. This is not the tree variety, but a bush called Siberian dogwood (*Cornus alba 'Siberica'*). It's particularly colorful against snow, which we hope won't accumulate here.

Another good bet is leatherleaf mahonia (*Mahonia bealei*), an evergreen shrub with stiff, spiny leaves that grows 3 to 4 feet tall. In late winter, leaf clusters are topped by yellow flowers, which develop into bluish–black berries in spring. The berries can remain all summer, but birds usually gobble them as soon as they ripen. This mahonia species may be labeled Oregon grape holly.

One of the earliest winter–blooming shrubs is witch hazel (*Hamamelis x intermedia*), which can survive the coldest temperatures in this area. It grows as a small shrub–tree, with short-stemmed clusters of pale–yellow flowers. The petals do strange twists and turns, and the most delightful benefit of witch hazel often is its fragrance.

Newcomers to our area are usually surprised by winter jasmine (*Jasminum nudiflorum*), which they often believed is early–blooming forsythia because its yellow blossoms appear before the leaves. One difference from forsythia is the green vinelike stem, which grows to about 5 feet. Winter jasmine is attractive when planted where it can form a cascading mound.

Another winter bloomer is wintersweet (*Chionanthus praecox*). It also has forsythia–like blossoms with an intensely sweet aroma. This plant typically goes unnoticed the rest of the year, so it could be tucked away among others. But in cold weather, it shines. Branches get heavy with blossoms, which have a waxy coating that helps them survive.

Another sweet-smelling plant is the fragrant Tea Olive (*Osmanthus fragrans*). It looks like holly but has tiny aromatic blooms in early November.

Other winter bloomers include winter daphne (*Daphne odora*), winter honeysuckle (*Lonicera fragrantissima*) and Japanese apricot (*Prunus mume*). They're all prolific bloomers and not a bit choosy about their growing conditions.

Fall is an ideal time to put any or all of these plants into your lawn or garden. You may have to look hard for them because some are not regularly stocked by nurseries. Calling ahead may save you driving time. Any one of them can help brighten gray winter days.

Great Coverups Replace Lawns

It's difficult to eliminate all the expletives in a homeowner's discussion about lawns. Either the grass is too long or too short. It always needs cutting when you want to fish or play golf. Or, it won't grow at all.

While everyone suffered from high temperatures, humidity and glaring sun in summer, your grass probably was the hardest hit. So, why don't you do yourself and your lawn a favor and admit defeat? Then plant a ground cover.

Grass just won't thrive in places like these: under dense trees such as cedar; under shallow-rooted trees such as magnolia; in hard clay soil; or, on banks where it's difficult to start grass.

Ground covers can be used not only to cover bare areas, but also to prevent soil erosion on slopes and banks. Among their many uses are helping to vary the landscape, regulating foot traffic when used as edging for paths, and linking unrelated shrubs and flower beds in the lawn or garden.

When you plant a ground cover, be aware that some degree of maintenance is required, but not nearly as much as a lawn. This bit of truth often is overlooked when homeowners decide to abandon grass for an alternative. And it is crucial to select the proper plant for a specific purpose. Plant size is important. Here are some suggestions and indications of what to expect:

Rockspray (*Cotoneaster horizontalis*): A semi-evergreen plant, this ground cover will grow about 3 feet high and 4 feet wide. It really becomes a bed or thicket, so don't plan on growing anything among it. Once established, it's easy to grow and keep healthy. It has red berries in fall.

Creeping juniper (*Juniperus horizontalis*): This plant creates a dense horizontal mass. It can be used almost as a rug in sunny, seashore–type areas.

Hosta, all species: The hostas create a vertical effect, growing 10 to 15 inches tall and round in dimension. They do best in shade.

Phlox subulata: It offers a combination of a fine–textured evergreen ground cover and bright color (purple, pink or white) in spring. Requires full sun.

English ivy (*Hedera helix*) and other varieties of ivy provide interesting effects and are easy to grow but hard to control. When planting, place it nearest the sunny areas and it will grow better toward the trunk of the tree. It thrives in shade.

Japanese spurge (*Pachysandra terminalis*): This plant prefers an acid soil that is sandy and coarse. It will not spread in heavy clay. Much of it is grown in this area, but it does best at the beach in deep shade.

Rose moss (*Portulaca grandiflora*): This annual is often not considered a ground cover but can be used as one. It will do better in poor but well–drained soil. Although an annual, it usually will reseed.

Periwinkle (*Vinca minor*), or myrtle: It's all the same plant and a good ground cover for this area. Bright–purple blooms add color in the spring. It grows in shade and hugs the ground closely.

Ajuga is another ground cover that flowers heavily in spring with a purple bloom and grows in the shade. But it must be controlled. Make sure there are definite edges for the beds where you plant ajuga and don't fertilize it. That often kills it.

Lily–turf (*Liriope muscari*): This grasslike evergreen perennial grows to 12 inches tall and does well in heat, dryness, intense sun or deep shade. How can you beat that? Leaves are dark, dark green and flowers are purple. It even produces berries. It forms a dense mat from which small divisions can be made to plant new areas. Also comes in a variegated variety. Also a new white.

Mondo Grass (*Ophiopogon japonicus*), or monkey grass: A low-growing form of liriope and less colorful but just as dependable. Never needs mowing.

You can find all of these ground covers at your favorite nursery or garden center. Often a friend who wants to divide his or her own plants will give you a start, and it won't cost you a thing!

Forcing Paper-whites For Christmas

Flowers in bloom make a wonderful holiday gift. Those you grow yourself offer a personal touch.

A perfect present would be a container filled with Paper-white Narcissus. If you start them at the beginning of November, they can be in bloom just in time for Christmas. Their white flowers add to the purity of Christmas, and their fragrance perfumes an entire room.

Many bulbs can be forced into bloom indoors, but the easiest and quickest is Paper-white. Buy bulbs from any large garden center that stocks a wide variety. If you can't find them, they can be ordered by mail.

Plant the bulbs as soon as possible after bringing them home, and follow these simple instructions:

Take a bowl large enough to hold the desired quantity. Three bulbs in one bowl is enough for a nice gift. Place small pebbles, gravel or bulb fiber in the bottom of the bowl so the bulbs are about 2 inches from the top. Then stand the bulbs on the pebbles and fill the space between and around them with more pebbles or bulb fiber. Keep the bulbs upright. The rooting medium will help anchor the plants. Add fresh water, and always keep the level of water just below the base of the bulbs.

Then put the bowls and bulbs in a cool, dark place. A refrigerator in the garage that you seldom open is ideal. Keep the temperature not more than 48 degrees F, and let them sit there for four to six weeks. You'll find that they soon start to sprout, and by the time you bring them out into the house, the foliage will be 6 to 8 inches tall. Put the bowl in a light, airy place in the house with an even temperature. A sunny window is ideal to produce blooms in a hurry. The less sun, the slower they will be to bloom. Do not put them near intense heat such as an open fire or radiator.

Within two weeks, each bulb will throw out one or more stems filled with beautiful white perfumed flowers. It's so easy to do, you'll wonder why you haven't grown them every Christmas.

The Paper-white Snowflake is the most popular, but if you prefer a yellow bloom, they're available in the Grand Soleil d'Or variety. Try either, or both.

A bulb can be forced into bloom only one time. But if you do it right, once is enough.

Gardening Reminders for November

Early month

Lawn care

➤ Keep falling leaves off your lawn, or they'll smother the grass. A leaf blower causes far less damage to the lawn than a rake.

Maintenance

➤ Clean gutters that are clogged with leaves and twigs.

➤ Remove debris such as dead plants, from vegetable gardens.

➤ Mulch fig trees. Many gardeners complain about figs dying during severe winters. Water them well from now until the ground freezes. Put a heavy mulch of ground–up leaves, pine straw or shredded bark around them and hope for the best. Figs like alkaline soil, so apply lime if you haven't done so recently. Sprinkle a cup or two around the bush and rake it into the soil. While you're at it, apply lime to clematis and lilac, too.

➤ Cut back and destroy all dried–up perennials and annuals. Divide perennials that have grown too thick. Don't divide chrysanthemums until spring. The Rule of Thumb is: "Blooms in spring, divide and replant in fall. Blooms in fall, divide and replant in spring."

➤ Neatly saw off stubs from limbs broken by storms. Seal the wounds with pruning paint. The value of pruning paint is debatable, but at least it improves the looks of the wound.

➤ Consider buying a leaf mulcher. The machine sucks up the leaves and grinds them into an excellent mulch. Use all the downed pine needles to mulch your shrubs and trees for the winter ahead.

➤ Listen to weather reports for the first frost, and be ready to protect tomatoes and fragile flowers.

➤ Send trees and shrubs into winter with at least 1 inch of water a week, which you must supply if nature does not.

➤ Be sure to dig sweet potatoes before the first frost. Use a spading fork, but take care not to bruise them. Undamaged potatoes will cure and store much better. Cure sweet potatoes in a warm, moist place where the temperature is 85 degrees and humidity is about 90 percent. Leave them there five to 10 days, and then you can store them in any area with a 55–degree temperature. The more humidity the better.

Miscellaneous

➤ Be prepared to see azaleas and camellias get out of cycle in their blooming. These shrubs may bloom in unseasonably warm weather. A freeze will spoil it all, but there's not much you can do. They'll get back in step when the weather returns to normal.

Pest and disease control

➤ Use slug and snail bait, if they're a problem at your house. They're easier to spot now with most foliage gone.

➤ Continue to spray roses for black spot and other diseases, but do not apply fertilizer. They're ready for dormancy.

Planting

➤ Transplant any shrubs or small trees that need moving. If it's in the wrong place, don't put off moving it. Now's a good time.

➤ Now is the time to plant pansies for winter and early spring color. Plants should be spaced 8 inches to 12 inches apart in loose, organic soil. They prefer full sun. Mix 8–8–8 fertilizer into the soil before planting, and once more in the spring.

➤ Fall is best for planting lilies. They are one

of the most underused flowers and are so easy to grow. Buy or order some lily bulbs now, and get them into the ground at once. If you plant in a well-drained spot with full sun, lilies will reward you with lots of blooms. Protect from rabbits with a fence since rabbits will strip them of all foliage.

➤ Want to grow fruit? This is a good time of year to set out apple, peach, cherry, pear and nectarine trees.

Pruning

➤ Trim bramble fruits and blueberries. Raspberries and blackberries produce on new or first-year canes, so it's important to cut back the old ones, advise experts at the University of North Carolina Botanical Garden. Plants should be cut within an inch of the ground, especially any containing suckers. If bushes have become extremely dense, they are best taken back to only six or eight canes, which will increase berry production next year. Be sure to wear long-sleeved shirts and gloves to avoid the brambles. Then put slow-release fertilizer, decomposed manure or compost around each plant and repeat the application in spring.

Midmonth

Maintenance

➤ When your fall crops of leaf lettuce, spinach, Swiss chard, collards, kale, mustard or turnips get big enough, pick the outer leaves. Doing so allows the center of the plant to keep producing leaves. If you grow horseradish or salsify, wait until after the first light frost to dig because the flavor will be better.

➤ Dig and store caladium bulbs now. Foliage has wilted, and you should lift tubers, wash and allow them to dry. Pack in peat moss or dry sand, and store in a cool location or hang in a nylon stocking until planting time in April or May. Do not allow tubers to freeze. About half of them come back when replanted next spring.

➤ If okra, squash or tomatoes seemed stunted this year and yielded poorly, pull them up now and check the roots. If there are knots on their roots, you have nematodes. One effective chemical product for eradicating nematodes was a liquid called Vapam, but it is not currently available. An organic control is ground-up crab shells. You can find them at most garden centers. Follow directions carefully.

Planting

➤ If you haven't done so already, plant daffodil bulbs immediately, advises Brent Heath of The Daffodil Mart in Gloucester. If you're unable to plant, at least open the bag so air can get to the bulbs, or spread them out in a dry place. Bulbs are perishable. The best place for them to be is in the soil. Once a bulb has made roots, it will not freeze, even in sub-zero weather. The correct depth for planting daffodils is three times the height of the bulb, usually 6 inches to the bottom of the bulb. Tulips prefer a colder situation, so you can store them in your refrigerator to plant later. But plant daffodils, as well as crocus, right away. Do not put fertilizer into the bed when planting, but fertilize immediately afterward and again in midwinter with a 3-9-18 or 5-10-20. Any fertilizer low in nitrogen and high in potash is ideal.

➤ When you buy a tree or any plant in a container, check for girdling roots. They circle the soil ball as the plant becomes pot bound. If left undisturbed, they will enlarge as the plant grows. This can choke off the expanding trunk or root system and cause the plant to grow poorly, even die. So be sure to cut through them. When you take your tree or plant out of the container, slash the sides of the ball with a sharp knife to cut the outer roots. Dig the planting hole twice the width of the container and bend the circling roots into a more natural position in the planting hole. Hold them in place while you fill soil around them. Then be sure the plant gets 1 inch of water a week.

Pruning

➤ Prune roses down to about 2 feet high now that they're losing their leaves. This helps keep them from blowing in high winds and becoming loose in the soil.

Late month

Lawn care

➤ If you haven't seeded your fescue grass for fall, you're too late. About all that will germinate now is rye grass, if we have some warm days. It's time for the second or third application of fertilizer, depending on what you've done to date. At least apply the second feeding before cold weather.

Maintenance

➤ Put away hoses before water freezes in them and causes cracks. It's a cumbersome job but worth the effort. Drain them and store in a warm, dry place.

➤ Gardeners often question this, but it works. Geraniums can withstand cold weather, but before a heavy freeze, dig them up. Shake off all the dirt from their roots. Then hang them, one per large paper bag, upside down in a cool, dry place. I've put them in the attic or garage. In spring, take them down, cut their dry foliage back to 8 or 10 inches, replant and water. You'll be surprised at how fast they grow back and bloom – usually bigger and better than the prior season. And you have saved the cost of new plants.

Pruning

➤ Check boxwood. If they become so compact that little light and air reaches the center of their crowns, then interior shoots may die and the plant may weaken, warn Virginia Tech horticulturists. Pruning or picking out some of the inner branches will help open the plant to admit light to the interior. This will encourage the growth of green leaves all the way up the stem. If you don't do some annual thinning, you're asking for boxwood trouble. Also at least once a year, clean out all the leaves and twigs that accumulate in the center of a boxwood. Without such cleaning, fungus growth on leaves and twigs is promoted. Then water thoroughly. Add mulch, and your boxwood should be ready for winter. They also can be pruned in spring.

DECEMBER

Winterize Your Garden

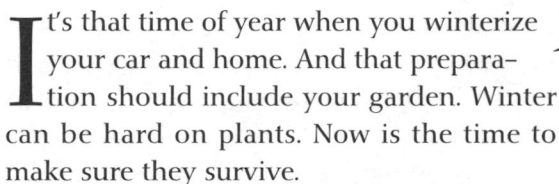

It's that time of year when you winterize your car and home. And that preparation should include your garden. Winter can be hard on plants. Now is the time to make sure they survive.

In the mid–Atlantic states where we live, plant roots systems continue to grow late into fall and winter. They may grow all winter if the weather is mild. Newly planted shrubs and trees tend to have limited root systems, so they need abundant water during their first growing season.

Winter damage may include: Drying (desiccation) of the leaves of evergreen plants and the twigs and stems of deciduous plants; damage by snow and ice loads on shrubs; and root damage from frost heaving. There also is the problem of mice and rabbits feeding on plants and causing girdling of the bark, which can kill the plant the next summer.

Here are some tips to help you prepare:

➤ Many plant losses blamed on a hard winter can be attributed to a lack of water during fall. Newly transplanted trees and shrubs should be watched carefully and watered regularly and deeply. Do this until the ground freezes, which is usually mid–January. Evergreens, particularly the broad–leaved ones such as rhododendron and shallow–rooted ones such as holly, continue to lose moisture from their foliage through the winter, so send them into winter well watered. And many narrow–leafed evergreens such as yews, juniper and arborvitae are located close to the house where they don't receive the full benefit of rain. Always thoroughly water all plants under a building overhang.

➤ Stake newly planted trees to help them withstand strong winds. Whether a tree needs support depends on its size and exposure to wind.

➤ When setting out broadleaf evergreens, such as ligustrum, holly and rhododendron, avoid windy, exposed sites.

➤ If you have plants that are not adapted to this climate, such as silver dollar eucalyptus, give them added protection. This includes extra mulch or building a canvas or burlap tent around the plant, leaving only the top open.

➤ A light snow isn't anything to worry about because it helps insulate plants. But if a heavy snow hits, remove the snow as it accumulates or build structures to protect the plant from a heavy load. If snow slides off a roof onto a plant, it can break limbs. When you remove snow from evergreens be sure to work from under the branches and out from the trunk so that you won't apply additional weight to the plant as the snow falls.

➤ If you have rhododendrons that get wind–

burned, many gardeners spray them now and again during a winter thaw with Wilt–Pruf or Cloud Cover. Wilt–Pruf is an anti–transpirant that slows down water loss from plant leaves.

➤ Take steps to prevent frost heaving, which often hurts perennials. Apply mulch around those plants. By now, most plants have quit growing and can be cut down to ground level. Then apply about 3 inches of bark or pine-straw mulch.

➤ Protect trees and shrubs from gnawing rodents. For rabbits, guards made of one–half–inch mesh hardware cloth, or taste repellents such as Thiram, are useful. If there's snow, make sure the deterrents rise above the snow line. Rabbits prefer azaleas, roses and Indian hawthorn (*Rhaphiolepsis*).

Cleaning up the garden

Some flowering annuals still might look perky this month, but you can be sure they won't last. One universal gardening law is that, eventually, a killing frost will wipe out flowers and vegetables. Then comes cleanup.

Tidying up the garden helps prevent infection of spring plants by insects or diseases that typically live through our mild winters. Do not recklessly plow under the dying garden. Instead, remove all rotten foliage and burn it or throw it in the trash. Do not use it for compost; otherwise, you'll be preserving numerous pests and fungi that could plague your entire garden. Powdery mildew, rusts and other leaf and stem–disease organisms could generate lots of problems come spring.

Be aware that some diseases will remain in the soil no matter how well you dig, rake and till. If you suspect problems, then treat the soil with ground–up crab shells this fall or early spring before planting. Root–knot nematodes should be eradicated by removing and destroying the infected plant's roots at the time of harvest. Then apply a fumigant or an organic substitute. Plant viruses that normally are a problem in vegetables and ornamentals are destroyed when the host plant dies.

Dead vines and foliage left on your garden provide luxury accommodations to insects. If we have a mild winter, they'll get an early start munching on next year's garden.

Also remove all weeds because they, too, attract viruses that will survive the winter.

African Violets: Friend or Foe?

With winter at the doorstep, it's time to think about house plants. One that provides more color than most any other – but also requires more care – is the African violet. "They sulk when they're dry or cold," comments Virginia Tech horticulturist Diane Relf.

One of the big problems with African violets is getting them to rebloom. Many indoor gardeners buy a plant in beautiful bloom, but when they are unable to get it to repeat its blooms, they throw it out in disgust. African violets flower best in bright light, but not in extreme heat or humidity. East or

west windows are best, or under fluorescent lights. Their preferred daytime temperature is 72 degrees F, and night temperatures should not be below 62 F.

African violets are extremely sensitive to

dryness. Check soil moisture daily and water them when the soil feels dry to the touch and before it becomes hard. Never use cold water. It causes irregular-shaped, white-colored spots on foliage. Use lukewarm water only. Despite what you've been told, you can water them from the top or bottom. Just keep water off leaves and make sure the plant is watered deeply when doing it from the top.

When watering, excess water should flow out a drainage hole in the pot. Be sure to pour off excess water. If watering from the bottom, remove the pot from its saucer as soon as you see soil at the top of the pot turn wet. If you leave the pot standing in water, it can cause the soil to become saturated and eliminate air spaces essential for healthy root growth.

Relf recommends that if you normally water from the bottom, switch to top watering occasionally. This helps prevent the accumu-lation of crusty, white salts on the soil surface and edge of pots. Leaf stems can become soft or discolored if they lie on soluble salts on the pot rim. This problem occurs most often when the plant is in a clay pot. If you want to avoid constant watering, use a self-watering wick system. They can be purchased in garden centers or by mail.

You must have a good soil mix for African violets, especially one that provides good drainage. Relf recommends two parts peat moss to one part Perlite.

African violets need a regular supply of plant food. Use a special liquid African violet fertilizer, applied every two to four weeks. But the most important requirement of all for African violets is proper light. If yours have not done well, keep moving them around until you find the spot they like best. Then they'll reward you with blooms and more blooms.

For the Birds

Want to watch a bright-red cardinal visiting just outside your window? Or how about a chorus of golden yellow finches against the backdrop of a gray day?

A broad palette of feathered friends will brighten your garden nearly every day if you treat them right. The best way to get their attention is through their stomachs. Wild birds have appetites like a dog or cat, eating daily. Don't expect regular visitations if you set out a spread only once or twice a year.

After big snowstorms or icy spells, birds need food the most and find it the hardest to get on their own. Putting out a little extra at that time will be much appreciated. Berries, insects and seeds won't appear until spring, so the birds need your help until they can fend for themselves.

Once you start feeding, birds become de-pendent and will stay all winter long. So don't let them down when natural food supplies run out.

Now is the time to get out your feeder. In planning a winter oasis, remember that the essentials are water, shelter and food. Feeders should be sheltered from prevailing winds. If possible, place your feeder on the south or east side of your home so the birds will be protected from west and north winds. And make sure you can see it from a favorite kitchen or family room window.

Feeders should be within 5 feet of some kind of cover – shrubs, trees, or both – that offers a retreat from cats or other threats. It's also helpful to provide a gradual approach route for shy birds and a convenient perch for opening sunflower seed. Squirrels are always a problem, but there are "squirrel-proof" feeders on the market.

When first setting out a feeder, advertise it by scattering some seed around it on the ground. It's important for birds to sight the seed easily. Be patient in waiting for the first visitors. It may take a couple of days or even weeks.

The type of seed you use determines which birds you will attract. A wild bird seed with lots of black-oil sunflower seed and white millet, but not much else, is ideal, according to Lee Carey of Princess Anne Farmer's Service in Virginia Beach.

Some birds are called "woodland look-alikes." These include sparrows, red-breasted and white-breasted nuthatches, bald-capped and Carolina chickadees, purple and house finches.

Goldfinches, sometimes seen around this area, are attracted best to special feeders and special food. The long, clear tubes with many perches seem to be their favorite. Their preferred food is niger seed, usually called thistle seed. It's a tiny black seed that comes from India and Africa and is expensive.

Smaller birds prefer black-oil sunflower seed and thistle seed, Carey said. Finches, chickadees and titmice don't like fighting large birds, so they prefer a hanging feeder that's burglar-proof. Cardinals, which are shy, need more privacy and time to feel at home in your yard.

Open "bird tables" draw many seed-eating birds. They offer easy access and are readily visible to birds. The disadvantages of open tables or platforms include the lack of protection from the elements and raids by hawks, crows and squirrels.

Covered feeders have the advantage of protecting the feed from the elements and are not as easily accessible to predators.

Large seeds such as sunflower seeds attract cardinals and grosbeaks. Smaller seeds and cracked corn draw sparrows and juncos.

You can discourage house sparrows, cow-birds, blue jays and grackles by offering safflower seeds, which attract mourning doves and cardinals.

Suet, the chunks of fat cut from beef and mutton, is a good supplement during the winter, said Gary San Julian, extension wildlife specialist at North Carolina State University. Birds prefer beef suet above other kinds. It's inexpensive and may be purchased at a grocer's meat counter, or a butcher may give it away. Suet can be placed in a special feeder or melted and poured in a mold filled with grain such as wheat, barley, sorghum, millet or a birdseed mix. Commercial suet-seed cakes also are available. Suet attracts woodpeckers, flickers, chickadees and nuthatches. This provides them with body heat and will supplement the lack of grubs and other insects that make up their normal diet in warm weather.

For starters, buy one feeder that is squirrel-proof and 10 pounds of black sunflower seed. Remember that many of the birds you enjoy most prefer a hanging feeder. With one inexpensive feeder and black sunflower seed, you can enjoy some of your favorite birds for hours on end. I've found that black sunflower seed draws flocks of birds, much more so than wild bird seed.

Another necessity for seed-eating songbirds is grit. They must take grit or gravel into their gizzards to grind up the food they eat. Natural sources often are frozen in winter. You can help by scattering sand, ground oyster shells or eggshell near your feeders or using a seed mix that contains crushed oyster shells.

It is important to remove all moldy seeds from the feeder. Some molds produce byproducts that are toxic to birds. Molding occurs as a result of rain or other dampness, which means open feeders should be cleaned out after wet weather. Suet can become rancid in summer, so use it mainly during cold months

Favorite plants

The following list of shrubs will draw birds year after year in the fall and winter. according to horticulturists at Virginia Tech. All hold their fruit into winter months.

• Bittersweet (*Celastrus*). It's not often seen in this area but will grow under certain conditions.

• Washington hawthorn (*Crataegus phuenopyrum*). Many of these are planted in highway median strips in Virginia Beach.

• Hawthorn, "winter king" is especially attractive to cedar waxwings.

• Euonymus is available in many varieties, but the Burning Bush and Spindle Tree varieties are especially attractive to birds.

• *Ilex opaca*, or American holly, is loved by birds, especially as the fruits ripen and ferment. You've probably seen robins clean out holly or pyracantha berries after they ferment in midwinter, and then stagger around, trying to recover from a cheap drunk.

Other recommended plants include: Winterberry (Ilex verticillate); several varieties of juniper, including red cedar; native bayberry; native sumac (Rhus glabra); Viburnum of many varieties with berries; roses (for the rose hips); crabapple trees; and dogwood (*Cornus florida*).

Evergreen trees and shrubs also are important for an inviting bird habitat. Their dense branches offer shelter from severe weather.

Bird houses should be put up by March so potential occupants can scout for a nesting spot.

Finally, when you take down your Christmas tree, follow a custom that goes back to the 16th century. Put the tree outdoors and on it place strings of peanuts, popcorn and cranberries. Also hang stale donuts, or little baskets made from orange rinds, filled with seeds, raisins and nuts. Birds love pine cones dipped in melted suet or smeared with peanut butter. Add banana and chunks of other fruits. Or, try marshmallows and apple slices, hung on strings. Believe it or not, even dog biscuits will draw a crowd.

All these tips may seem like a lot of work, but the resulting pleasure is well worth the time and trouble. You'll add a new dimension to your garden.

Indoor Blooms Brighten Dull Winter Months

Flowering house plants triumph over lethargic philodendrons this time of year. Rather than waiting for spring, you can spend from $2 to $40 a plant for a range of winter-busting bloomers. They're available at most garden centers, even grocery stores.

Before buying, you should know what to expect. Some plants are able to flower year-round, such as begonias, if given the right attention. Those that bloom for just a few weeks or months include kalanchoe and orchids.

Some plants, such as gloxinia and cyclamen, require a dormant period. And others – tulips, hyacinths, Narcissus – put on a one-time show.

Here is a sampling of different plants. Unless otherwise indicated, most do well in bright indirect or sheer curtain-filtered light. A fertilizer high in phosphorous is recommended.

African violet: Fertilize with one-quarter strength fertilizer once a week when watering. Don't let them get too dry. Alternate watering from the top and bottom. Avoid splashing water on leaves to prevent water spots.

Azaleas: Forced azaleas bloom only once indoors because they require a six-week cold period every year. Fertilize with a high-acid solution once a month. Keep soil most. Prune just after blooming. They can be planted outside in shade or semishade after the frost danger has passed. They also make beautiful bonsai plants, if you have the time and expertise.

Cineraria: It has large daisylike flowers clustered in the center of bright-green, furry leaves. Colors are vibrant: magenta, purple, blue, pink. Generally, they don't need fertilizer. They're best treated as annuals and tossed out when done blooming. Plants like cool, sunny locations.

Cyclamen: This plant, grown from a bulb, blooms in fall, winter and early spring. Water when soil feels dry and fertilize once a month. Don't be alarmed when it dies back in mid-spring and remains dormant for a few months. It needs a rest. In late summer, begin fertilizing full-strength.

Gardenia: For a whiff of spring, try one of these. Gardenias need lots of light and should be placed out of drafts in a 60- to 80-degree climate. Keep soil moist; if they get too dry, foliage will drop. Fertilize lightly with an acid fertilizer. Trim blooms when they fade. They tend to be prone to pests, so keep plants healthy to deter them. This type is not winter-hardy, meaning it won't survive outdoors.

Gloxinia: Like the African violet, the gloxinia also has velvety leaves. Trumpet-shaped flowers are white, pink, red or purple. But instead of blooming year-round, it requires a dormant period. The tuber can be dried off in autumn and replanted in spring. It requires bright indirect light. Water when the soil feels dry. Trim faded flowers.

Hibiscus: The greenhouse variety will bloom year-round. Fertilize once a month in winter, biweekly in spring. Give it direct sun or bright indirect light. Choose from yellow, orange, pink, white or red. It will grow into a small tree, or you can prune it to table-top size.

Kalanchoe: This colorful succulent remains in flower for about three months. Colors range from pink through red to yellow through orange. It like a sunny or bright location. Allow soil to dry one-third the depth of the container between waterings. Feed once a month. Clip out faded blooms.

Phalaenopsis orchid, or "moth orchid": This lovely plant, the most popular orchid, may be more expensive than most house plants, but it will bring years of beauty. Fertilize twice a month with a special orchid fertilizer (high nitrogen, such as 30-10-10). Soak the soil when watering, but allow the water to run through the bottom of the container (preferably at the sink). Don't allow the plant's roots to stand in water. To help provide a moist environment, set the container on a bed of pebbles in a shallow dish. Keep enough water in the dish to almost cover the pebbles without touching the roots. Other favorite orchids are cattleya, oncidium and dendrobium.

Primrose: For instant gratification, you can't beat the perennial primrose. It blooms from Christmas until summer in vibrant colors with bright-green foliage. Place a bunch of them together in a basket in a sunny window, and water from the bottom when the surface feels dry. Prune out faded blooms. Feed monthly in winter, biweekly in spring and summer. After they finish flowering indoors, plant them outside.

Wax begonia: A profusion of white, pink or red flowers appear from spring through winter and can be planted outdoors in warm weather. Plants like a warm, sunny spot indoors. Fertilize every two weeks in spring and summer.

Gardening Reminders for December

Early month

House plants

➤ Give poinsettias as much light as possible. Fertilize once a month. Water weekly.

➤ It's time to prepare Paper-white Narcissus if you want them in bloom for Christmas. It takes about three weeks from planting to bloom. Paper-whites can be planted simply on pebbles in water. But better results and longer-lasting flowers can be expected if you plant them in a special potting mixture. The newest trend is to sow ryegrass seed around their base for a ground-cover look.

Maintenance

➤ Before the first hard freeze, protect spinach, lettuce, broccoli and other cold-weather crops by covering them with a special garden fabric, available at local garden centers.

➤ Kiwi-picking time is here. The longer they're on the vine, the sweeter they'll be. But be sure to harvest them before a freeze.

➤ Now is a good time to take soil samples from lawns and vegetable gardens. Take small amounts of soil from each area, mix together and dry it out. Mark on each container what you plan to grow in that soil. Some local garden centers offer soil testing analysis for a small fee.

Miscellaneous

➤ Get the family together and buy your Christmas tree early. It will be a lot better off in a bucket of water in your back yard than standing on a tree lot drying out. To test for freshness, bounce the tree on the ground. If needles drop, move on to the next tree, or the next lot. After buying a tree, take it home and saw an inch or two off the trunk and immediately place it in a bucket of water in the shade until it's time to bring it indoors. A variety of products are available to help prevent needle drop once the tree is inside. Here's a recipe from the Virginia Cooperative Extension Service: Mix a gallon of hot water with one-quarter cup horticultural iron chelate, 2 cups light corn syrup and 4 teaspoons chlorine bleach. Be careful not to spill the mixture on carpets because stains are permanent.

➤ Try this if your Christmas greens were a dull green last year: Cut evergreen branches during the first two weeks, being careful to prune so as not to harm the future shape of the tree or shrub. Soak the greens in water for several hours and then place them in plastic bags. Close the bags tightly, and store them in a cool place. At Christmas, you'll find these early cut greens will be richer in color than those cut later. Many decorators spray their greens with Wilt-Pruf.

➤ If you're decorating an outdoor Christmas tree for the birds, don't use cranberries and popcorn because they won't be touched. Birds like plain white bread, says Dot Wilbur at the North Carolina Botanical Garden. Cut out stars and bells with a cookie cutter for each slice of bread. Poke a hole through the shapes for hanging and toast them lightly in the oven. Hang on the tree when cool. Wilbur says birds also like "glop," a mixture of 1 cup peanut butter, 4 cups cornmeal, 1 cup shortening and 1 cup white flour. Blend the ingredients with your hands and spoon into shortened paper cups, coconut halves, orange-peel cups or scooped-out apple halves and hang them on the tree. Or, let the kids slather peanut butter and lard or bacon grease on pine cones, roll them in seed mix and tie the cones onto the tree. Birds also like suet, cornbread crumbs, whole oats, stale donuts, sliced apples and oranges, straw-berries, bananas, grape jelly, dog biscuits, cottage cheese, cooked potatoes, broken squash seeds, pecans, walnuts and pie crust.

Pest and disease control

➤ The Brooklyn Botanic Garden uses 1 tablespoon of Sunspray Ultra–Fine oil, plus one tablespoon of baking soda per gallon of water to control powdery mildew, blackspot and other fungal problems on roses, starting in early spring. Cornell University researchers say the same mixture can kill powdery mildew and three other vegetable diseases on contact. The baking soda treatment reduces the need for fungicides on pumpkins, squash and cucumbers. Some authorities recommend adding a tablespoon of liquid soap to provide better coverage.

Planting

➤ You still have a month left to plant tulips and daffodils. The recommended planting time for Southeastern Virginia–Northeastern North Carolina is between Oct. 1 and Jan. 1.

Midmonth

Fertilize

➤ Now that trees have lost their leaves and become dormant, it is an excellent time to fertilize them. Research proves that roots develop all winter, making for a stronger tree or shrub next spring. Tree food spikes are easy to use. There also are granular tree fertilizers, such as 12–6–6. If you can't find exactly what you want, 10–6–4 fertilizer will do the job. Research also has proven that most feeding roots are in the top 10 inches of soil, so there's no need to drill holes for food. Just sprinkle it heavily on top of the soil around the tree. For trees in grassy areas, spikes eliminate the possibility of burning the grass. Remember that when grass and trees compete for food, grass always wins.

Lawn care

➤ Keep leaves off the grass now, whether newly planted or established. Decaying leaves smother grass quickly. Maple leaves are especially harmful because they're small and tend to hug the ground.

Maintenance

➤ Cool–weather vegetables such as cabbage, broccoli and spinach can survive freezing weather if you cover them with a special garden fabric such as Reemay or Easy Gardener Blanket.

➤ Keep putting wood ashes from the fireplace on your garden, but do not use them around azaleas, camellias, blueberries and rhododendrons. Those plants prefer acid soil, and the ashes, because of their calcium content, tend to make the soil less acid. Use around bulbs, fruit trees and grapevines, as well as your vegetable and flower garden.

➤ Make sure shrubs and trees receive 1 inch of water per week from now until the ground freezes. If the season has been dry, you might want to spray evergreens, rhododendrons, camellias, azaleas and hollies with an anti-transpirant (Wilt–Pruf, Cloud Cover), which helps plant leaves retain moisture.

Miscellaneous

➤ Prune holly, boxwood and other shrubs for Christmas greens. For bright berries, use nandina, pyracantha and many hollies.

➤ To bedeck a mantel in greenery, enclose blocks of pre–soaked floral foam securely in plastic bags. Line the blocks along the mantel a foot or two apart. Cut the evergreen branches at a sharp angle so the stems will easily pierce the plastic bag and lodge securely in the foam. Then simply insert enough greenery to fill the mantel and conceal the foam blocks. Similar techniques can be used to make Christmas centerpieces and table arrangements, adding fresh flowers from time to time for color.

➤ Use baking soda to get the pine pitch or resin off your hands after putting up your

Christmas tree. Plain baking soda, rubbed on your hands and rinsed off, will get rid of resin.

Planting

➤ You can take hardwood cuttings of forsythia, spirea, Japanese quince, wisteria, mock orange, viburnum and other deciduous shrubs now if you want to root your own. Follow the same procedures used for rooting azaleas and camellias. (See July.)

Pruning

➤ Prune hardy waterlilies and other pool plants down to the crown, advise experts at Lilypons Water Gardens in Maryland. After a heavy freeze, prune all foliage, leaving none to drop to the pool bottom and foul the water. Small leaves will continue to be produced near the plant's crown; do not prune them. Do not fertilize again until early spring. Tropical water lilies will bloom right up until a freeze and, in this area, may bloom again during warm spells.

Late month

House plants

➤ Place your house plants where they'll receive the most natural light available. Water sparingly once a week from now until March 1. Most indoor plants need no fertilizer in winter unless they're actively growing under artificial light. Too much fertilizer and water and too little light and low humidity are the main reasons that house plants perform poorly in winter.

Maintenance

➤ You should be through with your lawn mower and other power tools for the year. If they're gasoline-powered, drain the fuel tank and run the engine dry, or fill the tank and add a fuel preservative. Check belts and spark plugs, and buy replacements. Tape the new parts to the equipment so you won't have to remember where you put them. Change oil, sharpen blades or tines, and clean off dirt and plant debris so equipment will need only a few minutes' attention when you're ready to go in the spring.

Miscellaneous

➤ Check the water regularly in your Christmas-tree stand. A fresh-cut tree usually soaks up extra water the first week it's in the house. Keep the container filled with water, plus a preservative, to help prevent drying.

Pest control

➤ Two problems are common in December: rabbit damage to azaleas, trees and other shrubs, and holes where squirrels have buried nuts and food. When you see the outer branches of azaleas stripped of their leaves and shorter limbs nipped off, rabbits are the culprits. Rabbits also like to eat rose bushes and peel the bark off apple trees and lilacs. Once a plant is girdled (bark eaten off all the way around the trunk), it seldom recovers. Human hair is a good deterrent. Ask your barber or hairstylist to save some for you, then scatter large amounts around beds, about 6 inches from plants.

➤ As for the inch-deep, quarter-sized holes in your lawn and beds, blame squirrels. Snare squirrels in a live trap, then drop them off at a park with lots of oak trees. Prevent damage to trees by using rodent guards: cylinders of one-quarter inch mesh hardware cloth, foil tree wrap, or chemical taste repellents. Chemicals may require reapplication during winter.

Planting

➤ Plant camellias, flowering trees, fruit and nut trees, shade trees and flowering shrubs whenever the ground is not frozen. The better time for planting in the home garden is winter, not spring, especially for those trees and shrubs that lose their leaves in winter. Camellias will still give out blooms this season.

➤ Plant radishes and spinach and put out onion sets if you want to have an extra early spring garden. Each of them will germinate and grow in December and January.

Reader Questions

Birds And Butterflies

Q. We have hummingbirds in our yard all summer because they are attracted to our scarlet sage. But I can't get them to use my hummingbird feeder. Are there any guidelines for good places to hang a feeder?

A. One of our reliable hummingbird advisers, Rebecca White of Norfolk, is a member of the Cape Henry Audubon Society. She says the feeders should be hung relatively low. She also recommends the book "Hummingbirds – Their Life," by Robert and Esther Tyrrell, Crown Publishers, N.Y. White says the book emphasizes the mixture, which should be one part sugar to five parts water. This closely resembles nectar. That's more important than the location of the feeder. Feeders with short trumpets attract birds better than those with long trumpets. The food should be colored red, but in experiments it's been proven that location is more important than color, for the birds would feed at the same location even when the color of the nectar was changed. We don't recommend doing that, however. White suggests that you put your feeder close to the scarlet sage and as you see the birds use it, gradually move it away, toward the location you want it to be permanently. They should follow the feeder. North Carolina State University horticulturists report that the more red and orange flowers you grow that have deep throats, the more hummingbirds you will attract. Some of these flowers are: canna, trumpet creeper vine, coral honeysuckle, cardinal flower, azalea, fuchsia, scarlet sage, gladiolus, phlox, weigela, columbine, nicotiana, coral bells, bee balm, petunias and verbena.

Q. After weeks of hearing a woodpecker in my back yard, I finally spotted it in a tree. However, it turned out not to be one bird, but two. There were two holes in a tree branch and one long, hollowed-out area. What can we do about woodpeckers, and what can we expect in the way of damage? We have 13 very large trees in our back yard and several smaller ones.

A. Sounds like you're going to be den mother to a family of woodpeckers. They won't damage the tree they're in, or any others. They eat insects found in the bark. Woodpeckers are not harmful, reports a spokesperson for the Cape Henry Audubon Society. The hole in your tree is a nest. The birds usually drill holes only in dead or diseased trees. So you might want to check the limb or the entire tree. Maybe that is why the birds found insects in it. Woodpeckers are protected birds, and many gardeners would love to have a nest of them in their yards.

Q. Please tell me what flowers are native to Hampton Roads and will attract butterflies. I have a butterfly hibernation house and am eager to have some tenants.

A. Julia Bristow, founder of the Virginia Butterfly Society, suggests these: *Asclepias tuberosa* (butterfly weed), *Buddleia* (butterfly bush), lantana, Homestead purple verbena, cosmos, penta, single pink zinnias, Mexican sunflower and native purple phlox. There is disagreement among experts on whether hibernation or other butterfly houses work. A good book on the subject is "Gardening for Butterflies in Hampton Roads," by Jeanne Pettersen and Connie Sale. It costs $4.95, mailed to P.O. Box 2884, Chesapeake, Va. 23327-1686.

Q. My house on the Outer Banks is constantly attacked by birds pecking at shingles, making destructive holes. When I'm there, I can chase them away but they seem to always attack when no one's home. What can I do?

A. This is a tough question, but here are answers provided by others with a similar problem: Put a loud ticking clock inside where they attack; that seems to drive them off. Hang aluminum pans or strips of aluminum on fishing line in areas where they peck. Allow plenty of line, so the pans, etc. will blow. Or use Mylar tape - silver strips with red on the backside, available in garden centers - in lengths of 3-5 feet which usually drive birds away.

Q. I see large caterpillars eating my parsley. They are supposed to hatch into butterflies. What should I do?

A. If you want butterflies, you need caterpillars. Plant enough parsley, which the caterpillars love, for you and the worms.

Q. I'm interested in planting hedges that provide food and nesting for birds, especially bluebirds and robins. Can you give some suggestions?

A. Birds like berries, so any shrub that produces them is good for attracting birds. And they like bushy shrubs, where they can hide, especially timid birds such as cardinals. Bluebirds are rare in this area, however, and nest only in houses made especially for them. Here are the common names of a few shrubs and small trees to consider: shadblow, red chokeberry, spicebush, Washington hawthorn, cotoneaster, Russian olive, flowering dogwood, inkberry holly, American holly, red cedar, honeysuckle, flowering crabapples, wax myrtle and bayberry. Many of these are easy to grow, and fall or early spring is an excellent time to plant them.

Bulbs

Q. I have jonquils, daffodils, and narcissus that need dividing. I prefer not to dig, dry them and then replant this fall. Can they be dug and replanted in the spring? How deep should I plant the bulbs?

A. Not everyone agrees on this, but the easiest method is to dig bulbs while you can see them, after they bloom in the spring. Dig a clump of earth with the bulbs, divide the clump and replant. The other method is to dig them, shake off the dirt, wash the bulbs and dry thoroughly. Then store them in your refrigerator and replant in the fall. The problem with digging in the fall is that there is no foliage, and you can't find the bulbs. You could, of course, mark the spots with flags in the spring so you could find them in the fall. Either way, replant the bulbs 6 to 8 inches deep.

Q. I'm anticipating a move for our family in the future. I need advice on which flower bulbs I can take with me. I have glads, tulips, Dutch iris, amaryllis, crocus, snow flowers, hyacinths, star–of–David, windflowers, lily–of–the–valley, dahlias, cannas, daffodils, anemones, grape hyacinths, plus many others.

A. Your spring-blooming bulbs such as tulips, Dutch iris, crocus, snowflowers, hyacinth, star–of–David, windflowers (anemones), grape hyacinth and lily–of–the–valley all can be dug as soon as their tops die down. Store them in your refrigerator until you move. Then replant them in September. Amaryllis can be kept in the house until you move. If you have them set outside, they can be dug any time of year. Dahlias, cannas and glads all have to be dug and stored during the winter if you're moving up North. If your move is not until late summer, leave the dahlias and cannas until ready to move. Then dig them up with a good clump of soil and replant at your new home site. My suggestion would be not to plant the gladiolas until you move. If they're already in the ground, you can either dig them now or when you move. Let the tops dry and then store in a cool, dry place and replant next spring

Q. What bulbs are sure to come back year after year in this area? I know that in the South, some do not.

A. Bulbs you can count on for years and years are daffodils and crocus. Tulips seldom if ever repeat. They should be considered annuals. Hyacinth are "iffy" in that some repeat and some do not. Scilla, anemones, snowdrops and chionodoxa will usually repeat and multiply.

Fruits And Berries

Apples

Q. I would like some information on planting and transplanting Delicious apple trees. Now that it's April, I want to get a golden Delicious apple to go with my red Delicious that I planted last August in my front yard on the west side. It lost all of its leaves and never put out any new sprouts. I don't think it's dead. Where is the best place to plant fruit trees? My back yard faces east.

A. Fruit trees need full sun and well-drained soil. To test if your red Delicious is alive, scrape the bark and see if it's still green. If it's green but hasn't leafed out, fertilize it slightly and leave it alone for a couple of months. It may be a slow starter. When you plant a fruit tree in August, you are putting every imaginable stress on it. It may have defoliated itself because of stress from heat or not enough water. Although some fruit trees are self-pollinating, it's usually smart to buy two varieties at a time so you'll be sure of proper pollination. Also remember that you must spray fruit trees regularly or you'll have lots of bugs and diseases and no good fruit.

Q. I have two dwarf apple trees, 3 years old. They bloomed beautifully last spring. When the apples got the size of a quarter, they started dropping, one by one, until they were all gone. Can you tell me what causes them to drop, and what I can do about it?

A. There are probably two problems causing the fruit drop. First, a minimum of seven sprays are required in this area for good fruit. You can get a spray schedule by writing to Virginia Tech, or send a self-addressed, stamped envelope to me at the newspaper.

The other problem is the need for thinning. The first fruit on a new tree makes a gardener feel so proud that he or she seldom removes any of it. Here's how it works: A dwarf apple tree requires 25 leaves to grow one big apple. So in early June, remove by hand all the excessive fruit and leave about 6 to 8 inches between the apples you leave on the tree. If you do that and spray as per the schedule, you should harvest apples this fall.

Berries

Q. I want to grow red raspberries in Suffolk, but I've been warned that Virginia winters are not cold enough to kill or control the virus that attacks raspberries. I've seen a new variety called Southland supposedly suited for warmer climates. But it's only "disease-resistant." It also produces suckers, or new plants, which I would not mind. However, other varieties such as Latham and Heritage are "virus free," but the literature does not say they are suited for the South. Which would you recommend? What other advice do you have on growing raspberries locally? And how many plants should I plant for a family of four who would eat them fresh only?

A. My source for raspberry information was the late Jim Mays. He said he tried to grow Southland and had no luck and then discovered it

was "not suitable for coastal areas." Whether Suffolk is a coastal area is debatable, but it's certainly on the fringe. Mays grew only Heritage, which he said is the only variety that small-fruit authorities at Virginia Tech recommend. Latham will grow here, but Mays did not try it. Most plants sold now are virus free. If you should order from the state of Maryland, they have a law where all berries must be tested and labeled virus free.

Last year, I planted three of the Titan varieties only because it supposedly is a climber and can be kept on a fence. Only one plant lived, so I have no growing history to report. For a family of four to eat fresh red raspberries, you probably need 10 plants.

Q. Can all juniper berries be used with food? Several recipes, such as sauerkraut, call for them. The berries I'm sending you came from bushes that are growing upright, not hugging the ground.

A. Experts at the Hampton Roads Agricultural Research Station in Virginia Beach say juniper berries are edible. And they insisted I eat some of your berries to prove it. They tasted like pitch. If you want better-tasting berries, sample some from western juniper.

Citrus

Q. In 1975, I started nine citrus trees in 6-inch pots. They are now in half barrels, and I don't know where to go from here, unless I dump them, do severe root pruning and call them bonsai! We pick an abundance of fruit from them. Ponderosa and Meyer lemons, plus Persian and Key limes. Our pineapple oranges are super. I have a small grapefruit tree that has not done its thing yet. We move them from the driveway into a south-facing garage each winter. It is getting too difficult to move them. What do you suggest?

A. Authorities at the Hampton Roads Agricultural Research Station say that as long as your citrus plants stay healthy, they do not need to be repotted. They suggest testing the soil in each container, especially for pH and soluble salts. When the salt level (residue from fertilizer) gets too high, leach out the containers by pouring a lot of water through the soil. Why not put the containers on platforms with casters, which would make it easier to push them around? With this procedure, your citrus trees should be able to grow to a ripe old age in their half barrels.

Grapes

Q. I recently planted two kinds of grapes with one at each end of an arbor. I'm now being told that they will grow but not produce. Please tell me if this is true. I'd also appreciate any help on grape growing.

A. Grapes are self-fruiting, which means they pollinate themselves. Stark Bros., a large mail-order nursery, says that when you plant different grape varieties close together, they're apt to cross-pollinate. But don't worry. This affects only the number of seeds, their size and shape and not the quality of fruit or the grapes. Muscadines, except Scuppernong and Jumbo, are self-fruiting. But if you grow these two, make sure to plant another Muscadine with them. American grapes will not pollinate Muscadine grapes.

Q. Can you solve the problem of my Concord grape vine? I've had this vine for years, and it grows profusely on my fence. Each spring it puts out bunches of miniature grapes. That's as far as it produces. One week ago I was thrilled to see all these bunches, more than ever before, thinking I would have grapes this year. Today I found all the bunches took on a different appearance, just as they have in the past. In the spring, it has lovely tiny grapes, but then one week later the shape changes and they never produce. The vine has abundant leaves and healthy foliage. Last year I found exactly four large grapes, and I mean single grapes, not bunches. I don't see any aphids or other insects that could have eaten them.

A. Virginia Tech experts say you have pollination problems. The grapes never develop because they are not pollinated properly. The experts also suggested talking with Virginia Beach grape authority Rob Mays. Mays says that your problem is typical and that you'll never successfully grow Concord grapes in Southeastern Virginia. He says you need a Fredonia grape, which looks and acts like Concord but tastes much better. You can keep the Concord as a vine on your fence. Mays sells Fredonia grape vines from Rob's Market at the Farmer's Market in Virginia Beach.

Peaches

Q. The last two years, I sprayed faithfully every seven to 10 days, from "green tip" to harvest with an insect–fungus combination. My peaches were still destroyed by black spot and brown rot. Would winter spraying correct this problem?

A. Although you followed the correct schedule, professional orchardists spray by the condition of the fruit rather than a set schedule that requires daily inspection. The professional also uses spray equipment that has much higher pressure and does a more adequate job. In recent years, black spot on peaches has worsened.

In home orchards, some years you'll get a crop and other years will be a disaster. That's the risk you take in trying to grow fruit at home. I know how disheartening it sometimes is. But when you're about to give up, you get a luscious crop, and that gives you enthusiasm to continue.

Q. Can you provide a schedule for pruning peach and apple trees?

A. You prune fruit trees just before new growth starts in the spring, which is usually late February. There is some debate about summer pruning, after the growth gets very full and flush. Some say you should prune more then to let the sun in to ripen fruit. Dan Milbocker at the Hampton Roads Agricultural Research Station maintains that if you prune then, you only force new growth.

Q. Last year we had two peach trees that produced about a bushel of peaches, but they were no good. The trees had a jellylike substance around them. Would you tell me how to care for peach trees?

A. It sounds like your peach trees have borers, probably in both the trees and the fruit. You can take a coat hanger and try to poke out the borer by hand. Some people use Lindane, an insecticide. The problem is that once the borer gets up into the tree, it is difficult to reach with any spray. Virginia Beach extension agent Randy Jackson recommends the old fashioned but often effective moth-ball method. Scrape soil away from the bottom of the tree and remove the protruding gummy sap above and below the soil line. Then pour moth crystals or moth balls in a ring around the trunk but far enough away not to touch it. Cover with soil and tamp down. This treatment works best in fall, but it can be done in the spring. The borer has a life cycle in which he goes up into the trunk and then comes down again. You must catch him near the soil surface for the fumes to exterminate him.

In addition to regular sprayings for insects and fungus, peach trees should be fertilized once a year in spring or fall. In fact, there is more and more research indicating that one of the best ways to prevent borers is to keep trees healthy by fertilizing regularly.

Q. Can you identify and suggest a cure for the bug pest I am sending you a sample of? The problem occurs when this bug appears on my fruit trees about the time of harvest. I am afraid to spray with anything toxic, lest I poison myself. The pest attacked my peaches and nectarines without apology. Spraying with Sevin did not seem to do anything except frighten them when the spray hit. Then they moved to my red Delicious apples. Needless to say, my backyard orchard suffered a green plight. I also had many peaches and nectarines with a small white grublike larvae next to the pit in the fruit. Could the bugs be the source of the larvae? They are very tiny, as if they have just started to form. I have been spraying according to schedule, using diazinon and captan, then switched to Sevin liquid to combat Japanese beetles closer to harvest. If these larvae and the pests I have seen are related, I need to find a way to break their life cycle. What do I spray in the early part of the season to kill all pests? Also, if the larvae are not related to the adult pest, when in my spray schedule should I change?

A. Entomologist Peter Schultz at the Hampton Roads Agricultural Research Station identified the bugs you sent as click beetles. They are adult beetles attracted to sweets. The larvae you found near the seed pit probably were wire worms. The small white grublike larvae on your plums were plum curculio. Schultz says you're doing everything right. Just keep doing it. Be sure to follow your spray schedule. The timing of spraying is important in growing fruit. Also, it often takes two or three seasons to get insects under control. I'm convinced that in growing fruit, a dormant oil spray such as Scalecide, used during winter months, is important.

Q. I have a peach tree that bears each season, but the peaches have black spots on them. What can I do?

A. The problem is a fungus, probably brown spot. You must spray regularly to grow fruit in this area. Otherwise, insects and disease will take over. Always in such cases, keep the rotting fruit picked off the tree and from the ground to prevent the disease from spreading. Buy a good all-purpose spray at any garden center and follow instructions on the label.

General

Q. My fig tree is plagued with ants, and I have been told that if I sprinkle black pepper around the roots of the tree, it will chase the ants away. Birds also eat the figs.

A. Virginia Tech recommends Sevin or diazinon to eradicate a bad case of ants. Red pepper probably would be the best alternative to try; however, I'm not sure that will cure the problem. According to a Virginia Agricultural Extension Service agent, the main cause of the ants is leaving rotted or half–eaten fruits on the bush. The same applies to strawberries. The ants and pills bugs are attracted to the fruit. Keep it picked. A net or strings of shiny tape wrapped around the tree will help keep birds away. You can find both at garden centers. Remember to close the net at the bottom to keep squirrels from climbing up the trunk.

Q. Is there any way to distinguish a male kiwi from a female?

A. Yes. After it flowers, the female has white pistils in the middle of the old bloom. The male has none.

Q. I have a problem growing watermelon. They get the size of a softball and then turn black and rot. My soil tested between 6 and 7 pH. I used a lot of compost on my garden. What is the problem?

A. Your soil pH is correct for watermelons, but they must be grown in well–drained soil, such as around Edenton, N.C., where many melons are grown. Your best bet may be to grow them in raised beds.

Herbs

Q. This is the second year I have spread pine bark mulch over a long bed that contains herbs, annuals and perennials. Among the herbs are basil, thyme, oregano and marjoram. This year my herbs don't look healthy. I'm wondering if the mulch has changed the composition of the soil. Is this possible, and should I take samples and have the soil tested?

A. Pine bark should not radically change the soil, but it's always smart to take a soil test. Do it at least once every three years. Herbs are Mediterranean crops and mostly prefer a hot, dry, sandy soil. I suspect the mulch is too much for them. They may be too wet, or their trunks and limbs are staying damp from the bark mulch. Remove the mulch from around them and see if they perform better. If you believe you must mulch, pine straw or even gravel might better suit their needs.

House plants

Q. Can you tell me what is wrong with my dwarf palm (Neanthe Bella) *chamaedorea?* The plant is not quite 7 years old and was repotted about three years ago. Now blackish–brown elongated spots are appearing all over the leaves. Also, are the older, bottom stems supposed to die? That has happened several times.

A. It's difficult to analyze palm problems, although the parlor palm is listed in houseplant books as one of the easiest to grow. Dan Milbocker at the Hampton Roads Agricultural Research Station said he has repotted his palm and it still is doing the same thing as yours. He suspects a calcium deficiency, which could be corrected with a small amount of lime. Usually, browning at the tips and edges of leaves indicates a hot, dry room or fertilizer injury. You might try running a lot of water through the soil to leach out some of the fertilizer, and then try a more humid location.

Q. Please tell me how to start a pineapple tree from a pineapple I bought in a store. Also, there's a way to make it produce fruit by putting it in a bag with an apple. I'm not sure when and how to do it.

A. Cut the top off the pineapple and set it in moist sand. In about three months, it will have developed roots. It probably will be two years before it blooms. Then put a plastic bag over it with an apple inside. With the apply supplying ethylene gas, it should produce fruit.

Q. I know you've had this question before, but how can I get a 2-year–old Christmas cactus to bloom? It grows very slowly and never shows signs of blooming.

A. This plant is often called Crabby Cactus because so many people have problems getting it to bloom. In spring, you should fertilize and water it regularly. Many folks put them outdoors in the summer in the shade, which they love. In late August, slack off on the water, and then the plant needs night temperatures of 50 to 55 degrees F and 13 uninterrupted hours of darkness every 24 hours. It will then set flower buds. Once you see the buds, bring it back into a room with heat and light and it should bloom at Christmas.

Q. Please tell me what I am doing wrong with a cactus plant. I bought it as a Christmas cactus, but it often buds anytime during the year. In fact, it recently was full of buds, but as before, they fell off. As yet, it has never had a full bloom. The plant is growing and looks healthy.

A. Christmas cactus are temperamental. They must be kept in a cool, dark room in the fall without any exposure to light at night. The optimum night temperature should be from 50 to 55 degrees. Poinsettias call for similar conditions. Bud drop usually is caused by giving them too much water. You may want to repot the plant in a coarse or medium soil mix. They always seem to do best if kept in one place, preferably a window.

Q. My Christmas cacti are sick and withered. I'm not neglecting them, so what's wrong?

A. Christmas cactus will wilt from too much or too little water. Most likely, it's too much. By the way, the best gift you can give your holiday cactus plants is to put them outside in the shade for the summer. The same goes for your other house plants.

Q. I am getting paranoid from mealybugs. They tried to take over my town home last summer. I washed the plants and brought some indoors for winter, but now mealybugs are spreading to my African violets. I used Orthene, alcohol and now a bug spray. I understand that mealybugs are spread by a white fly. Is that correct, or have they mutated into a new species like the local fleas?

A. Mealybugs are difficult to eradicate, particularly when you have as many as it sounds like you have. Try washing plants thoroughly with Calgon soap. Safer Insecticidal Soap also is recommended. Mealybugs are a common house–plant pest and are disseminated by ants, moving about infested plants.

An aerosol insecticide named resmethrin will eliminate mealybugs, as well as white flies. Other recommendations include washing off the plants with a strong spray from your hose, then spraying with malathion at a ratio of 1 tablespoon per gallon of water. But you'll need to spray two or three times a week for several weeks until you see no more signs of them. Malathion has a horrible smell, so be sure to do your spraying outdoors, and follow directions very carefully.

There also are systemic controls (absorbed through the roots) that can be applied to the soil. They're effective because mealybugs are sucking insects. Ask at a garden center for a systemic product in granular form that you can sprinkle on the soil.

Q. I had an elderly neighbor who had beautiful porch ferns. She kept all her used tea leaves and put them on the ferns. I have been emptying my tea bags and putting them in my vegetable and flower gardens. Do they help?

A. Tea leaves contain tannin and may provide some help to your plants, indoors and out. Grass clippings also contain tannin and would produce similar results outdoors.

Q. Several weeks ago, I was given an amaryllis bulb planted in a small pot of special peat. All I had to do was water the bulb faithfully and keep it at the proper temperature. I am now enjoying its beautiful blossoms. How do I ensure future blooms?

A. Keep your amaryllis in a warm spot until the weather is warm enough to set it outdoors. Then place it in semishade, where you can water it when nature does not. Feed it once a month. You'll notice its foliage growing and multiplying. In September, bring it indoors in a cool, dry place. I always turn the pot on its side so foliage will dry up. Let it rest, meaning no water or fertilizer, for about six weeks. Afterward, move it to a sunny spot and water and feed it. It should bloom again. Occasionally, it will skip blooming for a year. The amaryllis is temperamental, but most years it will rebloom. It likes being potbound, so do not repot until small bulbs grow around it. New bloom shoots are slow to form. If you want to speed up the process, put low heat under the pot, such as a radiator that's not too hot.

Q. Every Christmas I purchase a poinsettia plant but cannot get it to bloom again the next year. The plant has beautiful green leaves year-round and is healthy. Can you help me?

A. Your poinsettia will bloom again in time for the next holiday season with a little year-round care. The following poinsettia-care holiday calendar provided by the Society of American Florists, is a helpful way to keep track of what you should do and when you should do it.

Christmas Season: Select plants with tightly clustered yellow buds. Protect from hot or cold drafts, keep soil moist but not soggy, and place in a room with enough natural light that you can read a newspaper. Ideal temperature: 70 degrees day, 60 degrees night.

New Year's Day: Use an all-purpose house-plant fertilizer. Continue light, water and fertilizer and your plant will remain colorful for many weeks.

St. Patrick's Day: Remove faded and dried parts of the plant. Add more soil, preferably a commercially available sterile mix.

Memorial Day: Plant could be up to 3 feet high. Cut back all stems and branches one-half their length to promote side branching. Re-pot in a large container. You can move plant outside, first to indirect, then direct light.

Independence Day: Trim plant again to promote side branching. Make sure it has full sunlight. Slightly increase amount of fertilizer.

Labor Day: By now, your plant may have grown up to 4 or 5 feet. Move it indoors to a place where it will have six hours of direct light from a curtain-free window.

First Day of Autumn (Sept. 21): Give your plant 14 hours of uninterrupted darkness (i.e., in a closet, basement or under a box) and 10 hours of bright light each day. Keep night temperature in the low 60s. Continue to water and fertilize. Rotate the plant each day to give all sides even light.

Thanksgiving: Discontinue short-day/long-night treatment. Place the plant in a sunny area with at least six hours of direct light. Reduce water and fertilizer.

Christmas Holiday Season: Enjoy your "new" poinsettia!

Lawn Care

Q. Please tell me what to do about bare spots in a backyard lawn with numerous tree roots.

A. You don't say what kind of tree, but presumably the protruding roots are near the tree. Often, too much shade from trees will keep grass from growing. Protruding roots of a shallow–rooted tree such as magnolia usually sap up moisture before grass can get it. If that describes the problem, the best solution is to make a bed around the tree and plant a ground cover, such as vinca minor, ivy, mondo grass, liriope or pachysandra. Vinca and ivy are the easiest to grow, but vinca is a big favorite over ivy because it is covered with a lavender bloom in early spring. If you want something with height of 10 to 12 inches that's easy to grow, liriope is a good choice.

Q. How do I rid my lawn of crab grass? During the past three years, I have reseeded with Rebel II fescue and fertilized with 10–10–10. Crab grass still becomes prominent each year.

A. The only good way to control crab grass is with a pre–emergent crab–grass control in the spring, going over your entire lawn. It should be used before forsythia blooms fall. Do not walk or rake the lawn after application because it forms a seal that prevents crab grass seed from germinating. Crab grass regenerates in August, so your best bet is to use the same or a similar product in August to prevent another crop. Early next spring, use it again. The post–emergent liquid crab–grass killers available now do little good and often damage grass.

Q. I am sending you a sample of my biggest lawn problem. A fine short grass that spread through my yard was evident for three to four weeks in the spring and has been recurring. I have been told the only way to rid myself of this nuisance is to dig it out or poison it at the expense of the lawn's appearance. I tried digging/poisoning it in early spring but have even more of the mess. Is there no herbicide that will do the job without killing the fescue?

A. The sample grass you sent is poa annua, or annual blue grass. It is a pest of the first order and is terribly difficult to control. It grows all winter and especially in early spring, forming seed heads that will germinate and hassle you next year. It dies in hot weather and you no longer see it. Best control is the herbicide Betasan, which is found in some crab–grass control products and is pre–emergent. Golf courses use it regularly, but you may have trouble finding it. Call a golf course or garden center distributor to find out where to buy it. It can be applied dry or sprayed. The only other solution is to spray with Roundup, but that will kill everything it touches.

Q. Please give me a simple, step–by–step plan to refurbish a lawn this spring and summer. Mine is a cornucopia of weeds. What little grass exists feels spongy underfoot.

A. If you have full sun, your best bet is to grow Bermuda, Centipede, zoysia or St. Augustine, all warm–season grasses. Bermuda is invasive, but it can be kept under control with Roundup, a glyphosate. It is less expensive than zoysia. You can buy hulled seed in spring and see new grass starting in a few weeks. Water it thoroughly and often, and feed it 1 pound of nitrogen per 1,000 square feet from April through August. By next summer, you should have a good lawn. But remember, it browns out at the first frost and stays brown until next spring. St. Augustine must be planted in plugs, found at garden centers, and also browns out in winter. Zoysia is finer and non–invasive. Buy Pursely Cashmere zoysia plugs at a garden center. Set them about a foot apart, and by fall, you'll have a beautiful lawn. Feed and water it the same as Bermuda. It also browns out in winter. Centipede can be started by sowing seed in the spring.

Fertilize warm–season grasses in April and every month through September with a high–nitrogen fertilizer, such as 30–5–10. Apply at a rate of one–half to 2 pounds of pure nitrogen per 1,000 square feet of lawn. Centipede requires about half as much, applied only twice during the season.

If you choose fescue, which does stay green year–round, put up with the weeds this summer but spray the area with Roundup in August. Then seed the entire area in early September with Shenandoah or Rebel II fescue seed. Fertilize with 10–10–10 when you seed. Apply a slow–release, high–nitrogen fertilizer once a month for three months. Fertilize only once in spring. Keep it watered until fall. If your lawn is in full sun, you will constantly have to fight Bermuda.

But no matter which method you choose, have a soil sample taken to determine whether you need lime or plant food.

Q. We are trying to get St. Augustine grass established in our lawn and need a yearly maintenance plan. Can you help? We also have been battling crab grass and Dalis grass. Any suggestions you have will be greatly appreciated.

A. Your primary problem is that St. Augustine grass is not supposed to grow here because there's not enough rainfall to keep it looking lush. Also, our winters are too cold. As you know, you must start with plugs. It needs full sun and as much water as you can give it. Fertilize from April through August with a high–nitrogen fertilizer such as 30–5–10, applied in an amount to give it about 1 pound of nitrogen per month per 1,000 square feet. It also is a haven for many insects, so check regularly for them. Apply an insecticide if you find bugs, but make sure it is OK to use on St. Augustine. As for crab grass and Dalis grass, use a pre–emergent control early each spring, perhaps in March. Many crab–grass products also control Dalis grass. Again, make sure you get a product especially for St. Augustine or you'll harm it.

Q. I have had a good front lawn of St. Augustine for 10 years. But I can't get it to "take" in my back yard, probably because of too much shade. Do you have a suggestion for enhancing its growth? Does it like a more acid soil? Is it necessary to use lime? I have not limed for several years.

A. First, lime the area well. Turf authorities at the Hampton Roads Agricultural Research Station say St. Augustine wants a neutral soil the same as fescue. Virginia Tech recommendations include adding one pound of nitrogen per 1,000 square feet in the months of April through August. Many also fertilize the same amount in August but no later because the grass needs to harden off before winter. If your lawn is not better by fall, then you must have too much shade; however, St. Augustine grows better than any other warm–season grass in shade.

Q. I am trying to solve the problem of brown patch in my St. Augustine grass. I sprayed with Daconil, but the brown patch seemed to keep spreading. Should I spray the entire lawn or just the infected area?

A. Daconil, Chipco 26019, Bayleton, Fore, Banner or any of the other fungicides designed for brown patch don't really stop the disease. They help prevent it from spreading, so it's important to spray the entire area that might be infected. You usually need to do this every seven days. Brown patch is not an easy disease to stop, so it's best to start spraying in early July when days are hot and humid and the nights are just about as bad. But are you sure the problem is brown patch? Virginia Tech turf specialists say it's more likely the damage is caused by Southern chinch bug, a pest of St. Augustine grass.

You can check to see if you have chinch bugs by removing ends of an empty coffee can. Cut the rim off one end to produce a sharp edge, and push the can 2 to 3 inches into turf in an area where chinch bugs are suspected. Fill the can with water and wait a few minutes. Chinch bugs will float to the surface. The tiny red nymphs may be difficult to see. If you find chinch bugs, Virginia Tech specialists recommend a winter treatment of Sevin or a spring treatment of diazinon, Oftanol, Dursban or Merit insecticides.

Q. Please let me know how to stop the spread of clover in my yard. I have St. Augustine grass and don't want to damage it.

A. For most grasses, you would use an herbicide such as 33 Plus, Weed–B–Gon or Weedone, but most of these products cannot be used on St. Augustine without harming it. Read the label before buying. Fertiloam products, located in Bonham, Texas, should have a product for St. Augustine. Call around first before driving to garden centers. Another method is to fertilize St. Augustine every month from April through August with one pound of nitrogen per 1,000 square feet and get it so thick it crowds out the clover. Some people adore clover in a lawn. It does have the beneficial effect of adding nitrogen to the soil.

Q. We have a mulching mower, and when my husband mows the lawn, he leaves the grass clippings behind to provide nitrogen. My neighbor says that leaving them on the grass will kill it. Our grass is turning yellow in some areas. We have Rebel Jr. grass. Who is right?

A. Both are correct. Leaving the clippings on your lawn can reduce the amount of fertilizer needed by as much as one-third. But if you use a regular mower and the grass is tall, a dense layer of clippings can smother the lawn. Mulching mowers are handy and won't kill the grass. The yellowing you described may be brown patch, a common summer disease that occurs when days are hot and nights are humid. If you're a fanatic about your lawn, you might be able to prevent brown patch by applying Daconil or Bayleton. The other possibility is that you have some rye grass mixed in your lawn. It turns yellow and dies this time of year. Do not fertilize your lawn again until September, and then reseed it and apply fertilizer.

Q. Help! Help! The miserable weed I'm enclosing a sample of is taking over our lawn. One patch is 10–by–20 feet and spreading fast. What can I do?

A. Your weed is wood sorrel, or oxalis. There are several varieties, one of which is a plant sold as shamrock. All are difficult to kill because they grow from a bulb. You will need to spray with 33 Plus at least three times, 10 days apart, when the weed is growing in spring.

Q. My problem is with my handkerchief–sized lawn. It has sprouted numerous clumps of wild onions/chives since last fall. I started to dig up the clumps, but it is a daunting task because there is a clump every 3 square inches. How else can I get rid of them?

A. There are three ways to eliminate wild onions or wild garlic: 1) Spray with a glyphosate such as Roundup, but hit only the onions because it kills grass as well; 2) Use a weed killer such as 33 Plus or Weed–B–Gon and spray about three times, 10 days apart. Follow closely the directions on the container; or, 3) mow the onions very close, and they usually will die. In spring, fertilize your lawn lightly. Fertilize twice in fall, and reseed. This program will help thicken the turf and prevent such pests in the future.

Q. Each fall, I find many small holes in my lawn and beds. What are they and what should I do?

A. The holes are from mole crickets, voles or squirrels burying acorns. There's not much you can do to stop squirrels. If holes are 3–4 inches deep, they're mole crickets. Spreading diazinon will eliminate them. If holes go deep, they're voles. Put Ramik, a rat poison, in the holes.

Moles, Voles And Other Varmints

Q. How do I get rid of moles from my yard and flower borders? They are slowly killing my plants and shrubs by burrowing under them and leaving the roots exposed.

A. Supposedly, moles do not eat roots, but the runs they make are used by voles and mice as interstate highways, and the latter two do eat roots and bulbs. Moles live off insects in the soil, namely grubs. If you can eliminate the insects, the moles will leave. Most authorities say that you will always have moles if you live next to woods or an open field. Here are some suggestions: Tramp down all the runs; then, in a day or two, you'll know which are active by the ones that rise up again.

In active runs, punch a hole with a pencil every 3 feet. In one opening, put two sticks of Juicy Fruit gum, unwrapped and rolled into a ball. In the next, put castor bean seeds. And in the third, place poison peanuts. Use rubber gloves so the moles do not detect your human scent.

As I've said before, I don't know which of the three remedies works (maybe they all do), but they do help eliminate moles. You've got to keep at it, however, and look for new runs all the time. Don't use castor beans in pet and/or play areas because they're poisonous.

Another more expensive method is to put milky spore over the entire area. A bacteria grows and causes disease among the grubs, eliminating Japanese beetles, as well as moles. It takes about three years to become effective, but lasts for 20.

People who have spent $100 or more for vibrating mechanisms tell me they do not work. They just drive the moles 25 feet in another direction.

Tony Avent, a marvelous gardener from Raleigh, N.C., said one way to prevent vole damage to flower beds is to mix fine gravel in with the planting mix. He said it reduces or eliminates vole problems.

More on voles and moles: Voles are called, among other less-flattering names, "meadow mice." They spend their lives underground in an extensive trail system 1 inch to 2 feet below the surface. They damage stems and roots of azaleas, many trees (they prefer apple and pine), tulips and other flowering plants. If you see round holes about the size of a quarter, or up to 1-1/2 inches in diameter, in your lawn or garden, you probably have the pests. Ramik is in demand as a control for voles but is sometimes difficult to find. Owner Brent Heath of the Daffodil Mart in Gloucester recommends it. Heath places small bags of it under planks and woodpiles and voles seek it out. An alternative is to use mouse traps baited with apple slices, peanut butter or oatmeal. Check the traps every day. At first, the voles are cautious, but once they taste the bait, they get greedy and sloppy and you'll start catching them. Lots of them. If you happen to have a hawk, owl, fox, skunk, weasel, mink or snake wandering around, they like a vole or two for lunch.

The most recent mole control on the market is Mole-Med, a liquid based on castor oil. It has been tested by Michigan State and other universities. They report it not only repels moles but also voles, skunks, raccoons, rabbits and squirrels. It does not kill moles but drives them away. The animals named instinctively know that castor beans are poisonous and apparently the varmints leave the area. You mix Mole-Med with water and spray over your entire yard and garden. Then sprinkle the area to soak it down into the soil. Two or three applications per year may be required. I've found that it drives moles away but it has not chased off the many rabbits, squirrels and raccoons that want to make their home at my place. Mole-Med is available in garden centers.

Q. About a year ago, I wrote asking about holes in my yard. At that time, you said they were caused by voles. I have since been using pelleted mouse poison. I put pellets inside the holes and little piles of them in other places. I have probably spent $50 on that poison but have yet to see a dead vole. A few weeks ago, an exterminator told my neighbor that the holes are caused by mole crickets. I have 50 to 100 holes in my yard now. Please tell me that you think causes them and what I can do about it.

A. From the photo you sent, it looks like the holes were caused by voles. Don't expect to see dead voles after using the bait. They normally don't crawl out of their holes for you to watch them die. But the exterminator may be correct. Mole crickets, which are lawn pests, make similar holes. Dig down into the holes. If you have mole crickets, you'll find them in the soil. If so, use Sevin or parasitic nematodes to eliminate them .

Q. I have had problems with moles pushing up the ground in my yard. I tried putting out poison peanuts, gum and mothballs in their tunnels. I also set two mole traps, but I never got the first mole. Last year, I got a female cat, had her spayed and she killed at least 15 moles. My neighbor said her cat also kills moles.

A. I'm hearing from more and more readers who say cats are the best way to control moles and voles. But you must have a hungry cat. Fat house cats might resent being forced to catch moles. So other readers will know, the methods you mentioned will not work until you use milky spore, diazinon or similar products to eliminate grubs in your lawn. Once you get rid of grubs, moles will usually leave. The poison peanuts, etc., will usually take care of the few that come back. One reader introduced me to Giant Destroyers for mole control. They're like large firecrackers. They explode into a sulfur gas that is guaranteed to drive off moles, ground-hogs, skunks and a variety of pests that burrow in the ground. I gave some to a friend who liked them so much he bought more.

Q. Having lived on a dairy farm in New England most of my life, I found a simple solution to keeping varmints out of my garden. We had electric fences for cattle. I ran wires around my garden and attached them to the cattle fence to keep woodchucks, skunks, chipmunks and raccoons from raiding the garden. Since moving to Virginia's Eastern Shore, where we are blessed with a lack of skunks, woodchucks or chipmunks, I only use fence to deter rabbits and raccoons. I purchased a charger and use it for the raccoons. I place one wire about 4 feet from the ground and another at 12 to 15 inches. Obviously, you should vary the height depending on the animal. These charges transform 110 volts to 12 volts DC and have a make-and-break system, using a flasher similar to those on automobile directional lights. No animal or person receives a continuous shock. Once animals touch an electric fence, they won't come back a second time.

A. Thanks for the advice. Perhaps it will help the readers who have muskrats wrecking their gardens.

Q. A magazine I read had a notice about a squirrel deterrent. The product is called Scripton, a powder to be mixed with bird seed to keep squirrels out of the feeder. Its spicy taste will not deter birds but will annoy squirrels. One tablespoon to 4 pounds of seed is the proper amount.

A. Scripton is a botanical product that birds used to eat in the wild, according to a manufacturer's representative. It is a capsicum (pepper), and birds like it but squirrels do not. Some pet and bird stores carry it.

Q. I have found that regular screen wire can keep rabbits from chewing young fruit trees. Cut a piece of wire in the appropriate size and then use a desk stapler to secure it loosely around the tree. Let it extend 12 to 15 inches above ground. This will drop to rest at ground level and remain there for years. The tree has room to grow, and no replacement is needed.

A. Thanks for the idea to prevent rabbit damage. It seems like a quick solution.

More on rabbits: Set a jar of water in your garden about every 15 feet to keep rabbits away. Those who have used this method say it works, but they can't say why. Use a gallon jug or a clear glass container, such as a juice bottle. Fill it half full of water, and place one jar every 10 to 15 feet in your garden. If that doesn't work, a fence is the only other solution. Be sure to use 1–inch chicken wire up to 30 inches high or baby rabbits will go through it. You can try those "nature traps," but rabbits are tough to trap.

Q. How effective are nets at protecting fruit trees from being picked over by birds?

A. Several gardeners have told me that nets often are ineffective at protecting berries, apples, peaches, figs and pears. One man carefully netted his blueberry bushes, but a raccoon crawled under the net one night and stripped the bush. I netted my 10–foot Delicious apple tree, but then watched a robin walk under the net, fly up into the tree and pick at the ripening apples. A better deterrent might be a Mylar strip, which has a shiny glare and flaps in the breeze, scaring off pests.

Q. Isn't it a bit presumptuous of you to have a "plan for the universe?" The animals you want to eliminate have a purpose in life, even if they interfere with what YOU consider important! Aside from their many ecological purposes, they provide humorous antics for me and my 86–year–old mother, and we enjoy feeding them. We live in a very nice neighborhood, and most of my neighbors enjoy the same animals. I feel we humans should be able to live peacefully with our surroundings, and at the same time, have a nice yard. It's called co–existing with the environment. Who cares about a few holes or tunnels? Really, which is more important? I and many others say, "Phooey on you!" Why don't you go live on AstroTurf?

A. I don't mind a few holes or tunnels. But when raccoons and squirrels steal my apples and pears, as has happened the past two years, my love for animals diminishes. In the past two weeks, raccoons have pulled impatiens out of six of my hanging baskets for three nights in succession. Why? I don't know. I want to have a green world, but not one made of AstroTurf.

Q. I missed your column about the use of a Hav–a–Hart trap that one reader referred to in his question about baiting it for squirrels. As a wildlife rehabilitator, I am often asked how to deal with animals, usually squirrels and raccoons whose presence seems to cause problems. It is more effective to modify a habitat than to attempt to eliminate the unwanted animals or birds.

Whoever said "nature abhors a vacuum" was right. If you remove squirrels who find your back yard a suitable home, then other squirrels will move into the territory upon elimination of the first population. If you remove a large number of a population, those that remain will produce offspring at a higher rate than normal.

A more effective approach is modification of the environment. Find out what originally attracted the animals and change or remove it. If bird feeders are attracting squirrels, try to find a squirrel–proof feeder; or, better yet, give the squirrels their own feeder. They can be a lot of fun to watch.

There are instances when only one squirrel or raccoon out of the bunch has learned a behavior that makes him a particular nuisance. In such a case, it may be necessary to relocate this one animal. Do not do it during winter. A creature that suddenly finds itself in strange territory has a hard time finding food, water and adequate shelter.

Squirrels produce a litter of young in the spring and another in the fall. Relocating the mother will leave the babies to freeze or starve to death in the nest.

Since we are destroying so much natural habitat that once belonged to wildlife, we must learn to adapt to living with these critters, as many of them have already adapted to living in close proximity to humans.

While I am on the habitat subject, wood ducks, screech owls and other cavity dwellers are looking for nest sites now (late May). Just a reminder that this is a good time to cap a chimney if it has not been done.

A. Thanks for a different opinion and interesting information. There are probably as many readers who disagree with your theories as there are who agree. It appears to me that the critters are winning the war.

Q. I am 13, and every week I read about the problems people have with moles and voles in their yards. We had the same problem until my mother finally let me get a kitten. Fenway stays out every night to sleep, and the first year we found over five dead moles in our yard. All the mole tracks are gone, and our tulip bulbs no longer get eaten. My mother doesn't like cats, but she sure is glad we go Fenway!

A. Readers have written before that a hungry cat is the best vole control there is. What often happens, however, is that the cat becomes a house cat and gives up hunting voles for indoor comfort. Moles are 6 to 8 inches long and almost as big around so you need an elephant-sized cat to handle them. Fenway sounds like the kind of watch cat you need in every yard.

Perennials, Biennials and Annuals

Q. Please identify the plant I am sending you, and tell me how to care for it. Does it bloom? It came up in my flower beds last fall, has carrotlike leaves and is 36 inches tall.

A. Your plant is *Daucus carota*, or wild carrot. Most people know it as Queen–Anne's lace. It is a biennial, meaning it will grow two years, blooming the second, then die. It has fern-like foliage and clusters of small, white flowers with a dark–red flower in the center. It is attractive but spreads.

Q. When is the proper time to trim pampas grass?

A. If you don't like the natural look of brown grass in winter, then pampas grass should be pruned before new growth begins each spring. March is ideal. Because the plants are so large and thick, the job may require a chain saw.

Q. I have two beautiful hydrangeas in full bloom. I am interested in knowing how to dry their blooms. Is there any way for them to retain their color after they're dried?

A. Cut them off with the stem length you prefer and hang them upside down in a dry, cool, dark place such as a closet. In two to three weeks, they should be dry. You can use silica gel specially packed for drying flowers, but it's more work. Hydrangea blooms tend to turn green the longer they're on the bush. Prune the blooms when they reach the color you prefer. After drying, they eventually will lose their color.

A newer method for preserving hydrangeas is to cut them with the length stem you desire. Strip all the leaves off the stem and immediately stick them into boiling water for only 30 seconds. Then remove and put in a vase with 1 inch of water. They will gradually absorb the water in the vase and preserve themselves for winter bouquets.

Q. I have been trying to establish Oriental poppies – not the new variety but old-fashioned red ones – in my garden. I have a small garden in full sun. It is well-drained, and the soil is on the loamy side. First, I tried spreading seed. Next, I purchased what appeared to be healthy plants. The plants are still alive but don't look healthy. The latest plant sent up a healthy–looking flower pod, but it aborted before it fully opened. Can you give some advice on how to raise poppies?

A. Poppies are not easy to raise in this area. I know of more failures than successes. Experts at the Hampton Roads Agricultural Research Station say they need afternoon shade and well-drained soil. They are best grown from seed planted in the fall.

Q. I am sending you snapshots of my "moon vine" taken last summer. One shot is taken in daytime and another at night, to show how they are as pretty at night as in daytime. They are very fragrant, but they reseed and could become a nuisance. What is the botanical name?

A. Your photos prove the moon flower is an attractive plant, day and night. Moon flowers are a confusing group. Your plant, which is not a vine, is *Calonyction*, a member of the morning glory family. It is sometimes called *Ipomoea bonanox*. Moon vine, which is a morning glory, is *Ipomoea*, and it has vines. All have trumpet–shaped flowers.

Q. I planted moon flowers last spring and was fascinated by them. One night between 7 and 9 p.m., a beautiful hummingbird visited mine, and I hope to see it again this summer. What do you know about it?

A. I hesitate to get into moon flowers because there are so many different versions and opinions. I think you are talking about moon flower (*Calonyction aculeatum*), which has white scented flowers 6 inches across that open in the evening and stay open until noon the next day. It can climb up to 15 feet tall. Burpee sells the seed.

Q. Can you give me information on growing sweet peas?

A. Sally Dozier of Chesapeake is an expert on sweet peas (*Lathyrus latifolius*). She says it is a climbing perennial vine reaching up to 8 feet in one season. All summer long, it is covered with fragrant clusters of large rose, pink and white blooms. They are easy to grow if you sow seed in October. Growers say they get best results by planting the seed deep, about 4 to 6 inches. In late spring, new plants should be breaking through the soil. Another method is to start the seed indoors in late winter and then transplant into your garden. Sweet peas will bloom the first growing season and should multiply year after year. Annual sweet peas do not grow well in our area.

Q. Enclosed is a sample of a blue lilylike plant that is a volunteer in my yard. It has been growing for several years, but we have been unable to put a name on it. Will you kindly name the plant for us?

A. Experts confirmed that your plant is spiderwort. Specifically, it is *Tradescantia virginia*, usually called Virginia spiderwort. A native of eastern North America, it is a hardy perennial that grows 2 or 3 feet tall and has slim leaves with small clusters of flat, three–petaled blue flowers 1 inch across. There also are purple, pink, white and rose–colored varieties. Blooms open in the morning but close by midafternoon. It will grow in sun or shade in ordinary garden soil. The plant can develop thick roots that will crowd out other plants, so it always should be planted where it has plenty of room to spread out.

Pest, Disease and Weed Control

Q. During the past month, I have noticed small patches of a yellow gooey substance in areas around my shrubs. It eventually fades out to a light brown.
I also see it near my neighbors' shrubs. I have reapplied mulch this past
spring to my shrubs. Do you know what this substance might be?

A. It's most likely that a fungus brought in with the bark, according to Dan Milbocker at the Hampton Roads Agricultural Research Station. It won't
hurt anything, and the sun usually kills it.

Q. I have recently seen an ad (enclosed) for a "mosquito repellent plant." It sounds terrific,
but not being one to believe everything I read, I wonder what you can tell me about it.
If it is legitimate, is it available locally?

A. The ad you sent is from Michigan Bulb Co. Save your money. Nowhere in the ad is the
plant given its botanical name, so you don't know what you're buying. From a March
1992 issue of the American Horticulturist magazine, here is an answer to your questions: "The
plant is *Pelargonium x citrosum*. A July article in the New York Times quoted many satisfied cus-
tomers. However, research conducted (by a university) found the plant's impact on mosquitoes
was negligible. Researchers who rubbed lemon thyme on their hands were more successful in
avoiding bites. Another study indicates the plant contains almost nothing in the way of active
ingredients that would repel mosquitoes.

Plants that do contain active ingredients used in insect repellents and candles include lemon
balm, citronella grass and lemongrass. You probably can find these locally in garden centers,
or they can order them for you. They're also available from the following catalog companies:
Mellinger's, 2310 W. South Range Road, North Lima, Ohio, 444521; Kurt Bluemel, 2740 Green
Lane, Baldwin, Md. 21013; and Logee's Greenhouses, 55 North Street, Danielson, Conn. 06239.

Q. My yard is being taken over by my neighbor's ivy. How can I get rid of it? Spray? Or what?

A. Ivy experts report that it has become almost resistant to Roundup. My experience proves
that true, so spraying is not going to be very helpful. If you spray with Roundup, it's going to kill the grass in your yard. And three sprayings are likely to be required.

Here are other suggestions: Rake up or pull up the ivy by hand before it gets rooted and
discard it. That can be done, even though it doesn't sound realistic. You need a Great Wall to
prevent its spread. That can be done by cutting a trench at your property line, or building a
wall or fence lined with screen wire that ivy cannot crawl through. Anything that will force it
into the air makes it easy to prune. None of these solutions is easy, but they are about the only
way to control ivy.

Q. To keep roots from encroaching over the line of my neighbor's property, I used the method you suggested. Using a post–hole digger, I dug a trench close to the fence line, put in metal sides from discarded washing machines 12 to 15 inches deep, plus some heavy plastic sheets, and that combination keeps out the encroaching roots.

A. Thanks for the testimonial. The only sure way to keep weeds from traveling from one area to another is to dig a trench and line it with something roots can't penetrate such as solid sheets of plywood, heavy sheets of plastic or metal.

Q. Three years ago, we purchased several acres in the Northern Neck area north of Kilmarnock. An area near the road was closely cropped by grazing horses. Since then, it has not been grazed and is now densely covered with a vine, interspersed with poison ivy. It grow 2 to 3 feet high, and I'm sending you a sample to identify. What can we use to control it, other than Roundup?

A. The bush you describe is Japanese honeysuckle, a real pest in this area. It will crawl over, under and above everything, smothering plants as it grows. Weed authorities say the best control is Roundup. Spray two or three times while the plant is growing.

Q. In front of my town house, I have four boxwoods bordered by impatiens. In late September, I pruned the boxwood and pulled up the impatiens. Then I covered the area with additional pine bark mulch. The area already had a good layer of mulch, but I thought an additional amount would be good for winter protection. I also fertilized with Miracle Gro. Since all this was done, toadstools have been growing rapidly, and they are all purple in color. As soon as I dig them up, more appear. What is the cause of this, and how can I get rid of them?

A. Every fungus has its own toadstool. Bark carries a fungus that is the purple toadstool. It does not affect growth of plants and the toadstools may be beneficial. Usually this corrects itself after the bark is exposed to sun for a while. If you desire to eliminate the toadstools at once, spray with a fungicide.

Q. We are having a problem with bamboo. When we purchased our home three years ago, the bamboo was not bad, but this stuff has steadily spread. I contacted the City of Chesapeake because a ditch is full of it, and they said it was not their responsibility. Please help us get rid of this pest.

A. Most everyone who has bamboo has a problem. It is difficult to control unless planted in a concrete container. To try to contain your weed, dig a trench 2 feet deep at the edge of its growth and line that with heavy plastic sheets. By heavy, I mean impenetrable. Otherwise, use cement to line the trench. Some authorities advise cutting the plant off at the ground and then spraying it with full–strength Roundup when new growth appears. Doing that several times is supposed to stop its growth.

Q. Can you provide a list of garden plants that are poisonous? I have children and don't want to endanger them by planting the wrong thing.

A. It's important to identify poisonous plants and not let children near them. Each year, hundreds of thousands of poison cases are reported in the United States, a large portion of them children.

Never cut a branch from a bush you cannot identify to use for playing or cooking hot dogs over a fire. Obvious plants to avoid include poison ivy and its close relative, poison oak. Both may be a vine or shrub but have the characteristic three leaflets that warn us of their danger. You can become exposed not only by direct contact with the plant, but also by touching tools, animals or clothing that have been contaminated.

Poison sumac is another common plant that causes skin rashes and infections. The trumpet vine with its showy orange–red tubular flowers can cause skin inflammation and blisters.

Here's a short list of other plants that can be dangerous to people, as well as pets:

Hyacinth, **Narcissus**, **Daffodil bulbs**: May cause nausea, vomiting or diarrhea if in gested; may be fatal.

Oleander leaves or branches: Extremely poisonous if eaten; affects the heart and has caused death.

Dieffenbachia: All parts cause intense burning and irritation of mouth and tongue. The tongue swells and blocks air in the throat.

Seed of golden chain trees: Very poisonous for children.

Castor bean or rosary pea: A single pea seed has caused death. Two castor bean seeds are nearly a lethal dose for adults.

Mistletoe berries: Fatal to children and adults who eat them.

Lily–of–the–valley leaves and flowers: A dainty fragrant beauty in spring, but fatal when eaten. A small child died from just drinking water left over from a vase that had contained these flowers.

Bleeding heart, or **Dutchmans breeches**: Eating the foliage and roots has proved fatal to cattle.

Jimson weed: All parts are poisonous and have proved fatal.

Rhubarb: Never eat anything but the stems. Eating the leaves can be fatal.

Daphne berries, **wisteria seeds** or **pods**: Very poisonous for children.

Laurel, rhododendron and **azaleas**: All parts of these plants are toxic and can prove fatal.

Q. Two leaves from my rhododendron bush are enclosed. I've had it for three years but it only had one bloom this spring. Leaves are not dark green like my neighbors' and won't grow on the stems except at the tips. Can you help?

A. The leaves you sent have leaf spot. You need to spray with a fungicide such as Funginex to correct the problem. Is your plant in full sun? Rhododendrons need partial shade. They should also be mulched heavily and kept watered. Never let them dry out.

Q. For the past six years, my flowering hawthorn has been plagued with a rust and spot problem. Each year, it becomes worse. Last year, I cut it back after it blossomed. But new growth had rust and spots just as before. I have sprayed with Orthenex, and when that didn't work, I used Miticide to no avail. I live on the sound side of the Outer Banks, which might contribute to the problem.

A. Virginia Tech experts identify your problem as Entomosporium leaf spot. Other possibilities are rust and lacebug. Orthenex contains an insecticide and fungicide, but there are better ones for rust and leaf spot. Miticides are only for mite problems. Spray with Daconil 2787 regularly to eliminate the problem. Follow directions carefully. Helpful organic sprays include lime sulfur, copper and Bordeaux mix.

Q. I have a suggestion for the person who wrote you about a deer problem. I am a cosmetologist, and when I lived in Midlothian, Va., people from surrounding rural towns often came to the salon asking for bags of cut hair. They told me that they sprinkled it around their plants, and it repelled deer.

A. Thanks for the tip. I have used human hair to keep rabbits away from roses and find that it works until a few heavy rains. Then the rabbits begin to eat again. The same is probably true for deer, but I am so desperate to solve a rabbit problem that I called my barber when your letter arrived and asked him to save me a bag of hair.

Another idea recently came from Glen Ellen, Calif., in the Napa Valley, where vineyards are surrounded by 7-foot fences. Homeowners there use this recipe: one egg, whipped into 1 quart water, plus one-third bottle of hot sauce and some liquid soap (to help it spread). Spray on shrubs to repel deer. In arid climates, this solution may last three or four months. But in Southeastern Virginia and Northeastern North Carolina, you must repeat applications after heavy rainfall.

Q. I know you have written about bats for insect control. I am having a hard time finding bat houses. Can you point me in the right direction? And can you tell me the optimum location for them?

A. The problem is there's little evidence that North American bats use roost boxes, according to the American Bat Conservation Society. Your best bet is to send questions in a self-addressed, stamped envelope to the society: P.O. Box 1393, Rockville, Md. 20849. Ask for directions to make your own. Many mail-order garden catalogs sell them, as well as bird shops and shops in gardens and museums. The best location for a bat house is on the sunny side of houses and buildings, under the eaves, or on tree trunks 10 feet above the ground with no limbs below the house. Windy locations rarely are successful.

Q. What is punching holes in the outside edge of leaves on my roses? I never see the culprit. I spray with Isotox, malathion and Sevin, but the holes still appear.

A. Consulting rosarians Arnie Eggen and George Wilson of the Tidewater Rose Society looked at your leaves and diagnosed the problem as the carpenter bee. They say to leave it alone, and it will go away. The only problem it creates is damage to leaves, which looks bad if you plan to exhibit.

Q. What is the best chemical for killing grass in daylily beds?

A. Use a glyphosate, such as Roundup. But avoid hitting the foliage of the daylilies or they'll die. If that's impossible, try Poast, a product that will control Bermuda grass. For nut grass, Pennant is recommended.

Q. I have four miniature roses growing in containers, and I use diazinon for spider mites and Ortho Funginex for mildew. Are there any natural alternatives to either product? Or, should I even be concerned in view of the small number of plants I have?

A. All gardeners should be concerned about proper pesticide use. Many gardeners believe that hosing with a strong stream of water will scare off spider mites because they like hot, dry conditions. Others dispute that theory. If you want to use a chemical, kelthane is the one recommended for spider–mite control. For a natural pesticide, use an insecticidal soap in a spray bottle. It probably will have to be used more than once. For mildew control, there is adequate research now that shows that Wilt–Pruf, a product derived from natural pine oil, will prevent mildew, although the manufacturer does not claim such control. It is the only natural material I know of to control disease.

Q. What non–toxic product can I use to keep black spot off roses?

A. To prevent black spot, Cornell University recommends a solution of 1 tablespoon baking soda per gallon of water. Baking soda also can be used to fight powdery mildew. "We've found that sodium or potassium bicarbonate in combination with Safer Sunspray horticultural oil effectively controls powdery mildew on roses, cucurbits, herbs, zinnias and chrysanthemums," Cornell experts say. "Most effective treatment has been a weekly spray of 3 teaspoons of baking soda per gallon of water combined with 2 1/2 tablespoons of Safer Sunspray oil." Some gardeners now add 1 tablespoon liquid soap for better spreadability.

Q. I am a 74–year–old widow who does most all my own yard work. I have a problem with cat feces. My flower beds are messed up all the time. For easier upkeep, I put down black plastic with plenty of pine straw on top. I have used Scent Off pellets in the beds and Scent Off Twist–Ons on shrubbery. Both get expensive with repeated applications, and I do not think they are doing the job. Have you suggestions?

A. Most of the dog and cat repellents are based upon odor. Exposure to the weather, especially rain, makes them ineffective after a few weeks. Readers have told me that citrus peels scattered in beds repels cats the best.

Q. For the past couple of years, my flower beds have been taken over by something that looks like miniature lily pads. This weed has shallow roots but runs like a vine. It started in my front beds and showed up next in side and back beds. Can you tell me what it is, where it comes from and how I can get rid of it, without hurting the good plants?

A. Your weed is moneywort, a hydrocotyle. This group of plants thrive in or near shallow water. It is difficult to eradicate. Use a narrow–stream spray of Roundup or Kleenup to kill it, and be patient. It is an aquatic plant, so anything you can do to dry out the area will help eliminate this pest. On the plus side, it is often used in terrariums.

Q. I have a hedge of multiflora roses around my back yard. Behind the yard is a drainage ditch. The vine I've enclosed has overtaken my hedge of roses and other shrubs that get in its path. Please identify this pest and advise how to rid our yard of it.

A. Your weed has been identified as perennial morning glory, which could encircle the earth, given a chance. It's sometimes called "man of the earth." Roots are edible and, in some parts of the world, it is grown for its food value. Use Roundup or Kleenup to kill it. It dies down in the winter but should be sprayed in the spring when growth begins. Make sure you spray only the weeds and not any desirable shrubs.

Q. I have two very tall pine trees, which have ivy climbing to as high as 90 feet. I would like to remove it if it is threatening the health and life of these trees. Is there a simple solution to this problem, or should I be concerned?

A. The late Fred Heutte, a stalwart of the Norfolk Botanical Garden, once told me that ivy does not hurt any tree except the understory trees such as dogwood, holly, redbud, etc. For pines, oaks, poplars and other large trees, it does no harm. To kill ivy, cut it off at the base of the tree and wait for it to dry up enough so you're able to tear it off the trunk.

Q. How do you control green moss? We have patches all over our garden, and it's spreading.

A. Green moss on lawns, gardens, driveways and bricked areas is caused by lack of sunshine or lack of drainage or both. If you can provide more sunshine or do whatever it takes to get the area drained properly, the problem should solve itself. Sometimes lime will help, but test your soil first to see what's needed. Garden and home centers also sell products that eliminate moss only from structures, such as roofs, walkways, woodwork and fences.

Q. I have twice lost your recipe to get rid of crickets in the house. Please send me a replacement.

A. A reader offered this organic control for crickets: Mix 1/8 teaspoon boric acid and 1 tablespoon honey. Put the mixture in bottle caps and place them wherever you've seen crickets. Boric acid is available in most discount department stores and drug stores. To keep crickets outdoors in fall, put Borax (the laundry powder) around foundation shrubs and entryways.

Q. Spider mites are destroying my butterfly bushes. How do I get rid of them?

A. Many folks complain about spider mites during hot, dry periods in spring and summer. Mark Schneider, horticulturist for the Virginia Zoological Park, grows many butterfly bushes, and he says there are two secrets to good maintenance: proper pruning and using Sunspray horticultural oil. Adequate ventilation helps control the pest, so Schneider prunes to make sure limbs don't cross over one another. The other requirement is to spray early with Sunspray oil and to continue doing that all summer. Schneider, who prefers organic gardening, recommends Plants Alive for organic products. For a free catalog copy, write: Plants Alive, 5100 Schenley Place, Lawrenceburg, Ind. 47025.

Q. Japanese beetles bug me every year on roses, apple trees – everything. What can I do?

A. Sevin dust or spray is most often recommended. Do not use traps unless you place them far away from plants you want to save. The beetles go back into the ground in July. Then use diazinon, Merit or milky spore (not currently available) to eliminate them and that will help.

Rose Care

Q. I have a rose question that's bugged me for years. The pink climber Queen Elizabeth was highly recommended, so I purchased one. It failed to make more than two blooms for the first year. On checking with the garden center, they insisted that I must never prune this bush. Still no success, and a year or two later I moved. With misgivings, I bought another Queen Elizabeth because I heard so many favorable mentions of it. Again, only two to three blooms per year, and I never pruned it. Then our house was re-sided, and in consideration for the workers, I pruned the bush back severely. In response, this spring I had profuse blooms. Again, a different garden center had reiterated never to prune a climbing rose. What's the answer?

A. Every garden center should have at least one employee belong to the Tidewater Rose Society and insist they attend meetings regularly. Then they'd know there is no climbing Queen Elizabeth rose. The Queen Elizabeth is one of the best grandiflora roses, and it should be pruned down to 12 to 18 inches in late February. Then it will give you more blooms than nearly any pink rose you can grow.

Also, pruning advice about climbers was not proper. Every three to five years, complete canes need to be pruned out at ground level. That will rejuvenate the rose and it will throw out new canes that will bloom profusely. Two of the best climbers are red Blaze and pink New Dawn.

Q. What time of year can I plant roses?

A. Roses can be planted in October, November or February. If we have a mild winter, fall planting is best, because it gives roots a good start before spring. If we have a cold winter, it can devastate newly planted roses.

Q. How do fanatic rose growers keep their plants looking so perfect?

A. At the national meeting of the American Rose Society held in Norfolk in October 1991, growers from around the world revealed their secrets. Thomas Cairns of California, a past associate editor of The American Rose magazine, offered this monthly formula for growing prize-winning roses:
- First week. 1 tablespoon 20-20-20 fertilizer per bush
- Third week: Fish emulsion (1 tablespoon per bush).
- Fourth week: A high-nitrogen fertilizer (25 or more units of nitrogen) with guaranteed trace elements at a rate of 1 tablespoon per bush.

Each of these applications should be mixed with about a gallon of water and poured around each rose bush.

Q. As a novice gardener, I am confused about roses. Would you explain the difference between a floribunda and a tea rose. Is a grandiflora a type of tea rose? What different care is required for each kind? Do you have personal favorites to recommend?

A. A hybrid tea rose is the most popular. It is supposed to have one bloom per stem on long stems. A floribunda is a bush–type rose with lots of blooms that fall apart when they open up. They're generally not recommended for picking but good for a hedge. Several planted together make a good spot of color. Then the hybridizers bred a tea rose to a floribunda and created a grandiflora. It usually has several blooms on a long stem, but holds its blooms well and is good for picking.

As for care, a tea rose requires more care, more spraying. Floribundas are easiest to care for. Grandifloras, as you might expect, are in between in care requirements. All should be fertilized once a month from March through late August and sprayed weekly or as often as you can.

While on roses, don't forget climbing varieties. They are excellent and require little care. Old–fashioned roses are more fragrant and often hardier than newer varieties.

As for preferences, I'd plant Peace, Tiffany, Tropicana, Double Delight and Chrysler Imperial for tea roses, plus the grandiflora Queen Elizabeth. Europeana, Sunsprite and Charisma are favorite floribundas of many growers. In a climber, America and Blaze are best. I prefer to plant roses early in spring.

Q. Would you describe a typical spray to be used on roses?

A. Finicky roses require lots of chemical sprays if you want them to look unblemished. Many people are planting hardier old–fashioned roses, which are more fragrant. Organic gardeners use a pepper– or oil–based spray that contains dish detergent, among other things. But if you want fancy roses, protect your skin, clothes and lungs during spraying. Medal–seeking rosarians dress up like hazardous–waste removal workers to spray their precious plants. You'll find as many recommended spray solutions as rosarians. Here's one recipe contributed by the late G.H. Ferguson: Spray at least once a week and after every heavy rain. Begin when new growth first starts in spring. For black–spot prevention, add 1 level tablespoon of Phaltan or Daconil to 1 gallon water and mix. To prevent mildew, add the same amount of Benlate, also known as Benomyl, to the same solution. And to kill any insects that may start making trouble, add 2 tablespoons Isotox or 1 tablespoon malathion to the mixture.

Q. My neighbor spreads Epsom salts around her roses, and she has lovely flowers. What's the reason behind this practice?

A. Epsom salts is comprised of magnesium sulfate, one of the 13 plant foods needed for daily health. It's good for roses and tomatoes when they are setting fruit or blooms. Many rosarians use Epsom salts at a rate of 1 tablespoon per gallon of water. It should be watered in around the plant in spring and fall.

Q. Since relocating from Richmond, I have had problems with black spot and mildew on roses. I blame the high humidity of this area. Are there rose varieties that do better in this climate, or do you recommend a spray-and-dust routine?

A. Tidewater Rose Society former president Howard Jones says all roses are subject to black-spot and mildew, and there is no significant difference between varieties. He also says to forget dust and stick to sprays. Jones says old-fashioned garden roses are best to grow if you don't want to spray, but a lot depends on the summer weather. Organic gardeners are finding that a spray consisting of 1 tablespoon of horticultural oil (such as Sunspray) and 1 tablespoon baking soda per gallon of water prevents insects and disease.

Q. I bought four rose bushes last week, two climbing and two regular bushes. I don't know when or where to plant them in my yard. I have a fence on the southwest side of the house and would like to plant the climbing bushes there. I also have a fence on the northeast side. My house faces west. I want to plant them where they will grow best.

A. Your roses should be planted as soon as you take them home. If you purchased them in containers, you can plant anytime of year. If they were bare-root, soak the roots in a bucket of water with some plant-food crystals for several hours. Then use that solution around the roots when you plant. An ideal site for your climbing roses would be the southwest side against a fence. The other two can be planted wherever the soil is rich, well-drained and there is full sunshine.

Q. What kind of roses would grow well in a small garden?

A. Floribunda roses are excellent landscape plants, and some belong in every garden. They're especially suited to small gardens because they are short but have large blooms. Charles Turnbull, a consulting rosarian with the Tidewater Rose Society, recommends the following as best for today's gardens:

- **Europeana.** The richest dark red, it grows 2 1/2 to 3 feet tall.
- **Sexy Rexy.** One of the best pinks, it has enormous clusters of medium-pink blooms that are about 3 inches across on a medium-tall plant.
- **Sunsprite.** This yellow bloomer is winter-hardy. Flowers are about 3 inches across, and the bush grows about 3 feet tall.
- **French Lace.** One of the best creamy whites, it blooms continually with flowers about 4 inches in diameter. The plant grows about 3 feet high.

If you're looking for roses to provide color only, you may want to plant one of these two new roses. The first is Flower Carpet, a small ground-cover rose that grows not over 36 inches tall and spreads 3 feet wide. It's blooms are semidouble in a bright, deep pink color.

The other is Carefree Delight, a new All America selection. It spreads 5 feet wide, with carmine-pink blooms. It is highly resistant to black spot, mildew and rust.

Both of these new roses are said to require little or no spraying. Blooms are not meant for picking but to provide color in a garden.

Seaside Gardening

Q. We are troubled by brackish water that seeps into areas of our yard. When we have a high tide, accompanied by a northeaster, the Lafayette River floods North Shore Road and the brackish water floods a ditch that runs along the other side of our fence. Would you send a list of trees, shrubs and flowers, particularly perennials, that are resistant to brackish water?

A. When I lived on the eastern branch of the Lynnhaven River, I had the same problem. Plants that lived for 20 years under those conditions are: hardy hibiscus, the Fairy rose, cannas, daylilies, Vitex, lythrum, Japanese blood red ornamental grass, euphorbia (the ground cover), sedum 'Autumn Joy', tea roses, liriope, mint and wild ageratum.

Q. Can you help me save my 20-year-old dwarf evergreen? It's now about 4 feet tall and very full. It transplanted fine to the Outer Banks 15 years ago. Last summer, I noticed dead needles spreading down from the top. I cut them off, sprayed, watered and used some acid fertilizer, but it is still rapidly dying down. I inspect it often but find no trace of insects. I live in a remote beach area (Corolla, N.C.), and losing this plant is like losing a member of the family.

A. Your plant is sold as dwarf Alberta spruce, an attractive tree that is difficult to keep healthy. If yours has lived 20 years, you're about 15 years better off than most gardeners. They tend to become infested with spider mites, although the samples you sent showed no sign of them. Just in case, spray frequently with a strong stream of water, or use a weekly spray of Safer Insecticidal Soap or a spray containing kelthane. Once these dwarfs start downhill, it's difficult to stop the decline. Fertilize the tree lightly in December and again in late February. Be sure to water it all winter unless nature does it for you. But don't be surprised if your tree dies.

Q. Seaside gardening at Corolla consumes a lot of time. I am now halfway through my first five-year plan. Thanks to you and other good practitioners, I enjoy enhanced beauty while maintaining a naturalistic setting with no lawn. Arid weather and fierce winds caused many plants to fall by the wayside. Trial and error is a good teacher. Even though I was advised against certain plants, I still had to try. Large native plants, deck overhangs and small dunes, plus the use of containers, help create miniature eco-systems. Our soil is sandy, so we incorporate peat moss, pine bark, compost and mulch. The use of fertilizers is helpful, but nothing takes the place of Osmocote for nutrition.

To stabilize this site, we planted beach grass, put up snow fence and scattered native wildflower seeds. From 15 Japanese black pines, 12 are flourishing, but they are wider than they are tall. The native pine we transplanted never made it.

Next, we planted Blue Pacific juniper along the driveway and scattered daffodil and tulip bulbs to the extent our wallets could bear. Bulbs and perennials are our mainstay, with annuals used for fill-in color

Because of an injury, I wasn't able to visit the house from June to September one year. But despite no care and a very hot summer, the pines and juniper flourished. Other survivors include cotoneaster, hollies, yucca and pampas grass. Geraniums, gaillardia, gladiolas, iris, coreopsis, daisy and cushion mums all held up OK. Not surprisingly, annuals and vegetables died.

A. There are few places more difficult to garden than the Outer Banks of North Carolina. Thanks for your expert advice.

Q. What is the best time of year to cut down pampas grass?

A. Anything that is mowed down should be done when the plant is dormant. This would be during the late winter or early spring. If the grass starts sending out new shoots, it's too late. Shoots always come out of the root base, so you could still take some sharp shears and prune off the brown part, leaving just the new shoots.

Q. In a March column, you stated that pampas grass should be pruned before new growth begins each spring and that the job requires a chain saw. Why should it be pruned each year? The result of pruning pampas grass is an ugly bunch of stubble. Pampas grass requires a lot of elbow room. If the plant has become too large, then transplanting, not pruning, is best. If it is planted in a place where it is in the way, pruning will not solve the problem. If pampas grass is not pruned, new green leaves will emerge, mixed with the tall graceful foliage. The old foliage will gradually fade away. No butchering is needed, and certainly no chain saw is required.

A. I've never grown pampas grass and never intend to, unless I own a beach cottage. My information comes from university extension bulletins. I realize many landscape architects recommend leaving ornamental grass to stand all winter and not clipping it until spring, if at all. However, most homeowners seem to resent looking at brown foliage all winter.

Q. Our Russian olives are ailing this year. We live in Kitty Hawk, N.C., and have a hedge of them that has been doing well for five years. Now they're dropping yellow leaves, and small new leaves curl up and drop off. Nearby is an eleagnus of similar age. It was covered with blooms and filled with bees, but now a branch seems to be dying. On the other side of the yard, we have two sunburst locusts. One is full of new leaves. The other only shows leaf buds, which don't want to break out. Do you have ideas to help us?

A. It's tough to diagnose plant problems without seeing the patient. Virginia Tech horticulturists say your problem sounds like frost damage, probably from that last severe freeze in March. A severe wind storm carrying lots of salt from the ocean can cause similar damage. Eleagnus and Russian olive are usually considered the same plant. There are tree forms of Russian olive, and perhaps that's the way you identify them. Prune out all dead wood at once. Fertilize your plants and keep them thoroughly watered – at least 1 inch per week – all summer. By pruning, you'll force out new growth, which is what you want.

Q. I'm interested in finding out about trumpet vines. Would they help anchor sand? Where would I get them? What other vines would be suitable?

A. Trumpet vines will grow and anchor sand. They're available in many mail–order nursery catalogs. You don't need any select variety, and since it grows wild along the roadside in rural areas and around beaches, that's where I'd go to get some. Be sure to get permission if you find it on private beach property. Once trumpet vine gets going, it's tough and strong and can be hard to control. Creeping euonymus is another solution. Also, the highway department uses love grass for the same purpose, although it may be difficult to locate.

Q. I want to reply to the individual who wondered how she could establish and maintain a herb garden where occasional saltwater flooding occurred. Perhaps the best thing wold be to turn the salty plot into an asparagus bed.

A. Herbs are difficult or impossible to grow when flooded by saltwater. And asparagus is one plant that likes salt. It's worth a try.

Q. I'm a transplant from New Jersey, and I'm still trying to find out what grows well on the Outer Banks, where the winds do get fierce. We would like to plant some peaches, pecans and raspberries. What is the best way to care for raspberry bushes?

A. The late local berry authority, Jim Mays, said the only variety Virginia Tech recommends for our area is Heritage. North Carolina State University says Dorman and September Red will perform best in the eastern part of your state. The experts say to prepare the soil well and water plants thoroughly when setting them out, cutting back at least half the top growth. The best planting time is late fall or early spring. Fertilize after new growth starts with half a cup of 8–8–8, and do that again about July 1. Mulch the plants thoroughly, and remulch every year. Immediately after harvest, prune out old canes that have fruited because they die anyway. Thin out unhealthy plants so there is a healthy cane every 10 inches. When fruit begins to ripen, harvest every day. All fruit requires a lot of water, so make sure it gets plenty.

Q. I live at the beach, so the soil is sand, covered with pine straw. I have beautiful geraniums near the end of summer, but about that time, crickets invade my place. Something cuts off the plants at ground level. I blame it on the crickets because plants that are in planters are not affected. Do you think I'm right? If so, what can I use to protect them because I am getting ready to plant more geraniums in July.

A. Entomologist Peter Schultz at the Hampton Roads Agricultural Research Station says it could be pill bugs, shrews or voles, but crickets should not be blamed. Geraniums are not on their list of favorite foods. A dusting of Sevin will control pill bugs, but my suspicion would be voles or shrews, which would also account for those in window boxes not being affected. Either varmint can be destructive. If you see round holes about the size of a quarter, they are vole holes. Set a mouse trap, bait it with cheese or a peanut, cover it so other animals won't bother it and see if you can't catch some voles and/or shrews.

Q. I should like to grow something besides sand spurs at my cottage in Kill Devil Hills, N.C., preferably a garden that won't be too laborious, because I am a widow and do all the work myself. It would be nice to have a few flowers to pick, maybe even a veggie or two.

A. A few flowers that will grow in the sand are Chinese wisteria, Sweet Autumn Clematis, Hall's honeysuckle, artemisia, baptisia, chrysanthemum, euphorbia, liatris and goldenrod. Gaillardia, heuchera and iris also are possibilities, as are thyme and veronica. Vegetables are a tougher problem. Muskmelons and watermelons like sandy soil, and I have seen them growing in Nags Head. If you dig a hole and put some topsoil in before planting, you should be able to grow tomatoes and peppers. Just remember that with your sandy soil, water leaches out rapidly so water often.

Q. I live on the Outer Banks of North Carolina. Can you tell me what is a good soil mix for tomatoes?

A. Tomatoes like a soil with lots of leaf mold and peat moss. In the sand where you live, make sure you provide lots of that, plus a slow-release fertilizer and lots of water. You might want to try the Japanese or "ring" method. Put up a circle of fence and fill it half full with compost, and then set the tomatoes on the outer edge. As they grow in the compost, you can train them up the fence.

Q. I recently moved from Virginia Beach to Kill Devil Hills, one block from the ocean. What will grow here? I realize I need to work topsoil into the sandy soil, but will azaleas, gardenias or roses survive the climate here?

A. Azaleas are a poor bet to grow on the Outer Banks. They will need protection from the salt spray. Roses and gardenias should be OK if you can give them some shade from the afternoon sun. You will need to amend the soil with humus, such as pine bark, ground leaves or peat moss. Also plan on doing a lot of watering.

Dan Milbocker at the Hampton Roads Agricultural Research Station in Virginia Beach suggests Indian hawthorn, yucca, wax myrtle, euonymus and most hollies as better choices for your area. Acacia looks somewhat like a yellow-blooming crape myrtle and will grow in Kill Devil Hills.

Trees and Shrubs

Azaleas

Q. I would like to have azaleas in front of my house, but the area faces south and is in full sun until late afternoon. What do you recommend?

A. Dan Milbocker at the Hampton Roads Agricultural Research Station recommends that you grow the Southern Indica or Formosa type. One good variety that is rugged, as well as pretty, is named George Lindley Taber. Most nurseries stock them, but I'd wait until October to plant. You still might have problems if the heat reflected from your house is severe. Mulch heavily, and keep plants thoroughly watered.

Boxwood

Q. You said February was the month to fertilize boxwoods, and their one break of growth began each year in February. I have numerous large boxwoods that are much too large for the space they occupy. I want to trim them back. Is this the time to trim (March), and can they be cut back to bare wood? I am willing to have only the stump of the bush for a year or so if they will eventually put out new growth.

A. Pruning boxwood is tricky business. First, take the largest shoots and prune them out, down to inside the plant. This is done selectively, not by an overall shearing. Done properly, it will reduce the size of the bush by nearly one–third. But be sure to trim down inside the bush, and do it again next year. Do not go down to bare wood, for often a boxwood will not respond to such severe treatment. Pruning must be done selectively.

Q. Enclosed are leaves from my boxwood. Three of them have this problem of brown, rusty colored leaves. These three seem to be the worst. Can you tell me what to do about them?

A. Authorities at the Hampton Roads Agricultural Research Station inspected the leaves you sent and says that the rusty color is normal for boxwood in winter. They appear to be under some stress, so a light fertilization in spring with a shrub fertilizer containing long–lasting nitrogen or an application of cottonseed meal should be helpful.

Camellias

Q. Is it possible to move old camellias with trunks up to 5 inches in diameter?

A. It's not practical to move mature camellias unless you move a large ball of earth with each one. The best time of year for transplanting is October. Another suggestion is to air–layer your favorite plant. Then you can move the rooted air–layer to the location you desire.

Q. Please tell me how to air-layer camellias.

A. Air-layering of camellias is easy but should be done between March and July 1. Select a strong, upright branch that will make a good-looking shrub. At the point you want roots, scrape off all the bark, through the cambium layer, down until you can see white. Use a sharp razor blade and make a band about 2 inches wide. Dust the exposed area with Rootone. Then take spaghnum moss that has soaked overnight in water, and squeeze it thoroughly. Wrap that around your scraped area, being generous, for that is where the roots will form. Wrap that with plastic, tying it tight at the top to keep out rainfall but leaving the bottom loose enough so water that does get inside can drain out. Wrap again with tin foil and tie at both ends. Many gardeners then tie craft paper around the entire ball to prevent birds from pecking at the foil.

With a little bit of luck, your new air-layered camellia should be rooted by mid-September. Prune it off below your ball of spaghnum by Oct. 15 and before a freeze. Set the plant directly into the spot it will stay, or put it in a container of sawdust or peat moss for a year to allow further root development before planting.

When choosing a camellia to air-layer, be sure to choose an older, healthy plant because you'll be removing 12 to 18 inches from it.

Q. Please tell me how sasanqua camellias can be propagated. I'm interested in the cutting method, if possible.

A. Sasanqua camellias are propagated just like camellia japonica. Take cuttings of new wood in July or August. Strip the bottom leaves off. Make sure the cut is sharp and neat, using sharp tools to take it. Dip the cut end in Rootone and put it in a propagating mix of one-third each of sand, peat moss and Perlite. Put under plastic in the shade for the next six months. By spring, the plant should be rooted and healthy. Most folks have a nursery plot where they transplant such cuttings to help them grow larger before putting them in a permanent location.

Q. I'm sending you some leaves from a camellia bush in my yard. Please advise what the black soot is and what treatment is required.

A. Your problem is common with camellias. It's commonly called sooty mold, sooty blotch or black mildew. Aphids working on the underside of the leaves of your camellias excrete a sticky substance called honeydew, which clings to the upper side of the leaves below. A sootlike fungus grows in the excretion. Gardenias and crape myrtles also are susceptible. Virginia Tech recommends spraying in June or September with Orthene, malathion, Spectracide or Sevin to control the aphids, and you'll soon get rid of the sooty mold.

Q. What can be done about camellia buds rotting on the bush?

A. Camellias are relatively free from disease and insect problems, making them one of our easiest plants to grow. But if their buds turn brown and drop in winter, the cause probably is freezing weather. When temperatures take a dive, the buds go brown. The edges of flowers, if they open, also are brown. Early blooming varieties, such as Debutante, are particularly vulnerable to cold weather. If blooms have a blighted look, it is caused by petal blight. You can spray with a fungicide to prevent it from spreading. The best solution, however, is to remove and destroy all blooms that you believe have the blight.

Q. I have a beautiful camellia bush about 6 feet tall. Before the fall season, I pruned it down a lot. Then when the new leaves came back, most of them curled under, and it looks sick. Please tell me what is wrong and what I can do to help it.

A. First, you pruned at the wrong time of year. The only time to prune is after they bloom in the spring. When you prune in fall, you force new tender growth. Then winter weather causes the leaves to curl under as you describe. What you should do now is to scrape the bark on the bush to see if it is alive. If the stem is green under the bark, the plant is alive. Let nature correct it. The best thing to do now is to do nothing. If the plant is alive, it will come back to good health by itself. A year from now, after blooming, use some camellia fertilizer. Keep the plant watered this season and well–mulched to hold moisture in and fluctuating temperatures out.

Crape myrtle

Q. Our crape myrtle is about 6 feet tall. It has two main stems about 1 inch in diameter and about five smaller stems. It was transplanted from beneath a grown tree about five years ago. We would like to keep it as a bush, but it seems we prune off all next year's flowers each time. We seem to have this problem with many flowering shrubs in that we cut off the future blooms when we prune the shrubs to keep them small. Can you tell us when and how to prune so we don't cut off the blooms?

A. Crape myrtle blooms on new growth, so you can actually cut them to the ground every year and they'll grow back as a shrub with eight to 10 shoots and bloom. Many cities prune their crape myrtle back to stubs each year and they come back with new growth and bloom the following year. Dan Milbocker at the Hampton Roads Agricultural Research Station has one that he cuts back to ground level every year. As for proper pruning to get blooms, if you follow the rule to prune as soon as a shrub quits blooming (within two weeks), you can nearly always be sure that you'll not cut off next year's blooms.

Q. A crape myrtle I cut down began growing again last July. Now it looks like a small bush. How do I transform the bush into a tree with one strong trunk?

A. Pick the strongest erect branch that will make a good central stem. Then prune off all other branches at ground level. You'll soon have a crape myrtle that looks like a small tree. You must prune at the base of the trunk every spring, or it will become bushy.

Dogwood

Q. I have a dogwood in my back yard that is about 13 years old. It has bloomed only once. Can you tell me what to do with it?

A. Something is going wrong in late summer when the dogwood sets its bloom for the next season. Water it regularly in late summer to ensure flower set. Is it getting enough sun? Dogwoods have to have sun to bloom. If it's shaded by larger trees that have become thicker in the past 13 years, that could be a problem. After a drought, many dogwoods in this area may not bloom. I'd recommend feeding yours each fall after it goes dormant and watering it more often to see if you can prompt regular blooms.

Q. I have in my front yard a pink dogwood. The first year the tree had very pretty pink blooms. Last year, the blooms were more white than pink. This year, there were no blooms, and I thought it was a very good year for dogwoods. All my neighbors had trees loaded with blooms. Also, I have two white dogwoods 6 years old. They have never bloomed. Am I jinxed, or what? I have pine trees that give shade most of the day.

A. Yours is a tough question. First, the pink dogwood might be a bad graft. They are grafted on root stock from white dogwoods. Sometimes the pink graft dies, a shoot comes up from the roots of the white, and you end up with a conventional white dogwood. This causes the tree you sometimes see that is half white and half pink. Experts at the Norfolk Botanical Garden say to fertilize the tree this fall with a high phosphate fertilizer such as an 0-15-5, or perhaps just superphosphate. That may develop bloom buds on the tree. As to the whites that don't bloom, perhaps you have too much shade. They must have some sunlight to bloom. I've been told that they can go as long as 15 years before blooming. Fertilize them this fall using a special tree fertilizer on the whites, and then check to see if your dogwoods are getting sufficient sun.

Q. I am sending you a branch from a dogwood tree that is nearly 30 feet tall. For several years, the blossoms have been large, but at leafing time, the leaves are sickly looking. So the entire tree looks pathetic. What is the problem? Can a home spraying rig cure the tree? Is there a fertilizer routine for dogwoods? These trees have not been fed in years. Does this problem spread to surrounding trees and shrubs?

A. Experts at the Hampton Roads Agricultural Research Station says your dogwood has canker, a common disease of dogwoods. The limbs slowly die back. It often gets its start with "mower disease." A lawn mower blade hits the dogwood trunk and provides a place for the canker virus to enter the tree. From then on, it's downhill for the dogwood. Many dogwoods in Hampton Roads are suffering from the same problem. About all you can do is keep the tree watered and try to keep it healthy. Fertilize it every fall – after it drops its leaves – with a special tree fertilizer or tree food spikes.

Pecan trees

Q. The enclosed leaf came from our very old, very large pecan tree. It had good nuts for three or four years. But last year, we had none. A year or two before that, the few nuts we were able to gather did not have firm or "fat" meat. Hoping to have better results, we ordered beneficial insects (Trichogramma) from Gardens Alive catalog, which we have used twice. We are due one more shipment. There were numerous blooms this year, and I can now see some fruit forming. Leaves like the one enclosed concern me. Can you tell me what might be going on?

A. Virginia Tech authorities say your leaves show no insect problems. The black on the leaves may be minor nutrient deficiencies. Pecans like zinc, so you may want to try adding some under the drip line of your tree. It's available at feed–and–seed stores. Your tree is either not setting pecans or squirrels are getting them. As I've written before, pecan trees offer many challenges to homeowners, making the trees marginal as an investment.

Q. Many pecans from our tree had black spots on them. Upon observation, half of a nut would look fine, and the other half would be dry and black. Is there any way to prevent this?

A. Retired director Ed Borchers of the Hampton Roads Agricultural Research Station is a pecan expert, and he says there's not much you can do. If you find black spots scattered over kernels, the problem is an insect called stink bug. But when half the nut or kernel is black or all black, he says, it's a fungus. Spraying is not recommended because pecan trees get too large for homeowners to spray. Borchers also says timing of the spray is critical, and homeowners are not able to detect exactly when spraying should be done. Only commercial pecan orchardists have that expertise.

Q. I have a problem with my pecan trees. The meat of the nut has black bitter spots on it. Another tree blooms a lot, but the nuts get about one-quarter inch in size and drop off. I also have bugs that circle around small limbs and cut them off. Also, my trees have bagworms. I sprayed them in the spring, but it doesn't help.

A. A pecan authority told me that stink bugs cause black spots on the nut meat. They also attack lima beans and black-eyed peas. Spraying won't help much. His philosophy is "take what you can get" when growing pecans. The dropping off of the small nuts is natural. It's called "thinning" because the tree can't hold and grow that much fruit into maturity.

As for the bugs that cut off limbs, they're twig girdlers. They cut round and round a limb from the bark inward. Damage might be severe for young trees, and the fruit might look deformed. You also might get fewer nuts. Gather up all the fallen branches in late fall and destroy them. That's when the eggs and grubs are forming.

General

Q. Some of my photinia are throwing out very long branches, but I don't want tall bushes. What season can they be pruned?

A. Photinia grow fast and furious. You can prune them about any time you want, but early spring is recommended. You'll probably have to prune them more than once a season. They seem to look best when kept at about 6 feet tall. It's difficult to keep them shorter.

Photinia throughout Southeastern Virginia and Northeastern North Carolina is suffering from leaf spot, a disease that blackens the foliage before leaves drop off. The plant is then nude and often dies. North Carolina State University is recommending that no more photinia be planted. Virginia Tech says do not prune in the summertime, or you'll spread the disease. The only known cure is to start spraying early in the season with Daconil and spray every week all season long. You may want to yank yours out if it looks bad and replace with Anise or Ligustrum, both good substitute shrubs.

Q. Seven years ago, I bought a purple plum tree. At first, the blooms were pink or purple. But for the past three years, they have been white. Why? Does the soil need something?

A. There are several possibilities. First, it could be that the leaves shade the blooms so much that they don't get enough sun to brighten up to a pink-purple. Or, a sucker from the roots, which would have been a wild plum, has come up and produced white blooms. Or, sometimes the first blooms are pink and then fade to white in the sun. These suggestions come from experts at the Hampton Roads Agricultural Research Station in Virginia Beach. Observe the tree closely to determine the reason. Check for suckers from the roots at once, and cut them off at the ground.

Q. I am sending a leaf for identification, taken from a seedling growing in my yard. The leaves have a wonderful smell of peppery bayberry, and they stay green all year. Can you tell me about its care and habits?

A. You've correctly identified bayberry (*Myrica*), a group of deciduous shrubs with aromatic foliage and colorful gray or purple fruits. Its berries are used for scented candles. If you don't want your seedling where it is growing, you should move it in early spring or late fall. Bayberry requires little care. It can grow to 30 feet tall but normally stays 8 to 15 feet, growing in a floppy, informal manner. Fertilize it in early spring.

Q. My husband and I recently purchased property in Chesapeake. We have to clear both sides of the property to make drainage ditches. We would like to plant something on our property to regain our privacy. What type of tree or shrub do you suggest? We want something to look like Mother Nature had a hand in it; that is, something evergreen and fast-growing. The ditches should be completed by the end of August, which is not the best time for planting, so I'll appreciate some tips.

A. There are many good plants to solve your problem. For a hedge that looks as if nature put it there, wax myrtle (native bayberry), is hard to beat. It fits all your requirements and requires little pruning. Another excellent choice that is more formal is Leyland cypress, a tree. It can be pruned to a square shape or left to grow naturally. Yaupon holly is another native plant that would meet your needs. Other choices include sasanqua camellias and many varieties of holly. Although they won't be green in winter, many deciduous shrubs such as upright Tatarian honeysuckle can be purchased bare-root from mail-order nurseries. The cost is much less that way. October is ideal for planting. Water every other day after planting, but do not fertilize them until late winter or early spring.

Q. My neighbor has a fig bush from which I would like to get some cuttings and root them. How do you go about it?

A. You can root a fig most anytime of year. Dan Milbocker at the Hampton Roads Agricultural Research Station in Virginia Beach says one of the easiest ways is to lay a limb of the bush on the ground and hold it down with a brick or some other weight. Cover it with some soil or mulch, and in a few weeks it will be rooted. Then cut it off from the mother plant and set it wherever you want. Another method I have used is to divide a fig bush when it is dormant, preferably in the fall, and plant the new division where you want. Figs like a lot of sun and perform better with plenty of mulch under their limbs.

Q. What is the forsythia that blooms in winter? The branches are dark green and not as stiff as other forsythias.

A. The plant you refer to is not forsythia but winter jasmine (*Jasminum nudiflorum*), a tolerant, low-growing shrub with pendant-like branches.

Q. How do you prune deutzia, kolkwitzi, mock orange and flowering quince bushes? I know when, but get confused on how because there are so many branches. And why does my flowering quince lose its leaves in summer?

A. I had to look up kolkwitzi, which also is known as Beauty Bush. All these bushes bloom in spring, so they're pruned immediately after they complete their blooming. After that, they begin to set buds for next year. Always prune from the inside out. Thin it so the wind can blow through the plant to help prevent disease and insect problems. Trim it selectively so it has a graceful look. Even if you foul up, the plant will recover eventually. It's best to prune every year so you don't have to do so much at one time. Deutzia does get very thick and needs a lot of attention. The quince loses leaves as a matter of habit. Many people believe the thorny bush is more attractive without leaves so they don't complain about the loss. Quince seldom keeps the few leaves it has for very long. Fireblight is about the only disease that bothers quince, and that may cause leaf drop. Cut out any cankers you see and use a preventive spray.

Q. I have lovely Nandina but no red berries. My neighbors' plants all show beautiful red berries. What am I doing wrong?

A. Researchers at the Hampton Roads Agricultural Research Station say any one of several causes may be your problem. The newer dwarf-type Nandina rarely has berries, or very few. Too much shade will prevent berries. Or, you may be cutting them back too severely, or at the wrong time of year, which is most likely the problem. Use the "Bob Matthews method" in early spring. (He is the retired superintendent of the Norfolk Botanical Garden.) In early spring, prune three stalks at a time. Prune one completely down to the ground, the second halfway down and leave the third one alone unless it's too tall, in which case prune it down to a desirable height. Proper pruning should produce a nicely shaped plant and abundant berries.

Q. Have you informed your readers about hazardous trees and major storms, such as hurricanes? Research shows that certain trees are more likely to cause damage to your property if they fall in a storm. If you have large trees in your yard with potential targets, they should be evaluated for hazards. Trees that have been pruned properly hold up better. If you have a tree or trees that you are concerned about, call a certified arborist to have them evaluated. For a minimal fee, he or she can advise you on your potentially hazardous trees. Also, if you are planning to build a house and have valuable trees on your property that you would like to save, consult a certified arborist. A few simple steps can be taken to protect your trees and keep them healthy during construction and avoid unnecessary loss. A certified arborist has passed a comprehensive exam and will gladly provide you with proof of liability insurance, workmen's compensation insurance, business license and references.

A. Thanks for an informative and helpful letter. I agree with your recommendations.

Q. I am sending you a branch from an old, slow-growing compact shrub. I have not seen one like it in any of numerous catalogs I receive. Can you identify it?

A. Your plant is curly leaf ligustrum, properly named *Ligustrum lucidum corioceum*. It is a slow-growing evergreen shrub. It has shiny but very curly leaves and creamy white flowers. I have not seen it listed by mail-order nurseries, but Hampton Roads nurseries carry it.

Q. My pittosporum, planted last spring, looked good until March. Then some top sections of leaves started to turn yellow. They have not returned to the green color they once were, yet they are now putting out some new growth. Leaves have stopped dropping off. Could the damage be due to a freeze? Or too much water? Also, the bushes are in a foundation planting. Should I provide a more acidic soil? I've enclosed leaves for your examination.

A. Pittosporum are "iffy" in Hampton Roads and usually will winter kill in a severe winter. Horticulturists at the Hampton Roads Agricultural Research Center examined your leaves and suspect your plants were damaged by a drought. If they are throwing out healthy new leaves now, then they are recovering. The best policy is to feed them early in the spring and water them regularly all summer. They are not particular about their soil, so I would not be concerned about soil acidity. Keep them well mulched for protection in both summer and winter.

Q. Where can I buy bald cypress (*Taxodium distichum*) trees for transplanting? Will they grow in a marsh 1,000 feet from the ocean that is not connected to a saltwater inlet? Are they slow growing?

A. Check with local nurseries, who may be able to order it for you. One source is Tree Transplanters of Virginia. Owner Jack Wilkins also has willow oaks at his 100-acre tree nursery in Windsor, Va. His address is P.O. Box 4753, Virginia Beach, Va. 23454. Virginia Tech authorities say bald cypress should grow in a marsh if protected from being hit regularly with salt spray. The tree grows faster than a pine, which is rated as fast growing.

Q. My hydrangea was doing well until last year. Before that, it grew and had so many blossoms that I tied it up. When I cut the blooms, I cut branches back to about 18 inches. But those branches did not come out last year. The ones that were not cut back greened and blossomed. In August, I noticed it was wilting, although I kept it watered. Now it appears to be dead with only one green branch. Do you think I trimmed it too short? It does not get an abundance of sunshine.

A. A hydrangea will often do what you describe. It should return this spring from the one shoot and throw out more shoots from its roots. Don't prune it too severely, and don't prune too early in the summer. Pruning should be done only after you can see green buds in the spring. Hydrangeas bloom on new growth from the previous year's branches, so prune carefully.

Q. I read about preserving eucalyptus in your column. I had a silver dollar eucalyptus for three years, and it grew so large, I had to cut it down. I had good success in preserving the branches and still have homemade arrangements and wreaths. The leaves turned brown but stayed very soft and pliable. Here is the recipe I used from a friend who preserves flowers and makes arrangements.

Glycerin method for preserving foliage: First, wash foliage in cool water to remove dust and dirt. Cut out defects in leaves and pound lower 2 inches of stem with a hammer so fiber and bark are split. Next, stand material up in a jar containing a well-mixed solution of two-thirds water to one-third glycerin. It needs to reach 3 to 5 inches or so up the stems. Hot water mixes best. Let the material remain in the solution until full absorption has taken place. This takes at least two weeks. You can tell by looking since leaves will change color a little.

A. Thanks for the recipe. The same day a note arrived from horticulturist JoAnne Gordon, which reads: "I have eucalyptus growing in my yard. I cut them, then put in a vase with hot water. The stems soak up the water, and I did not replace the water. It dried nicely and still has a slight fragrance." That's an easy method to try without using glycerin.

Q. We moved to this area last fall and have two large trees in the front yard. I am enclosing a leaf from one of the trees. Some of the leaves were first getting rustlike spots, and now many are turning yellow and falling. If this is not normal, could you please advise a treatment for the trees?

A. Your leaf is from a magnolia tree. They shed leaves all year long and create a constant messy problem. You have two choices: either let the limbs grow completely to the ground and do not clean up under the tree, or keep limbs pruned to head height and constantly rake up the falling leaves. Another problem with the magnolia is that they have shallow roots and you'll often have roots protruding from the ground. You'll then have trouble getting grass to grow. Magnolias especially shed their leaves after periods of stress, such as excess rainfall or drought. Despite the many poems, songs and essays written about their waxy leaves and ivory blooms, they are a nuisance to have in a garden.

Q. Please advise on caring for a lilac bush that is at least 20 years old. It is 20 feet high and 2 1/2 feet in diameter at its base, spreading to 6 feet at the top. I know it needs pruning and shaping but don't want to chance losing it. It did not bloom as profusely this year as in past years.

A. Virginia Tech horticulturists recommend "renewal pruning," which means to cut out the oldest limbs at ground level. This forces new shoots to come out each spring. To shape, you can prune as much as you want after the lilac blooms. Fertilize it in early spring, which is also a good time to do your renewal. Just make sure to keep it watered if the weather is hot and dry.

Q. I want a privacy screen of fast-growing plants along the back of my yard. Photinia would be OK, but there are too many being planted around here now. I have seen bamboo used for privacy, and I like it. But I've also heard horror stories about how it takes over. Can I contain bamboo? Or what type of plants do you recommend?

A. Experts say the surest way to start a fight with your neighbor is to plant bamboo. And I agree. Under few circumstances is it ever recommended. Here are alternatives for what you need:

Eleagnus: It's the plant used in the median on Northampton Boulevard and Interstate 64 toward Williamsburg. It's thorny and keeps everything out, but is so rambunctious that it must be pruned regularly.

Rhaphiolepsis (*Indian Hawthorn*): Sometimes called cherry laurel, it's a good plant. Most sold on the local market is the dwarf variety, so make sure you get the larger plant.

Pyracantha: This plant fits all your specifications and makes a good hedge but not such a good privacy screen.

Heavenly bamboo, or **Nandina:** Planted close, it will grow to 6 feet tall and would give you privacy.

Wax myrtle: It can be an informal, fast-growing evergreen hedge.

Holly: Burfordi makes a good hedge. The drawback, however, is that it would be expensive for as many as you'd need for a hedge.

My overall choices would be Nandina for a low-cost, narrow hedge and wax myrtle for a wide, informal and inexpensive one.

Q. Please tell me what is wrong with my 5-year-old maple tree. About 6 inches from the ground, the bark has cracked open. Some of the bark is peeling, and the sap has been running out several places on the trunk. All the leaves were red in June, when they should not be that color until fall. Can you tell me what to do?

A. When tree foliage changes color prematurely, you can be sure the tree is under stress, mostly likely during its dormant stage. The bark problem is caused by last winter's severe weather. Many trees and shrubs suffered the same problem. Most likely your tree will die because of bark injury. You can cut it off at ground level now. If there is life in the roots, they will send out new shoots. Let them grow for a couple of months until you can find the strongest and straightest shoot. Then trim all the others off and you will have one straight shoot for a new tree. If the shoots do not come out, you'll need to replace the tree.

I've been asked often how to get the old roots out of the ground after a tree has died or been removed. I don't try. I just dig a hole as close to the old roots as possible and leave them alone to gradually rot away. When a tree is large and you want to get rid of the stump, check the classified ads for landscape services and you'll find the names of people who can help.

Vegetables

Tomatoes

Q. Last spring, you recommended an early, tasty, problem–resistant tomato. I bought whatever it was and had great luck. I know I wrote down the variety, but now I can't find it. Please list the variety in your column again.

A. I believe the one you're thinking of was Centennial, one of the best. The last issue of McDonald's Garden Center Greenleaves newsletter recommends three early varieties: Early Girl, First Lady (very disease resistant) and Quick Pick. Remember most early yielding tomatoes tend to have small fruit.

Q. What can I do to save my tomatoes from frost in October?

A. October is Save Your Tomatoes Before the First Frost Month. The date of the first killing frost in Southeastern Virginia is about mid–November, but the fateful day could arrive much earlier inland. Tomatoes that are allowed to ripen on the vine are more flavorful and nutritious because they've had time to accumulate sugars, minerals and vitamins produced by the plants. To avoid losing flavor in your tomatoes, experts recommend protecting them from frost for as long as possible. Creating a buffer of dead air space around the plant will protect it from light frosts. Something simple like a plastic trash–can liner placed over the plant at night will help. If a heavy frost is expected, it's nearly impossible to save your tomatoes, so pick the fruit while it's green and carry it into the house. Horticulturists warn gardeners that grandma's method of ripening tomatoes on the windowsill is outdated. Tomatoes ripened in a bright, sunny window won't be of the best quality because the sun will dry them out and sap their flavor. Cooling tomatoes in a refrigerator will delay ripening and can cause flavor loss.

A better method is to put green tomatoes in a paper bag and place them in a shaded area. You'll find that they ripen just as fast in the dark. To speed up the process, put a slice of apple in the bag along with the tomatoes.

Select only sound, full–sized fruit, free of wounds and spots. You can reduce after–harvest rot by soaking green tomatoes in a diluted chlorine bleach solution. Use a mixture containing one part bleach to 20 parts water. This is equal to three–quarters of a cup of bleach in one gallon of water. Soak tomatoes in the diluted bleach solution for 10 to 15 minutes. Then rinse and dry them carefully. Spread them out on a flat surface and store in a cool, well–ventilated basement or closet to ripen. Wrapping in newspapers is unnecessary. Inspect the ripening fruit regularly and throw out any that show signs of rot. Winter squash, pumpkins and gourds will be less prone to rot if given the bleach treatment before storage. As for green peppers, they won't ripen indoors. They should be harvested before the first frost and used promptly, or they can be frozen.

Q. How about some tomato advice? I have tested tomatoes for quite a few years and have found that Kotlas is the earliest tasty tomato. At 2 ounces, it is not as large as I would like. Husky gold, a very attractive, potato–leaf, golden–orange tomato is also very early and delicious. However, when hot, dry weather comes, these plants require a lot of help. Oregon Spring is another that is hard to beat. It requires no staking, sets fruit in cold weather, has few seeds, tastes great, bears all summer and into late fall. I started eating them the first week of June. Equally remarkable is Sun Gold, a small cherry type, voted the sweetest tomato. Sun Gold ripens at the same time as Oregon Spring.

A. Thanks. Tomato aficionados should take note of these varieties when buying seed.

Q. One November, on a trip to Lynchburg, our car broke down in Chesterfield County. A man took us to his home to wait for help. I observed that every window sill was lined with ripening tomatoes. Because all my tomato plants long had been gone, I asked him if he had grown them. He took me outside, and on one side of his home, he had six of the largest tomato plants I have ever seen. All were running up a wooden trellis with many green tomatoes still on them. I asked if they were a special type of tomato, and he said they were not. Then he explained that the way he grows tomatoes is to break up the ground thoroughly, then fertilize the soil using five or six fish per plant. He uses a post–hole digger to make a hole about 10 or 11 inches deep. He places gravel at the bottom. Then he places a plastic pipe 3 inches across and 14 inches long at the side of the hole. He takes a healthy tomato plant and sets it in each hole, filling in with rich soil. He said never to water a tomato plant from the top, as the roots will always turn upward to find the water. He waters his plants every second day by filling up the pipe. This method causes the roots to grow down toward the gravel, producing a stronger plant. I have not tried this, but I have seen the results and I am a believer. When you can have tomatoes like this gentleman had on Nov. 2, you're doing something right.

A. Thanks for sharing this information. Fish as fertilizer is what you'd call the Indian method of growing. As for the plastic pipe, there are some variations of this method, but they all involve using a pipe and watering the plant at its roots. Those who have tried it say you're exactly right. The tomatoes are the best ever.

Q. How many cubic feet of soil is needed to grow plants in pots, such as hybrid tomatoes, and how deep does the pot have to be for proper root development?

A. For plants in pots, about 3 cubic feet of soil is needed to grow a tomato properly. The deeper the pot the better.

General

Q. My brother gave me some beans from Korea. No one has been able to identify them. They have purple blooms resembling morning glories. I am sending two beans to you and a branch off the bush. Can you identify them and advise if they are edible?

A. My Virginia Tech friends at the Hampton Roads Agricultural Research Station identify the bean as *Canavalia ensiforms*, or horsebeans. The beans are the size and shape of lima beans. They are available in white or pink. Pods are 12 inches long, and they are edible. But don't ask for a recipe!

Q. Due to a water shortage, I am trying methods in the garden to avoid penalties on my water bill. I have an 18-gallon washing machine and wonder if I can drain the water from the rinse cycle onto my garden. There would be some detergent residue but no bleach in the water.

A. You can use water from your washing machine on flower and vegetables gardens without harm. If it contains bleach, let it set at least 24 hours. Also use your bath water for the same purpose.

Q. I'm eager to start my summer vegetable garden. Even though it's late April, I'm worried about lingering cold weather. When is it OK to plant?

A. Someone once told me that "when you can sit bare-bottomed in your garden and it's comfortable, it's time to put lima beans, peppers and eggplant in your garden." Ready to take that test?

Q. I grow several vegetables in my garden each year with great success. However, I am having trouble growing okra. I planted seeds in my small hothouse and kept the plants there until the nights were warm. I planted them with a mulch of grass clippings and garbage and a sprinkling of 5-10-5 fertilizer. They grew like magic up to a height of 3 feet, producing one or two green pods. Then they began to wilt and die. After they died, I pulled them and examined the roots. They had small knots on them but no insects.

A. Knots on your okra roots indicate nematodes. When okra gets knee high and starts producing but then wilts, curls up and slowly dies, that usually means fusarium wilt. The nematodes help carry it. Split one of the stems; if it has dark streaks, that's a sure sign of fusarium.

It's not going to be easy to eradicate. Plant your okra in a different spot this year. The fusarium fungus can live in the soil for 20 years, so rotation isn't the answer. Try growing them in the back of your flower garden.

Nematodes usually will not kill a crop but do prevent it from producing fully. One method of control is applying Clandosan (ground-up crab shells), which is supposed to control them.

Q. How about another comment on your question about suggestions for using Swiss chard? It's attractive while it grows and would not be unpleasing in a flower bed if one's space is limited. We simply remove the outer ribs as they mature enough to eat, clean them well, cover the chopped ribs and leaves with water and cook until the stalks are tender. I always put the stalks in the pot and cook them a few minutes before adding the leaves. It's best eaten with onions chopped in vinegar, chow-chow or pepper relish but delicious plain as well. If it will grow here, gardeners owe it to themselves to try kohlrabi, a member of the cabbage family, with an edible turnip-like stem at the base. It is a rather odd-looking plant but delicious raw as a snack, sliced in green salad, added to soup or cooked as a turnip. I much prefer it raw, however.

A. I've never had so many people praise one vegetable so much as Swiss chard. It's now planted in my garden. I just hope it tastes as good as you say (and a lot of other people). As for kohlrabi, it also will thrive here. It tastes like a cross between a turnip and a cabbage. It certainly won't win any beauty prize, but it may appeal to gardeners who want to try something different.

Q. My cabbage grows almost into a head and then withers and dies. The leaves then dry up. Now my collards and salad are doing the same thing. Please tell me something to stop this. I have a small garden that has been in my yard for years.

A. Yours sounds like a disease problem. Examine the roots of your cabbage. If they have growths on them, you probably have club root. Once it gets in a garden, it is difficult to control. Best solution is to rotate where you plant your vegetables in the garden. Try to plow or spade it in the fall and leave the soil exposed to winter weather. If that doesn't work, fumigate in early spring or summer with a chemical spray that will eliminate disease, nematodes, weeds and insects.

Q. We garden totally organic, using the same technique on flower beds as on our vegetable and melon garden. We put down grass clippings, leaves and organic trash. These compost naturally. Leaves are available only in the fall, so we use clippings from spring through autumn and organic trash year-round. Organic trash includes banana peels, orange peels, melon rinds, nut shells, grape stems and certain food scraps. We throw the leaves and clippings onto the garden bed where they're most needed. We use no chemicals, only organic fertilizer, bought commercially, for our lawn. We have a bird feeder for aesthetic reasons and to control the insect population. We also have several herb plants in both the flower and vegetable garden for kitchen use and insect prevention. The end result is birds, flowers, herbs, plants, trees and fruit all living happily together.

A. Thanks. Your ideas should help start others gardening organically.

Q. My vegetable garden produces well, but the problem is that it also gives me an abundant amount of grass and weeds. Sometimes the weeds are higher than the crops I grow. In fact, my garden has better grass than my lawn.

I have tried just about everything: black plastic, burlap and newspapers. Still the grass and weeds grow through everything. I grind up leaves and mulch them into the garden, adding lime when needed, plus cow manure and peat moss. It would seem like I'm doing everything right. I now have some Roundup but no instructions on how to use it. When and how do I use it? Do you recommend grinding the leaves in the ground whole or after chopping them up first? Or, should I burn them and till them into the ground?

A. Yes, you are doing everything right. I don't know how large your garden is, but one obvious solution would be to pull weeds before they get too big. If that seems impossible, use a glyphosate, such as Roundup. One gardener I know uses 5 1/2 tablespoons of Roundup per gallon of water to eliminate Bermuda grass. (The manufacturer recommends 6 oz. per gallon.) For Roundup to work, the weeds and grass must be green and growing. As soon as you see that happening, spray. Then every time you see a weed or sprig of Bermuda, spray it. Remember that glyphosate usually will not harm shrubs but it will kill grass, weeds and vegetables. It takes two weeks for the grass or weed to die after spraying, but you can plant immediately if you want. As for leaves, chopping them up and then tilling them into your garden is the best procedure.

Q. Last year, when I transplanted rhubarb, it grew rather well. But this year, it has disappeared. Is it not a simple matter to grow it in the South?

A. Rhubarb is difficult to grow in Southeastern Virginia because it requires excellent drainage and fertile soil, which we lack. Some gardeners manage to keep it alive. Yours probably died from root rot. Next time, plant it on a ridge. Mulch it in winter to prevent freezing.

Q. How can I grow red peppers? I buy the red bell pepper seeds but have no luck.

A. A red bell pepper is a green bell pepper that gets ripe. They all turn red late in summer and fall when they ripen. A few selected seed catalogs may offer a "red" bell pepper, but I am not aware of how they perform. They're not often found. There are other peppers that grow to be yellow, as well as purple. Let your peppers hang on the vine longer. Watch them closely so they don't become too soft.

Q. We have a vegetable garden problem. Nematodes are working over our cabbage and collard plants. We used mashed
crab shells on the garden after I read in the paper that they
would help. What can we do to eliminate the problem?

A. Experts at the Hampton Roads Agricultural Research Station
report that your plants have club-foot disease, spread by
nematodes. The best solution is to grow your cabbage and collards in a different part of your garden. It would be smart to rotate where you plant every year. Do not replant cabbage or collards
in the area you have the problem for at least four years.

Q. I have grown nice collards for years, but this year I had a new problem. Large leaves turned
brown in November. At first, it seemed to be the bottom leaves, but then they started
turning brown at the top as well. I kept cutting them off, but the browning continued. Can you
give me some advice?

A. Virginia Tech experts say they suspect it might be downy mildew, if yellowing of leaves
starts at the bottom. Check the underside of leaves and look for mildew. Another possibility is black rot, brought in on the seed. The best solution for that is to rotate every year where
you plant collards or other greens.

Q. I have a large amount of pine straw that I use to cover beds. Will it work well as a mulch
in my vegetable garden?

A. Pine straw is used by many excellent vegetable gardeners to mulch their gardens. It does
a good job. The only problem is that it's not easy to till under when you plow your garden next season. Because of it's spiny character, pine straw does not compost quickly.

Q. Somewhere I read that asparagus will tolerate a salt condition that controls most weeds.
I cannot find the amount of salt to add to 1 gallon of water. My two 25-foot rows are into
their second growing season, and the weeds have been an awful problem.

A. There's no set formula for the amount of salt to control weeds in asparagus. Virginia Tech
authorities advise experimenting. Try water from the Ocean or Bay, and see if it contains
enough salt. If not, make some homemade ice cream in an old hand crank freezer using rock
salt. The water you pour off will keep weeds down but not harm the asparagus.

INSECTS, DISEASES AND OTHER HOUSEPLANT PROBLEMS

Insects	Causes	Symptoms	Suggested Solutions
APHIDS	Small pear–shaped insects, also called "plant lice". May be black, green, yellow or reddish. Found on undersides of leaves, in buds and flowers, or on shoots. Suck plant juices and may transmit viruses.	Curled or deformed leaves or blossoms. Leaves sticky with honeydew, secreted by the aphids. Leaves may be coated with black sooty mold.	Wash plants with soapy water (2 tsp. of a mild dish detergent in 1 gal. of water). Spray with insecticidal soap, acephate, resmethrin or tetramethrin.
BLACK VINE WEEVILS	Black insects that chew the foliage. Creamy–white grubs destroy root system.	Notches or holes in leaves, or wilted plants.	Usually these weevils attack landscape plants, but may become bothersome on houseplants summering outdoors. If houseplant roots are found to be infested with grubs, try washing off the roots and repotting. Pick off and destroy adult weevils. They are not normally found in large numbers.
CYCLAMEN MITES	Minute creatures, barely visible with a magnifying glass, that suck juices from the leaves and buds.	Crown of plant distorted, new leaves and flowers deformed. Plants stunted. Typically on African Violets and Cyclamen.	Discard infected plants. Use Kelthane as a spray or dip.
MEALYBUGS	White cottony insects that have sucking mouthparts. Found on leaves, in leaf axils and on stems.	White cottony masses on plants. Yellow, sickly plants. Sticky honeydew in some cases.	Clean foliage with water or soapy water. Dip a cotton swab in ordinary isopropyl alcohol and gently swab off the insects. Spray with insecticidal soap, acephate, resmethrin or pyrethrins and rotenone.
SCALES	Small, soft or hard-bodied insects that may be black, brown, white or reddish in color. Suck juices from the plant.	Scab-like insects attached to midribs of leaves and twigs or stems. Plants are generally unthrifty. Honeydew is often present and sooty mold may coat leaves.	Remove by hand. Pick off severely infested leaves. Spray with insecticidal soap, acephate or resmethrin.
SPIDER MITES	Tiny arachnids that suck plant juices.	Sickly, yellow or bronzy foliage. Very fine webbing between leaves. Foliage appears dried out and plant may be stunted.	Discard severely infested plants. Spray with insecticidal soap, Kelthane, acephate or resmethrin.
WHITEFLIES	Snowy white flies that have sucking mouthparts.	Whiteflies fly up in "clouds" if plants are disturbed. Foliage may be yellowed, plant sickly. Sooty mold may be on leaves.	Spray with resmethrin or acephate in a pressurized can or use insecticidal soap.
Diseases	**Causes**	**Symptoms**	**Suggested Solutions**
BACTERIAL LEAF SPOT	Bacteria	Brown spots, "water-soaked", with a yellow halo, on leaves. May spread to stem.	Remove infected parts, avoid getting leaves wet, improve air circulation, don't crowd plants, and destroy severely infected plants.
BOTRYTIS BLIGHT (Gray Mold)	Fungus; wet, humid weather.	Gray fuzz or mold on leaves, flowers and stems.	Use sterile potting mix, remove fading leaves and flowers, avoid wetting flowers, improve air circulation. Apply benomyl once after these practices.
POWDERY MILDEW	Fungus	Whitish, powdery coating in spots on leaf surfaces.	Practice plant sanitation, improve air circulation, apply benomyl and repeat applications as needed.
ROOT ROT	Fungal or bacterial disease	Wilting, roots dark, may be soft or rotting. Leaves may be light or yellow.	Avoid over watering. Use well–drained, sterile potting soil, increase lighting. Throw away quickly declining plants.
SOOTY MOLD	Fungus, grows on honeydew coated leaves	Black, sooty coatings on leaves, resulting from buildup of honeydew secreted by sucking insects.	Control insects such as whiteflies, aphids, etc. Wash leaves.
Other Problems	**Causes**	**Symptoms**	**Suggested Solutions**
NUTRIENT DEFICIENCIES	Distorted growth, poor growth, reddening, interveinal chlorosis or chlorosis of entire leaf.		Apply a water soluble house plant fertilizer as per label directions.
OVER WATERING	Drooping, wilting plants. Yellowing and falling leaves.		Reduce watering frequency and empty saucers of excess water.
POT BOUND PLANTS	Water runs right through pot and out drainage holes. Roots protruding through draining holes and are present on soil surface.		Remove plant from pot. Loosen rootball and repot into the next larger size pot.

Cooperative Extension Service, Cornell University

INDEX

Abelia 22
Acidic soil 22, 27
Acorn sprouts 40
Aerated lawn 23
Aerator 86
African violets 114–115, 117, 132
African violets, proper light 115
Ageratum 50
Air–layering camellias 159
Ajuga 63, 108
All America roses 13
Allamanda 82
Alternative fertilizers 57
Aluminum sulfate 58
Amaryllis 133
Ambush bugs 11
American holly 117
Amsonia 74
Anemic Plants 71
Annual herbs 46
Anthracnose 31
Anti–transpirant 15, 27, 62, 114, 120
Aphids 52, 64, 106
Apple trees 72, 78
Apples 34, 126
Arbor Day 40
Arborists 4
Artemisia 63
Arthritis 70
Ash tree 78
Asiatic jasmine 89
Asparagus 27, 103, 156
Assassin bugs 11
Automatic sprinklers 62
Azalea caterpillars 79, 93
Azalea varieties 20
Azaleas 9, 15, 19–20, 27, 39, 59, 82, 101, 110, 118, 158
Azaleas, poor bet 157
Bacillus thuringiensis (Bt) 79, 93
Bacterial wilt 82
Bad bugs 11
Bag Balm 17
Bagworms 41, 59, 79, 103, 163
Baking soda 82, 120

Bald cypress 63, 166
Bamboo 145, 168
Barberry 89, 91
Bark mulch 19, 25
Basic Pruning Techniques 5
Bat houses 147
Bayberry 77, 164
Bayleton 81
Beach Gardens 67
Beans from Korea 171
Beauty Bush 165
Bedding plants 50
Beef suet 82
Beefmaster tomato 48
Bees 82
Beetles 81
Beets 43, 80
Begonias 50, 82
Beneficial insects 11
Beneficial nematodes 12
Bensulide 39
Bermuda grass 40, 51, 71, 81, 85
Berries 126
Best time to plant trees 98
Betasan 39
Better Boy 48
Biennial herbs 46
Biological pest controls 57
Bird and grass seed 101
Bird houses 117
Bird tables 116
Birds 7, 11, 82, 115–116, 123–124
Bittersweet 117
Black rot 174
Black spot 82, 148, 153, 163
Black spot control 120
Black swallowtail butterfly caterpillar 48
Black–eyed peas 163
Black–eyed Susan 74
Black–oil sunflower seed 116
Blackgum 76
Bleach 17
Blossom End Rot 28, 49
Blue to purple perennials 97
Bluebeard 21
Blueberries 42, 88, 111

Boltonia 75
Borers 32, 81, 93 129
Botanical tulips 105
Botrytis blight 41, 106
Boxwood 36–37, 145, 158
Boxwood questions 36
Boxwood root rot 36
Brackish water 154
Bradford pear 27
Bramble fruits 111
Broad leaf evergreens 113
Broccoli 72, 79–80
Brown patch 26, 71, 81, 86–87, 136
Brussels sprouts 80
Buddleia 21, 82
Bug Chow 11
Bugs 96
Bulb Booster 106
Bulbs 25–26, 40, 51, 92, 125
Bush beans 44
Bush–type cucumbers 40
Butterflies 123–124
Butterfly Bush 21, 54, 150
Butterfly rose 13
Butterfly weed 74
Cabbage 72, 79–80, 172, 174
Cages 49
Caladiums 50, 52, 59
Callicarpa 76
Camellia reticulata 9
Camellias 9–10, 15–16, 28, 82, 89, 101, 110, 121, 158, 159–160
Cantaloupes 82
Cardinal bush 1
Cardinal flower 75
Carefree Delight 13
Carolina allspice 54
Carolina jessamine 75
Carolina Yellow jasmine 34
Carpenter bee 148
Carrots 80
Caryopteris 21
Cat feces 149
Catalogs 6
Caterpillars 78, 81
Cauliflower 72, 79
Centipede grass 51–52, 81, 85
Certified arborists 165

INDEX

Chaste Tree 22
Cherries 34
Cherry tree 78
Chickweed 26
Chinch bugs 136
Chinese cabbage 80
Chinese hollies 89
Chinese pistache tree 63, 89
Christmas greens 119–120
Christmas tree for birds 119
Christmas trees 119
Christmas-tree stand 121
Chrysanthemums 59, 71,
    89, 96
Cineraria 118
Citrus 127
Citrus peels 149
Clay 23
Clean gutters 110
Clematis 33
Clemfine fescue seed 86
Clerodendrum bungei 54
Clethra alnifolia 22, 76
Climbing hydrangea 75
Cloud Cover 114, 120
Clover 136
Club root 172
Club-foot disease 174
Coleus 50
Collards 79–80, 174
Collect rainwater 62
Color combinations 50
Colorful Trees 107
Compost 19, 23, 45,
    49, 56, 80
Compost leaves 102
Compost pile 92
Conserve water 62
Control weeds 103
Cool-season crops 39
Coral honeysuckle 75
Coreopsis 74
Cornelian cherry 89
Cornell University 120
Cornell University
    solution 148
Cornus florida 31
Cornus kousa chinensis 32
Cosmos 28
Cotoneaster 108
Cover crops 103

Crab grass 24, 26, 124
Crab grass–prevention 39
Crape myrtle 29, 39, 53,
    63, 89, 160–161
Creeping euonymus 156
Cricket control 102
Crickets 156
Crickets in the house 150
Crinum lily 74
Crocus 105–106
Crossfire fescue seed 86
Cucumber beetle 82
Cucumber vines 71
Cucumber yields 52
Cucumbers 71, 82
Curly leaf ligustrum 166
Cut flowers 72
Cutting mums 102
Cyclamen 117–118
Cygon 3, 26, 39
Cypress vine 82
Daconil 27, 87 53, 81–82
Dacthal 39
Daffodil foliage 58
Daffodils 71, 105–106, 120
Dahlias 83
Dahoon holly 2
Damaged tomatoes 81
Damsel bugs and flies 11
Dandelion digger 93
Daphne 107
Darwin hybrid tulips 105
Daylilies 55–56, 81, 89,
    96, 101–102
Dead bloom stalks 81
Dead plants 110
Dead vines and foliage 114
Deadheading 71
Deadline 51
Deer problems 147
Delphiniums 101
Desiccation 113
Determinate tomatoes 48
Diazinon 79–80, 92, 102
Discouraging rabbits 15
Disease control 16, 41, 82
Diseases 114
Dividing cannas 27
Dividing coreopis 27
Dividing irises 71
Dividing mums 51

Dividing perennials 96
Dividing phlox 27
Dog and cat repellents 149
Dog urine 101
Dogwood 9, 31, 32, 77, 161
Dogwood anthracnose 32
Dormant oil spray 6, 28
Downy mildew 174
Drainage 22, 95
Dried flowers 69
Dried up annuals and
    perennials 110
Drip irrigation 62
Drought-resistant
    choices 63
Drought-tolerant garden 62
Drought-tolerant plants 61
Dusty miller 82
Dutch bulbs 93
Dwarf Alberta spruce 154
Dwarf trees 35
Early blight 49
Early blooming Azaleas 20
Early Girl Tomatoes 48
Early morning watering 63
Easter lilies 26
Easy to grow plants 89
Easy-to-dry flowers 69
Easy-to-grow herbs 47
Eatherleaf mahonia 107
Eggplant 81
Eleagnus 91, 168
Endive 52
English ivy 33, 108
Enriching soil 22
Epsom salts 28, 49, 152
Euonymus 117
Evergreens 6
Fall Vegetable Garden 79, 93
Fall webworm 78
Falling leaves 110
False yew 89
Feeding fish 17
Fern fronds 41
Ferns 73, 132
Fertilizing 3, 6–7, 15–16,
    23, 26–27, 38, 71, 81,
    92, 101, 120
Fertilizing crocus, daffodils,
    tulips, hyacinth 26
Fertilizing fruit trees 29, 35

INDEX

Fertilizing hollies 26
Fertilizing lawns 23
Fertilizing roses 92
Fertilizing trees 16, 27
Fertilizing warm–
    season grasses 51
Fescue 23, 52
Fescue blends 86
Fescue lawns 85, 88
Fig bush 164
Fig trees 41
Fig trees 41, 110
Figs 88, 130
Finale 26
Fish as fertilizer 170
Floral masses 50
Floribunda roses 152, 153
Flotox 53
Flower and vegetable
    gardens 28
Flower borders 7
Flower Carpet Rose 12
Flowering house plants 117
Flowering plum 27
Flowers that grow in
    sand 157
Flying insects 82
Forest tent caterpillar 41
Forsythia 27, 39, 52, 89, 164
Fosteri holly 2
Foundation plantings 3–4
Fragrant plants 54
Freezing seed 40
Fringe tree 77, 89
Frogs 12
Frost 28–29, 79
Frost heaving 114
Fruit bandits 35
Fruit tree problems 35
Fruit trees 34, 88
Fungicides 40, 80, 82
Funginex 29, 41, 53, 82
Fusarium blight 26
Galax 73
Galls 42
Garden soils 101
Gardenias 54, 72, 118
Gardening organically 173
Garlic 15, 26, 47, 90
Geraniums 28, 50, 72,
    82, 156

Germination ability 86
Getting the soil right 56
Gibberellic acid 10
Ginger lily 54
Girdling roots 111
Gladiolus 40
Gloxinias 117–118
Glycerin method for
    preserving foliage 167
Glyphosate 15, 86
Goldenrod 75, 92
Good bugs 11
Gourds 82, 103
Grafting camellias 28
Grandiflora 152
Granular tree fertilizers 120
Granulated lime 23
Grapes 127
Grass and weeds 173
Grass seed 102
Grasses 6, 15, 51, 97
Gray water 62
Green moss 150
Green tomatoes 83, 169
Green–striped
    mapleworms 79
Grinding leaves 173
Grit 116
Ground covers 63, 73,
    108. 134
Ground-up crab shells 171
Grouping plants 50
Growing fruit 111
Growing Garlic 90
Growing prize–
    winning roses 151
Gumpo azaleas 21
Gutters 40
Hanging baskets 52, 81, 88
Hardwood bark 25
Hardwood cuttings 121
Hav–a–Hart trap 141
Hawthorn 63, 117, 147
Hazardous trees 165
Healthy plants 50
Heavenly bamboo 168
Hedge clippers 3
Hedge shape, ideal 5
Hedges 164
Helianthus 89
Herbal fungicides 47

Herbs 46, 83, 130
Heritage roses 13
Hibiscus 118
Hickory tree 78
High–maintenance
    plants 88
High–nitrogen fertilizer 81
High–quality bulbs 105
Hollies 2, 3, 63, 76, 91, 168
Holly berries 26
Holly leaf miner 3
Honey bees 52
Hornets 82
Horseradish 27, 111
Horticultural Oil 6, 39
Hosta 51, 89, 108
House plants 6–7, 15–17, 26,
    51, 71, 102, 119, 121
Household bleach 27, 81
How grasses stand up 24
Human hair to deter
    rabbits 147
Hummingbird feeders
    41, 102
Hybrid azaleas 21
Hybrid lilies 54
Hydrangea colors 41, 58
Hydrangea petiolaris 33
Hydrangea pruning 77
Hydrangeas 16, 89, 142, 166
Ice 113
Impatiens 50
Improper watering 22
Improved fescues 85
Improving soil 62
Indeterminate tomatoes 48
Indian hawthorn 15, 61
Inkberry 75
Insect control 59
Insecticidal soap 57
Insecticides 80
Insects 39
Integrated Pest Mgt. 39
Intensive gardening 45
Iris 93, 96
Iris borer 93
Iris cristata 74
Iron 3
Iron chlorosis 87
Iron deficiencies 87
Irrigate efficiently 62

INDEX

Irrigation 89
Ivy 144, 149
Jack-in-the-Pulpit 74
Japanese apricot 107
Japanese beetles 59
Japanese black pine 60–61
Japanese cryptomeria 89
Japanese honeysuckle 145
Jasmine 54
Jessamine 34
Joe-pye weed 74
Juniper 108
Kalanchoe 117–118
Kale 80
Kentucky 31 fescue 81, 86
Kerria 76
Killing frost 80
Killing grass 148
Kiwi 33, 119, 130
Kohlrabi 80, 172
Lacebark elm 89
Lacebug 147
Lack of iron 71
Lack of water 113
Ladybugs 11
Landscape timbers 45
Lantana 82
Larkspur 101
Late blooming azaleas 21
Late-summer flowering
    trees 21
Laundry bleach 27
Lawn care 6, 15, 17, 26,
    39–40, 51–52, 58–59,
    71, 81–82, 101–103,
    110, 120, 134
Lawn cleanup 23
Lawn grass 88
Lawn mower 32, 39, 121
Lawn watering program 58
Lawns 23
Leaf miners 79
Leaf mold 32
Leaf mulcher 110
Leaf spot 147, 163
Leaky hoses 62
Leaves 6, 15
Leaves smother grass 120
Leeks 80
Lettuce 43, 52, 80
Leyland cypress 63, 164

Liatris 74
Light snow 113
Lilac bush 167
Lily-of-the-valley 42
Lima beans 59, 163
Limb up 32
Lime 9, 58, 87
Liming lawn 23
Limit turf areas 62
Liquid iron 36
Liquid soap 82
Liriope 15, 27, 40, 89, 108
Live oak 76
Loblolly bay 76
Longleaf pine 76
Lysol 17
Magnesium 28
Magnolia trees 167
Maintenance 15, 17, 26–27,
    41, 51–52, 58, 60,
    71, 92, 101–103,
    110–111, 119–121
Maintenance-free plants 95
Malathion 81, 92
Mallow 82
Maneb 92
Maple tree 168
Marigolds 50
Marsh marigold 73
Maypop 75
Mealybugs 132
Melons 71
Mice 113
Midseason blooming
    azaleas 20
Mildew 64, 153
Mildew control 148
Mildew-resistant
    cultivars 65
Milorganite 38
Miniature roses 148
Misting 16
Mock orange 54, 76
Moist soil 79
Moldy seeds 116
Mole crickets 139
Mole-Med 138
Moles 106, 138–139
Monarda 74
Mondo grass 40, 109
Moneywort 149

Moon flowers 143
Moon vine 143
Morning glory 149
Mosquito repellent
    plant 144
Moss 81
Mountain laurel 75
Mower blade 24, 58–59, 71
Mulches 3, 6, 32, 62,
    87, 89, 92, 96, 144
Mulching mower 137
Mulching trees and
    shrubs 25
Multiflora roses 149
Muskmelons 157
Nandina 89, 165
Narcissus myth 102
Native garden 73
Native plants 73, 77
Natural approach for
    growing herbs 47
Natural approach to
    insect and disease
    control 57, 58
Nectarines 34
Nematodes 37, 111, 171, 174
New lawns 85
New Roses 12
New sod 58
Newly installed shrubs 62
Newly planted shrubs
    and trees 53
Nicotiana alata 54
Niger seed 82
Nitrogen 24, 38
Non-toxic spray 82
Oak-leaf hydrangea 76
Obedient plants 75
Oil spray 26
Okra 171
Old-fashioned roses 152
Onion sets 39, 121
Orange-striped
    oakworm 41, 79
Orchids 117
Organic fertilizer 38, 92
Organic Gardening 56
Organic matter 23,
    27–28, 49
Organic sources 38
Organic spray 28

Organic substitutes 57
Oriental poppies 142
Ornamental grasses 89, 97
Orthene 79
Orthenex 29
Osmanthus 77, 107
Overgrown shrubs 41
Owls 72
Oxalis 137
Pachysandra 73, 89, 108
Packing peanuts 39
Palms 131
Pamela Harper 95
Pampas grass 97, 142, 155
Pansies 16, 27
Paper-white
    Narcissus 109, 119
Parsley 47
Partridge berry 73
Peach tree problems 35
Peach trees 129
Peaches 34, 128, 156
Peas 27, 43
Peat moss 23, 25, 32, 49, 102
Pecan trees 162-163
Pecan trees 7, 78, 156
Pendimethalin 39
Peonies 41, 96
Peppers 17, 71
Perennial flowers 27
Perennial herbs 46
Perennials 93, 95, 101
Periwinkle 89, 108
Persimmons 78, 88
Pest and disease
    control 102, 110, 120
Pest control 6, 15, 28,
    39, 51, 52, 58, 60,
    72, 81-82, 103, 121
Pesticides 11
Petal blight 40, 160
Petunias 50
PH scale 22, 77
Phalaenopsis orchid 118
Phaltan 53
Philodendrons 117
Phlox carolina 74
Phlox subulata 108
Photinia 40, 88, 163, 168
Phytopthora cinnamomi 37
Pinch off flowers 50

Pinching plants 5
Pine bark 10
Pine needles 10, 19
Pine pitch 120
Pine straw 25, 174
Pineapple 131
Pink dogwood 33, 161
Pink to red perennials 97
Pinus thunbergiana 61
Pittosporum 63, 166
Plant container removal 40
Plant pests 82
Plant protection 119
Planting 6-7, 15-17,
    27-29, 39-40, 42,
    52, 59-60, 72, 82-83,
    101-103, 110-111,
    120-121
Planting azaleas 20, 21
Planting camellias 102
Planting cool-weather
    vegetables 27
Planting corn 40
Planting daffodils 111
Planting Dogwood 32
Planting fruit trees 35
Planting lilies 110
Planting Method For
    Roses 14
Planting pansies 110
Planting roses 39, 151
Planting trees and
    shrubs 101
Plants failing to flower 58
Plants For Wet Places 90
Plugs 85-86
Plumbago 82
Plums 34
Poa annua 134
Poinsettia 6, 71, 93, 119, 133
Poinsettia re-blooming 133
Poison ivy 145
Poisonous bulbs 106
Poisonous plants 146
Pollination 2
Pollination of fruit trees 34
Poplar tentmakers 79
Poppies 142
Portulaca 108
Potash 24
Potting soil 22

Powdery mildew 53, 82,
    87, 92
Powdery mildew
    control 120
Praying mantis 12
Preserving eucalyptus 167
Preserving hydrangeas 142
Preventing needle drop 119
Primroses 118
Privacy screens 168
Problem plants 88
Problem-resistant
    tomato 169
Propagating sasanqua
camellias 159
Propagation 7, 72, 82
Proper drainage 19, 44
Proper pruning of
    hydrangea types 77
Proper Tree Planting 99
Pruning 3-4, 6-7, 16-17,
    19, 27, 29, 39, 41,
    52-53, 59-60, 72,
    83, 102, 111, 121
Pruning azaleas 7
Pruning boxwood 158
Pruning crape myrtles 64
Pruning Deciduous
    Shrubs 5
Pruning fruit trees 35
Pruning holly 120
Pruning hydrangeas 41
Pruning paint 4, 110
Pruning roses 16, 29, 112
Pumpkins 82
Purple coneflower 74
Purple plum tree 163
Pyracantha 91, 168
Pyrethrum 57
Quality plants 96
Queen Elizabeth Rose 151
Queen-Anne's lace 142
Quince 27, 165
Rabbit damage 121
Rabbits 15-16, 21, 113,
    140, 147
Raccoons 106, 141
Radishes 43, 121
Ragweed 92
Raised beds 45, 89
Raphiolepis 61, 168

INDEX

Raspberries 28, 156
Rebel II fescue seed 81, 86
Recommended fruit
   trees 35
Recommended tulips 105
Red pepper spray 47
Red peppers 173
Red-humped caterpillar 79
Red-stemmed dogwood 107
Redbud 63, 77
Reemay fabirc 80
Refurbishing lawns 135
Removing Heavy Limbs 5
Renewal pruning 167
Repelling deer 147
Repelling cats 149
Replanting iris 83
Repotting plants 39
Reseeding 85, 93
Retirement grass 51
Rhododendrons 27, 52, 146
River birch 76
Root damage 113
Root prune 32
Root stimulator 20
Root systems 113
Root-knot nematodes 114
Rootone 72, 82
Rosa chinensis
   'Mutabilis' 88
Rose blooms 82
Rose care 14
Rose varieties 153
Roses 9, 12-13, 33, 88, 153
Roses, bare-root 27
Roses, best climbers 29, 151
Rotate planting sites 80
Rotate plants 43
Rotenone 81-82
Roundup 26, 144
Rubber snakes 72
Rudbeckia 63, 74, 89
Russian olive 91, 155
Rust 147
Rye grass 85
Salamanders 12
Salsify 111
Salt 15
Salt-tolerant trees 63
Sand 23
Sasanqua camellias 40

Satsuki series 21
Saucer of soil 35
Scale 39, 59
Scalecide spray 10
Scilla 106
Scotts Pro Lawn 87
Seashore mallow 74
Seaside Gardening 66-67,
   154
Security Shrubs 91
Sedum 89
Seed 15
Seeding lawn 23
Seeds 82
Selecting a fertilizer 38
Setting out new shrubs 39
Severe freeze 155
Sevin 79, 81-82
Shadbush 77
Shade 44
Shade Lovers 74, 97
Shenandoah fescue seed 81
Shrews 157
Shrubs 6, 75
Shrubs that draw birds 117
Side dressing 81
Sidewalks 27
Silver-bell tree 77
Slug bait 81, 110
Slug damage 51
Slugs 50, 96
Small fruits 7
Snail bait 110
Snail damage 51
Snails 50, 81, 96
Snap beans 29, 59
Snapdragons 28, 50
Snow 15, 26, 113
Snowdrops 106
Sod 85
Soda 71
Soil 22, 44-45
Soil acidity 22
Soil alkalinity 22
Soil crusting 23
Soil Enrichment 22
Soil environment 57
Soil mix for tomatoes 157
Soil needed to grow
   plants in pots 170
Soil preparation 22

Soil samples 119
Soil tests 23, 27
Soldier beetles, bugs 11
Soluble fertilizer 81
Sooty mold 16, 159
Sophora japonica 77
Sourwood 77
Southern Belle
   fescue seed 86
Spacing plants 63
Sparkleberry holly 2
Spectracide 26, 102
Spent blooms 9, 71
Spider mites 72, 103, 150
Spider-mite control 148
Spiders 11
Spiderwort 75, 143
Spike fertilizer 33
Spinach 52, 80, 121
Spireas 89
Spraying apples 51
Spraying cherry trees 35
Spraying mums 92
Spraying fruit trees 34-35
Spraying peaches 51
Spraying pears 51
Spraying plums 51
Spraying roses 82, 110, 152
Spraying schedule
   for fruit trees 35
Spraying weeds 51
Spreaders 86
Sprigs 86
Spring bulbs 92, 105
Spring fertilization 40
Spring-blooming
   clematis 33
Squash 71, 81-82
Squash borer 60
Squirrel deterrent 140
Squirrel-proof 116
Squirrels 106, 121, 141
St Augustine grass 40, 52,
   71, 81, 85, 135-136
Staking taller perennials 96
Staking trees 98, 113
Starter fertilizer 86
Starting seeds 39
Starting seed indoors 7
Stella D'Oro daylily 55
Stewartia 76

INDEX

Stink bugs 81, 162
Stokesia 75
Storing caladium bulbs 111
Straw 87
Strawberries 42, 51
Strawberry beds 60
Strawberry bush 76
String trimmers 40, 92
String-trimmer damage 32
Styrax 89
Suckers 64
Suet 116
Sulfur 9
Summer Annuals 50
Summer Sweet shrub 22
Summer tub plantings 82
Summertime stress 92
Sun 95
Sun Lovers 74, 97
Sun or shade lovers 75
Sun-loving trees and
    shrubs 21–22
Sundrops 74
Sunlight 44
Swamp sunflower 75
Sweet alyssum 28, 50
Sweet autumn clematis 33
Sweet corn 44
Sweet gum tree 78
Sweet peas 143
Sweet potato plants 60, 110
Sweetshrub 76
Sweetspire 76
Swiss chard 80, 172
Tachinid flies 11
Tanglefoot 93
Tea family 9
Tea leaves 133
Tea rose 152
Tent caterpillar 78
Testing soil 22
Thatch 24
Thinning 4
Thinning fruit trees 35
Thistle 82
Thistle seed 116
Ticks 51
Tidying up the garden 114
Toads 12
Toadstools 145
Tomato advice 170

Tomato hornworm 59
Tomato plants 81
Tomatoes 28, 48–49, 71,
    157, 169–170
Tools 3
Topping 4
Transition zone 86
Transplanting 2, 28
Tree choices 98
Tree crotch 4
Tree food spikes 120
Tree growth 100
Tree maintenance 15
Trees 4, 6–7, 76, 92, 98
Trees And Shrubs 158
Trifoliate orange 91
Trumpet vine 156
Tuberose 54
Tulips 105, 120
Turnips 79
Twig girdlers 163
Valentines day roses 16
Varmints 138–139
Vase water 58
Vegetable gardens 43,
    45, 173
Vegetables 80
Verbena 50
Vermiculite 80
Viburnum 89
Vinca major 50
Vines 33
Vining crops 44
Vining vegetables 40
Vitex 22, 63
Voles 106, 138–139, 157
Warm-season grasses 23,
    71, 85
Warm-season vegetables
    43, 52
Warm-soil vegetables 59
Washington hawthorn
    91, 117
Watering gardens 102
Water shortage 62
Water-saving plants 62
Watering African violets 26
Watering the plant at
    its roots 170
Watering thoroughly 62
Waterlilies 121

Watermelons 82, 130, 157
Wax begonia 118
Wax myrtle 63, 77, 164, 168
Wear-resistant grass 24
Webworms 78
Weed killers 23, 32, 82, 85
Weeding 59
Weeds 45, 87, 92
Weigela 89
White cultivars 33
White oak 76
White to silver foliage 96
White wild-indigo 74
Whopper tomato 48
Wild ageratum 75
Wild berries 103
Wild cherry trees 78
Wild ginger 73
Wild olive 77
Wild onions 15, 26, 39
Wild red columbine 74
Wild-bird seed 116
Wildflowers 73
Willow oak 76
Willow tree 78
Wilt-Pruf 15, 114, 120
WIN 38, 40
Winter Aconite 106
Winter damage 113
Winter honeysuckle 107
Winter jasmine 107, 164
Winter protection 113
Winterize garden 113
Wintersweet 107
Wisteria 33, 59, 75, 88
Witch hazel 76, 89, 107
Wood ashes 6
Woodpeckers 123
Woods poppy 74
Xeriscaping 61
Yaupon holly 63, 77, 89
Yellow jackets 58, 82
Yellow leaves 3
Yellow perennials 97
Yellow-necked caterpillar 79
Yellowing grass 87
Yellowing of leaves 101
Yucca 76
Zinc 162
Zinnias 50
Zoysia 40, 52, 71, 81, 85